1986

Corner House Publishers

SOCIAL SCIENCE REPRINTS

General Editor MAURICE FILLER

MERCY WARREN.

THE WOMEN

OF THE

AMERICAN REVOLUTION.

BY

ELIZABETH F. ELLET,

AUTHOR OF "THE CHARACTERS OF SCHILLER," "COUNTRY RAMBLES," ETC.

VOL. I.

CORNER HOUSE PUBLISHERS
WILLIAMSTOWN, MASSACHUSETTS 01267
1980

Entered, according to Act of Congress, in the year 1848, by

BAKER AND SCRIBNER,

In the Clerk's Office of the District Court for the Southern District of New York.

REPRINTED 1980

BY

CORNER HOUSE PUBLISHERS

ISBN 0–87928–106–5

Printed in the United States of America

TO

MY MOTHER,

SARAH MAXWELL LUMMIS,

THE DAUGHTER OF A REVOLUTIONARY OFFICER,

THIS WORK

IS RESPECTFULLY AND AFFECTIONATELY INSCRIBED.

LIST OF PLATES.

CONTENTS OF VOL. I.

PREFACE.

In offering this work to the public, it is due to the reader no less than the writer, to say something of the extreme difficulty which has been found in obtaining materials sufficiently reliable for a record designed to be strictly authentic. Three quarters of a century have necessarily effaced all recollection of many imposing domestic scenes of the Revolution, and cast over many a veil of obscurity through which it is hard to distinguish their features. Whatever has not been preserved by contemporaneous written testimony, or derived at an early period from immediate actors in the scenes, is liable to the suspicion of being distorted or discolored by the imperfect knowledge, the prejudices, or the fancy of its narrators. It is necessary always to distrust, and very often to reject traditionary information. Much of this character has been received from various sources, but I have refrained from using it in all cases where it was not supported by responsible personal testimony, or where it was found to conflict in any of its details with established historical facts.

Inasmuch as political history says but little—and that vaguely and incidentally—of the Women who bore their part

in the Revolution, the materials for a work treating of them and
their actions and sufferings, must be derived in great part from
private sources.   The apparent dearth of information was at
first almost disheartening.   Except the Letters of Mrs. Adams,
no fair exponent of the feelings and trials of the women of
the Revolution had been given to the public ; for the Letters
of Mrs. Wilkinson afford but a limited view of a short period
of the war.   Of the Southern women, Mrs. Motte was the
only one generally remembered in her own State for the act
of magnanimity recorded in history ; and a few fragmentary
anecdotes of female heroism, to be found in Garden's collection, and some historical works—completed the amount of
published information on the subject.   Letters of friendship
and affection—those most faithful transcripts of the heart
and mind of individuals, have been earnestly sought, and
examined wherever they could be obtained.   But letter-
writing was far less usual among our ancestors than it is at
the present day ; and the uncertainty, and sometimes the
danger attendant upon the transmission of letters were not
only an impediment to frequent correspondence, but excluded
from that which did exist, much discussion of the all-absorb-
ing subjects of the time.   Of the little that was written, too,
how small a portion remains in this—as it has been truly
called—manuscript-destroying generation !   But while much
that might have illustrated the influence of woman and the
domestic character and feeling of those days, had been lost
or obscured by time, it appeared yet possible, by persevering
effort, to recover something worthy of an enduring record.
With the view of eliciting information for this purpose, application was made severally to the surviving relatives of women
remarkable for position or influence, or whose zeal, personal

sacrifices, or heroic acts, had contributed to promote the establishment of American Independence.

My success in these applications has not been such as to enable me to fill out entirely my own idea of the work I wished to present to the reader. Some of the sketches are necessarily brief an meagre, and perhaps few of them do full justice to their subjects. There is, also, inherent difficulty in delineating female character, which impresses itself on the memory of those who have known the individual by delicate traits, that may be felt but not described. The actions of men stand out in prominent relief, and are a safe guide in forming a judgment of them; a woman's sphere, on the other hand, is secluded, and in very few instances does her personal history, even though she may fill a conspicuous position, afford sufficient incident to throw a strong light upon her character. This want of salient points for description must be felt by all who have attempted a faithful portraiture of some beloved female relative. How much is the difficulty increased when a stranger essays a tribute to those who are no longer among the living, and whose existence was passed for the most part in a quiet round of domestic duties!

It need scarcely be said that the deficiency of material has in no case been supplied by fanciful embellishment. These memoirs are a simple and homely narrative of real occurrences. Wherever details were wanting to fill out the picture, it has been left in outline for some more fortunate limner. No labor of research, no pains in investigation—and none but those who have been similarly engaged can estimate the labor—have been spared in establishing the truth of the statements. It can hardly be expected that inaccuracies have been altogether avoided in a work where the facts have to be drawn from numerous and sometimes conflicting authorities ; but errors, if discovered, may be hereafter corrected.

The sketches contained in the first volume, illustrating progressive stages of the war, are arranged with some observance of chronological order; while those in the second do not admit of such a distribution.

Many authorities, including nearly all the books upon the Revolution, have been consulted, and reference is made to those to which I am under special obligations. For the memoir of Mrs. Bache, I am indebted to the pen of Mr. William Duane, of Philadelphia, and for that of Mrs. Allen, to Mr. Henry R. Schoolcraft, of Washington. My grateful acknowledgments are due also to Mr. Jacob B. Moore, Librarian of the New York Historical Society, for valuable advice, and for facilities afforded me in examining the books and manuscripts under his charge ; and to Dr. Joseph Johnson, the Rev. James H. Saye, and the Hon. Judge O'Neall, of South Carolina, who have obligingly aided me in the collection of authentic particulars connected with the war in that State.   Others have rendered valuable assistance in the same way, and in affording me an opportunity of examining family papers in their possession.   To them all— and to those numerous friends who have encouraged me by their sympathy and kind wishes ,in this arduous but interesting task—I offer most heartfelt thanks.   If the work whose progress they have cherished should be deemed a useful contribution to American History, they will be no less gratified than myself that its design has been accomplished.

E. F. E.

THE WOMEN OF THE REVOLUTION.

ALL Americans are accustomed to view with interest and admiration the events of the Revolution. Its
scenes are vivid in their memory, and its prominent
actors are regarded with the deepest veneration. But
while the leading spirits are thus honored, attention
should be directed to the source whence their power
was derived—to the sentiment pervading the mass of
the people. The force of this sentiment, working in
the public heart, cannot be measured; because, amidst
the abundance of materials for the history of action,
there is little for that of the feeling of those times. And,
as years pass on, the investigation becomes more and
more difficult. Yet it is both interesting and important
to trace its operation. It gave statesmen their influence,
and armed heroes for victory. What could they have
done but for the home-sentiment to which they appealed,
and which sustained them in the hour of trial and
success? They were thus aided to the eminence they
gained through toils and perils. Others may claim a
share in the merit, if not the fame, of their illustrious

deeds. The unfading laurels that wreathe their brows had their root in the hearts of the people, and were nourished with their life-blood.

The feeling which wrought thus powerfully in the community depended, in great part, upon the women. It is always thus in times of popular excitement. Who can estimate, moreover, the controlling influence of early culture! During the years of the progress of British encroachment and colonial discontent, when the sagacious politician could discern the portentous shadow of events yet far distant, there was time for the nurture, in the domestic sanctuary, of that love of civil liberty, which afterwards kindled into a flame, and shed light on the world. The talk of matrons, in American homes, was of the people's wrongs, and the tyranny that oppressed them, till the sons who had grown to manhood, with strengthened aspirations towards a better state of things, and views enlarged to comprehend their invaded rights, stood up prepared to defend them to the utmost. Patriotic mothers nursed the infancy of freedom. Their counsels and their prayers mingled with the deliberations that resulted in a nation's assertion of its independence. They animated the courage, and confirmed the self-devotion of those who ventured all in the common cause. They frowned upon instances of coldness or backwardness; and in the period of deepest gloom, cheered and urged onward the desponding. They willingly shared inevitable dangers and privations, relinquished without regret prospects of advantage to themselves, and parted with those they loved better than life, not knowing when they were to meet again.   It is almost impossible now to appreciate the vast influence of woman's patriotism upon the destinies of the infant republic.   We have no means of showing the important part she bore in maintaining the struggle, and in laying the foundations on which so mighty and majestic a structure has arisen. History can do it no justice ; for history deals with the workings of the head, rather than the heart.   And the knowledge received by tradition, of the domestic manners, and social character of the times, is too im- perfect to furnish a sure index.   We can only dwell upon individual instances of magnanimity, fortitude, self-sacrifice, and heroism, bearing the impress of the feeling of Revolutionary days, indicative of the spirit which animated all, and to which, in its various and multiform exhibitions, we are not less indebted for na- tional freedom, than to the swords of the patriots who poured out their blood.

" 'Tis true, Cleander," says a writer in one of the papers of the day,* "no mean merit will accrue to him who shall justly celebrate the virtues of our ladies! Shall not their generous contributions to relieve the wants of the defenders of our country, supply a column to emulate the Roman women, stripped of their jewels .when the public necessity demanded them?"   Such tributes were often called forth by the voluntary exer- tions of American women.   Their patriotic sacrifices were made with an enthusiasm that showed the earnest

* New Jersey Gazette, October 11th, 1780.

spirit ready on every occasion to appear in generous acts. Some gave their own property, and went from house to house to solicit contributions for the army. Colors were embroidered by fair hands, and presented with the charge never to desert them; and arms and ammunition were provided by the same liberal zeal. They formed themselves into associations renouncing the use of teas, and other imported luxuries, and engaging to card, spin, and weave their own clothing. In Mecklenburgh and Rowan counties, North Carolina, young ladies of the most respectable families pledged themselves not to receive the addresses of any suitors who had not obeyed the country's call for military service.

The needy shared the fruit of their industry and economy. They visited hospitals daily; sought the dungeons of the provost, and the crowded holds of prison ships; and provisions were carried from their stores to the captives whose only means of recompense was the blessing of those who were ready to perish. Many raised grain, gathered it, made bread, and carried it to their relatives in the army, or in prisons, accompanying the supply with exhortations never to abandon the cause of their country. The burial of friends slain in battle, or chance-encounters, often devolved upon them; and even enemies would not have received sepulture without the service of their hands.

When the resources of the country scarcely allowed the scantiest supply of clothing and provisions, and British cruisers on the coast destroyed every hope of aid from merchant vessels; when, to the distressed troops, their cup of misfortune seemed full to overflowing, and there appeared no prospect of relief, except from the benevolence of their fellow-citizens; when even the ability of these was almost exhausted by repeated applications—then it was that the women of Pennsylvania and New Jersey, by their zealous exertions and willing sacrifices, accomplished what had been thought impossible.   Not only was the pressure of want removed, but the sympathy and favor of the fair daughters of America, says one of the journals, "operated like a charm on the soldier's heart—gave vigor to exertion, confidence to his hopes of success, and the ultimate certainty of victory and peace." General Washington, in his letter of acknowledgment to the committee of ladies, says, "The army ought not to regret its sacrifices or its sufferings, when they meet with so flattering a reward, as in the sympathy of your sex; nor can it fear that its interests will be neglected, when espoused by advocates as powerful as they are amiable." An officer in camp writes, in June, 1780: "The patriotism of the women of your city is a subject of conversation with the army.   Had I poetical genius, I would sit down and write an ode in praise of it.   Burgoyne, who, on his first coming to America, boasted that he would dance with the ladies, and coax the men to submission, must now have a better understanding of the good sense and public spirit of our females, as he has already heard of the fortitude and inflexible temper of our men."   Another observes: "We cannot appeal in vain for what is good, to that sanctuary where all that is good has its proper home—the female bosom."

How the influence of women was estimated by John Adams, appears from one of his letters to his wife:

"I think I have some times observed to you in conversation, that upon examining the biography of illustrious men, you will generally find some female about them, in the relation of mother, or wife, or sister, to whose instigation a great part of their merit is to be ascribed. You will find a curious example of this in the case of Aspasia, the wife of Pericles. She was a woman of the greatest beauty, and the first genius. She taught him, it is said, his refined maxims of policy, his lofty imperial eloquence, nay, even composed the speeches on which so great a share of his reputation was founded.

"I wish some of our great men had such wives. By the account in your last letter, it seems the women in Boston begin to think themselves able to serve their country. What a pity it is that our generals in the northern districts had not Aspasias to their wives.

"I believe the two Howes have not very great women for wives. If they had, we should suffer more from their exertions than we do. This is our good fortune. A smart wife would have put Howe in possession of Philadelphia a long time ago."

The venerable Major-Spalding, of Georgia, writes, in reply to an application to him for information respecting the revolutionary women of his state : "I am a very old man, and have read as much as any one I know, yet I have never known, and never read of one—no, not one!—

who did not owe high standing, or a great name, to his mother's blood, or his mother's training. My friend Randolph said he owed every thing to his mother. Mr. Jefferson's mother was a Randolph, and he acknowledged that he owed every thing to her rearing. General Washington, we all know, attributed every thing to his mother. Lord Bacon attributed much to his mother's training. And will any one doubt that even Alexander believed he owed more to the blood and lofty ambition of Olympia, than the wisdom or cunning of Philip?"

The sentiments of the women towards the brave defenders of their native land, were expressed in an address widely circulated at the time, and read in the churches of Virginia. "We know," it says—"that at a distance from the theatre of war, if we enjoy any tranquillity, it is the fruit of your watchings, your labors, your dangers. * * * * And shall we hesitate to evince to you our gratitude? Shall we hesitate to wear clothing more simple, and dress less elegant, while at the price of this small privation, we shall deserve your benedictions?"

The same spirit appears in a letter found among some papers belonging to a lady of Philadelphia. It was addressed to a British officer in Boston, and written before the Declaration of Independence. The following extract will show its character:

"I will tell you what I have done. My only brother I have sent to the camp with my prayers and blessings. I hope he will not disgrace me; I am confident he will behave with honor, and emulate the great examples he has before him; and had I twenty sons and brothers they should go. I have retrenched every superfluous expense in my table and family; tea I have not drunk since last Christmas, nor bought a new cap or gown since your defeat at Lexington; and what I never did before, have learned to knit, and am now making stockings of American wool for my servants; and this way do I throw in my mite to the public good. I know this—that as free I can die but once; but as a slave I shall not be worthy of life. I have the pleasure to assure you that these are the sentiments of all my sister Americans. They have sacrificed assemblies, parties of pleasure, tea drinking and finery, to that great spirit of patriotism that actuates all degrees of people throughout this extensive continent. If these are the sentiments of females, what must glow in the breasts of our husbands, brothers, and sons! They are as with one heart determined to die or be free. It is not a quibble in politics, a science which few understand, that we are contending for; it is this plain truth, which the most ignorant peasant knows, and is clear to the weakest capacity—that no man has a right to take their money without their consent. You say you are no politician. Oh, sir, it requires no Machiavelian head to discover this tyranny and oppression. It is written with a sunbeam. Every one will see and know it, because it will make every one feel; and we shall be unworthy of the blessings of Heaven if we ever submit to it.   *   *   *   *   *   *

*   *   *   "Heaven seems to smile on us ; for in
the memory of man, never were known such quantities
of flax, and sheep without number.   We are making
powder fast, and do not want for ammunition."

From all portions of the country thus rose the expression of woman's ardent zeal.   Under accumulated evils,
the manly spirit that alone could secure success, might
have sunk but for the firmness and intrepidity of the
weaker sex.   It supplied every persuasion that could
animate to perseverance, and secure fidelity.

The noble deeds in which this irrepressible spirit
breathed itself, were not unrewarded by persecution.
The case of the quakeress Deborah Franklin, who was
banished from New York by the British commandant
for her liberality in relieving the sufferings of the American prisoners,was one among many.   In our days of tranquillity and luxury, imagination can scarcely compass the
extent or severity of the trials endured ; and it is propor-
tionately difficult to estimate the magnanimity that bore
all, not only with uncomplaining patience, but with a
cheerful forgetfulness of suffering in view of the desired
object.   The alarms of war—the roar of the strife itself,
could not silence the voice of woman, lifted in encouragement or in prayer.   The horrors of battle or massacre
could not drive her from the post of duty.   The
effect of this devotion cannot be questioned, though
it may not now be traced in particular instances.
These were, for the most part, known only to those
who were themselves actors in the scenes, or who
lived in the midst of them.   The heroism of the Revo-

lutionary women has passed from remembrance with the generation who witnessed it; or is seen only by faint and occasional glimpses, through the gathering obscurity of tradition.

To render a measure of justice—inadequate it must be—to a few of the American matrons, whose names deserve to live in remembrance—and to exhibit something of the domestic side of the Revolutionary picture —is the object of this work. As we recede from the realities of that struggle, it is regarded with increasing interest by those who enjoy its results; while the elements which were its life-giving principle, too subtle to be retained by the grave historian, are fleeting fast from apprehension. Yet without some conception of them, the Revolution cannot be appreciated. We must enter into the spirit, as well as master the letter.

While attempting to pay a tribute but too long withheld, to the memory of women who did and endured so much in the cause of liberty, we should not be insensible to the virtues exhibited by another class, belonging equally to the history of the period. These had their share of reverse and suffering. Many saw their children and relatives espousing opposite sides; and with ardent feelings of loyalty in their hearts, were forced to weep over the miseries of their families and neighbors. Many were driven from their homes, despoiled of property, and finally compelled to cast their lot in desolate wilds and an ungenial climate.* And while their

* The ancient Acadia, comprising Nova Scotia and New Brunswick, was settled by many of the refugee loyalists from the United States.

heroism, fortitude, and spirit of self-sacrifice were not less brightly displayed, their hard lot was unpitied, and they met with no reward.

In the library of William H. Prescott, at his residence in Boston, are two swords, crossed above the arch of an alcove. One belonged to his grandfather, Colonel William Prescott, who commanded the American troops in the redoubt at Bunkerhill. The other was the sword of Captain Linzee, of the royal navy, who commanded the British sloop of war—The Falcon, then lying in the Mystic; from which the American troops were fired upon as they crossed to Bunkerhill. Captain Linzee was the grandfather of Mrs. Prescott. The swords of those two gallant soldiers who fought on different sides upon that memorable day—now in the possession of their united descendants, and crossed—an emblem of peace, in the library of the great American historian—are emblematic of the spirit in which our history should be written. Such be the spirit in which we view the loyalists of those days.

I.

———————

MARY WASHINGTON.

THE MOTHER OF WASHINGTON! There needs no eulogy to awaken the associations which cling around that sacred name. Our hearts do willing homage to the venerated parent of the chief—

> " Who 'mid his elements of being wrought
> With no uncertain aim—nursing the germs
> Of godlike virtue in his infant mind."

The contemplation of Washington's character naturally directs attention to her whose maternal care guided and guarded his early years. What she did, and the blessing of a world that follows her—teach impressively —while showing the power—the duty of those who mould the characters of the age to come. The principles and conduct of this illustrious matron were closely interwoven with the destinies of her son. Washington ever acknowledged that he owed everything to his mother—in the education and habits of his early life. His high moral principle, his perfect self-possession, his clear and sound judgment, his inflexible resolution and untiring application—were developed by her training and example. A believer in the truths of religion, she inculcated a strict obedience to its injunctions. She planted the seed, and cherished the growth, which bore such rich and glorious fruit. La Fayette observed that she belonged rather to the age of Sparta or Rome, than to modern times; she was a mother formed on the ancient model, and by her elevation of character and matchless discipline, fitted to lay the foundation of the greatness of him who towered "beyond all Greek— beyond all Roman fame."

The course of Mrs. Washington's life, exhibiting her qualities of mind and heart, proved her fitness for the high trust committed to her hands. She was remarkable for vigor of intellect, strength of resolution, and inflexible firmness wherever principle was concerned. Devoted to the education of her children, her parental government and guidance have been described by those who knew her as admirably adapted to train the youthful mind to wisdom and virtue. With her, affection was regulated by a calm and just judgment. She was distinguished, moreover, by that well marked quality of genius, a power of acquiring and maintaining influence over those with whom she associated. Without inquiring into the philosophy of this mysterious ascendancy, she was content to employ it for the noblest ends. It contributed, no doubt, to deepen the effect of her instructions.

The life of Mrs. Washington, so useful in the domestic sphere, did not abound in incident. She passed through the trials common to those who lived amid the scenes of

2

the Revolutionary era.   She saw the son whom she had taught to be *good*—whom she had reared in the principles of true honor, walking the perilous path of duty with firm step, leading his country to independence, and crowned with his reward—a nation's gratitude; yet in all these changes, her simple, earnest nature remained the same.   She loved to speak, in her latter days, of her boy's merits in his early life, and of his filial affection and duty; but never dwelt on the glory he had won as the deliverer of his country, the chief magistrate of a great republic.   This was because her ambition was too high for the pride that inspires and rewards common souls.   The greatness she discerned and acknowledged in the object of her solicitous tenderness was beyond that which this world most esteems.

The only memoir of the mother of Washington extant, is the one written by George W. P. Custis, the grandson of Martha Washington, and published more than twenty years ago in his "Recollections" in the National Gazette. These reminiscences were collected by him in the course of many years; and to them we are indebted for all that is known of the life and actions of this matron. According to these, she was descended from the respectable family of Ball, who came to this country and settled on the banks of the Potomac.   In the old days of Virginia, women were taught habits of industry and self-reliance, and in these Mrs. Washington was nurtured.   The early death of her husband involved her in the cares of a young family with limited resources, which rendered prudence and economy necessary to

provide for and educate her children. Thus circum-
stanced, it was left to her unassisted efforts to form in
her son's mind, those essential qualities which gave tone
and character to his subsequent life. George was only
twelve years old at his father's death, and retained
merely the remembrance of his person, and his parental
fondness. Two years after this event, he obtained a
midshipman's warrant; but his mother opposed the plan,
and the idea of entering the naval service was relinquished.

The home in which Mrs. Washington presided, was
a sanctuary of the domestic virtues. The levity of
youth was there tempered by a well regulated restraint,
and the enjoyments rational and proper for that age
were indulged in with moderation. The future chief
was taught the duty of obedience, and was thus prepared to command. The mother's authority never
departed from her, even when her son had attained the
height of his renown; for she ruled by the affection
which had controlled his spirit when he needed a guardian; and she claimed a reverence next to that due to
his Creator. This claim he admitted, mingling the
deepest respect with enthusiastic attachment, and yielding to her will the most implicit obedience, even to the
latest hours of her life. One of the associates of his
juvenile years, Lawrence Washington, of Chotank,
thus speaks of his home:

"I was often there with George, his playmate, school-
mate, and young man's companion. Of the mother I
was ten times more afraid than I ever was of my own

parents; she awed me in the midst of her kindness, for she was indeed truly kind.   And even now, when time has whitened my locks, and I am the grandparent of a second generation, I could not behold that majestic woman without feelings it is impossible to describe. Whoever has seen that awe-inspiring air and manner, so characteristic of the Father of his country, will remember the matron as she appeared, the presiding genius of her well-ordered household, commanding and being obeyed."   Educated under such influences, it is not to be wondered at that Washington's deportment towards his mother at all times, testified his appreciation of her elevated character, and the excellence of her lessons.

"On his appointment to the command-in-chief of the American armies," says Mr. Custis, "previously to his joining the forces at Cambridge, he removed his mother from her country residence, to the village of Fredericksburg, a situation remote from danger and contiguous to her friends and relatives.   There she remained, during nearly the whole of the trying period of the Revolution. Directly in the way of the news, as it passed from north to south; one courier would bring intelligence of success to our arms; another, "swiftly coursing at his heels," the saddening reverse of disaster and defeat.   While thus ebbed and flowed the fortunes of our cause, the mother, trusting to the wisdom and protection of Divine Providence, preserved the even tenor of her life; affording an example to those matrons whose sons were alike engaged in the arduous contest; and showing that unavailing anxieties, however belonging to nature, were unworthy of mothers whose sons were combating for the inestimable rights of man, and the freedom and happiness of the world."

When news arrived of the passage of the Delaware in December, 1776, the mother received calmly the patriots who came with congratulations; and while expressing pleasure at the intelligence, disclaimed for her son the praises in the letters from which extracts were read. When informed by express of the surrender of Cornwallis, she lifted her hands in gratitude towards heaven, and exclaimed, " Thank God ! war will now be ended, and peace, independence and happiness bless our country !"

Her housewifery, industry, and care in the management of her domestic concerns, were not intermitted during the war. "She looketh well to the ways of her household," and "worketh willingly with her hands," said the wise man, in describing a virtuous woman; and it was the pride of the exemplary women of that day, to fill the station of mistress with usefulness as well as dignity. Mrs. Washington was remarkable for a simplicity which modern refinement might call severe, but which became her not less when her fortunes were clouded, than when the sun of glory arose upon her house. Some of the aged inhabitants of Fredericksburg long remembered the matron, "as seated in an old-fashioned open chaise she was in the habit of visiting, almost daily, her little farm in the vicinity of the town. When there, she would ride about her fields, giving her orders and seeing that they were obeyed." When on one occasion an agent departed from his instructions— she reproved him for exercising his own judgment in the matter; "I command you," she said; there is nothing left for you but to obey."

Her charity to the poor was well known; and having not wealth to distribute, it was necessary that what her benevolence dispensed should be supplied by domestic economy and industry. How peculiar a grace does this impart to the benefits flowing from a sympathizing heart!

It is thus that she has been pictured in the imagination of one of our most gifted poets.*

> " Methinks we see thee, as in olden time,
>   Simple in garb, majestic and serene,—
>   Unawed by 'pomp and circumstance'—in truth
>   Inflexible—and with a Spartan zeal
>   Repressing vice, and making folly grave.
>   *Thou* didst not deem it woman's part to waste
>   Life in inglorious sloth, to sport awhile
>   Amid the flowers, or on the summer wave,
>   Then fleet like the ephemèron away,
>   Building no temple in her children's hearts,
>   Save to the vanity and pride of life
>   Which she had worshipped."

Mr. Custis states that she was continually visited and solaced, in the retirement of her declining years, by her children and numerous grandchildren. Her daughter,

---

* Mrs. Sigourney, in her poetical tribute on the occasion of laying the corner-stone for the monument.

Mrs. Lewis, repeatedly and earnestly solicited her to remove to her house, and there pass the remainder of her days. Her son pressingly entreated her that she would make Mount Vernon the home of her age. But the matron's answer was : " I thank you for your affectionate and dutiful offers, but my wants are few in this world, and I feel perfectly competent to take care of myself." To the proposition of her son-in-law, Colonel Lewis, to relieve her by taking the direction of her concerns, she replied: " Do you, Fielding, keep my books in order; for your eyesight is better than mine : but leave the executive management to me." Such were the energy and independence she preserved to an age beyond that usually allotted to mortals, and till within three years of her death, when the disease under which she suffered (cancer of the breast), prevented exertion.

Her meeting with Washington, after the victory which decided the fortune of America, illustrates her character too strikingly to be omitted. "After an absence of nearly seven years, it was, at length, on the return of the combined armies from Yorktown, permitted to the mother again to see and embrace her illustrious son. So soon as he had dismounted, in the midst of a numerous and brilliant suite, he sent to apprize her of his arrival, and to know when it would be her pleasure to receive him. And now, mark the force of early education and habits, and the superiority of the Spartan over the Persian schools, in this interview of the great Washington with his admirable parent and instructor. No pa-

geantry of war proclaimed his coming—no trumpets
sounded—no banners waved. Alone, and on foot, the
marshal of France, the general-in-chief of the combined armies of France and America, the deliverer of
his country, the hero of the age, repaired to pay his
humble duty to her whom he venerated as the author
of his being, the founder of his fortune and his fame.
For full well he knew that the matron was made of
sterner stuff than to be moved by all the pride that
glory ever gave, or by all the 'pomp and circumstance'
of power.

   " The lady was alone—her aged hands employed in
the works of domestic industry, when the good news
was announced ; and it was further told, that the victor-
chief was in waiting at the threshold. She welcomed
him with a warm embrace, and by the well-remembered
and endearing names of his childhood. Inquiring as
to his health, she remarked the lines which mighty cares,
and many trials, had made on his manly countenance—
spoke much of old times, and old friends ; but of his
glory, *not one word!*

   "Meantime, in the village of Fredericksburg, all
was joy and revelry. The town was crowded with
the officers of the French and American armies, and
with gentlemen from all the country around, who hastened to welcome the conquerors of Cornwallis. The
citizens made arrangements for a splendid ball, to which
the mother of Washington was specially invited. She
observed, that although her dancing days were *pretty*

well over, she should feel happy in contributing to the general festivity, and consented to attend.

"The foreign officers were anxious to see the mother of their chief. They had heard indistinct rumors respecting her remarkable life and character; but forming their judgment from European examples, they were prepared to expect in the mother, that glare and show which would have been attached to the parents of the great in the old world. How were they surprized when the matron, leaning on the arm of her son, entered the room! She was arrayed in the very plain, yet becoming garb worn by the Virginia lady of the olden time. Her address, always dignified and imposing, was courteous, though reserved. She received the complimentary attentions which were profusely paid her, without evincing the slightest elevation; and at an early hour, wishing the company much enjoyment of their pleasures, and observing that it was time for old people to be at home, retired, leaning as before, on the arm of her son."

To this picture may be added another:

"The Marquis de La Fayette repaired to Fredericksburg, previous to his departure for Europe, in the fall of 1784, to pay his parting respects to the mother, and to ask her blessing. Conducted by one of her grandsons, he approached the house, when the young gentleman observed: 'There, sir, is my grandmother.' La Fayette beheld—working in the garden, clad in domestic-made clothes, and her gray head covered with a plain straw hat—the mother of 'his hero, his friend and

2*

a country's preserver!' The lady saluted him kindly, observing, 'Ah, marquis! you see an old woman; but come, I can make you welcome to my poor dwelling, without the parade of changing my dress.'"

To the encomiums lavished by the marquis on his chief, the mother replied: "I am not surprised at what George has done, for he was always a very good boy." So simple in her true greatness of soul, was this remarkable woman.

Her piety was ardent; and she associated devotion with the grand and beautiful in nature. She was in the habit of repairing every day for prayer to a secluded spot, formed by rocks and trees, near her dwelling.

After the organization of the government, Washington repaired to Fredericksburg, to announce to his mother his election to the chief magistracy, and bid her farewell, before assuming the duties of his office. Her aged frame was bowed down by disease; and she felt that they were parting to meet no more in this world. But she bade him go, with heaven's blessing and her own, to fulfil the high destinies to which he had been called. Washington was deeply affected, and wept at the parting.

The person of Mrs. Washington is described as being of the medium height, and well proportioned—her features pleasing, though strongly marked. There were few painters in the colonies in those days, and no portrait of her is in existence. Her biographer saw her but with infant eyes; but well remembers the sister of the chief. Of her we are told nothing, except that "she was a most majestic woman, and so strikingly like the brother, that it was a matter of frolic to throw a cloak around her, and place a military hat upon her head; and such was the perfect resemblance, that had she appeared on her brother's steed, battalions would have presented arms, and senates risen to do homage to the chief."

Mrs. Washington died at the age of eighty-five, rejoicing in the consciousness of a life well spent, and the hope of a blessed immortality. Her ashes repose at Fredericksburg, where a splendid monument has been erected to her memory.

II.

~~~~~~~~

ESTHER REED.

ESTHER DE BERDT was born in the city of London, on the 22d of October, 1746, (N. S.,) and died at Philadelphia on the 18th of September, 1780. Her thirty-four years of life were adorned by no adventurous heroism; but were thickly studded with the brighter beauties of feminine endurance, uncomplaining self-sacrifice, and familiar virtue—under trials, too, of which civil war is so fruitful. She was an only daughter. Her father, Dennis De Berdt, was a British merchant, largely interested in colonial trade. He was a man of high character. Descended from the Huguenots, or French Flemings, who came to England on the revocation of the Edict of Nantes, Mr. De Berdt's pure and rather austere religious sentiments and practice were worthy of the source whence they came. His family were educated according to the strictest rule of the evangelical piety of their day—the day when devotion, frozen out of high places, found refuge in humble dissenting chapels —the day of Wesley and of Whitfield. Miss De Berdt's youth was trained religiously; and she was to the end of life true to the principles of her education. The simple devotion she had learned from an aged

ESTHER DE BERDT.

E. DeBerdt

father's lips, alleviated the trials of youth, and brightened around her early grave.

Mr. De Berdt's house in London, owing to his business relations with the Colonies, was the home of
many young Americans who at that time were attracted by pleasure or duty to the imperial metropolis.
Among these visitors, in or about the year 1763, was
Joseph Reed, of New Jersey, who had come to London
to finish his professional studies (such being the fashion
of the times) at the Temple. Mr. Reed was in the
twenty-third year of his age—a man of education, intelligence, and accomplishment. The intimacy, thus
accidentally begun, soon produced its natural fruits;
and an engagement, at first secret, and afterwards
avowed, was formed between the young English girl
and the American stranger. Parental discouragement,
so wise that even youthful impetuosity could find no
fault with it, was entirely inadequate to break a connection thus formed. They loved long and faithfully—how
faithfully, the reader will best judge when he learns
that a separation of five years of deferred hope, with
the Atlantic between them, never gave rise to a wan-
dering wish, or hope, or thought.

Mr. Reed, having finished his studies, returned to
America, in the early part of 1765, and began the practice of the law in his native village of Trenton. His
success was immediate and great. But there was a
distracting element at work in his heart, which prevented him from looking on success with complacency;
and one plan after another was suggested, by which he

might be enabled to return and settle in Great Britain.
That his young and gentle mistress should follow him
to America, was a vision too wild even for a sanguine lover.   Every hope was directed back to England ; and the correspondence, the love letters of five
long years, are filled with plans by which these cherished, but delusive wishes were to be consummated.   How
dimly was the future seen !

Miss De Berdt's engagement with her American lover,
was coincident with that dreary period of British history, when a monarch and his ministers were laboring
hard to tear from its socket, and cast away for ever, the
brightest jewel of the imperial crown—American colonial power.   It was the interval when Chatham's voice
was powerless to arouse the Nation, and make Parliament pause—when penny-wise politicians, in the happy
phrase of the day, "*teased America into resistance;*"
and the varied vexations of stamp acts, and revenue bills,
and tea duties, the congenial fruits of poor statesman-
ship, were the means by which a great catastrophe was
hurried onward.   Mr. De Berdt's relations with Government were, in some respects, direct and intimate.
His house was a place of counsel for those who sought,
by moderate and constitutional means, to stay the hand
of misgovernment and oppression.   He was the Agent
of the Stamp Act Congress first, and of the Colonies
of Delaware and Massachusetts, afterwards.   And most
gallantly did the brave old man discharge the duty which
his American constituents confided to him.   His heart
was in his trust; and we may well imagine the alterna-

tions of feeling which throbbed in the bosom of his daughter, as she shared in the consultations of this almost American household; and according to the fitful changes of time and opinion, counted the chances of discord that might be fatal to her peace, or of honorable pacification which should bring her lover home to her. Miss De Berdt's letters, now in the possession of her descendants, are full of allusions to this varying state of things, and are remarkable for the sagacious good sense which they develope. She is, from first to last, a stout American. Describing a visit to the House of Commons, in April, 1766, her enthusiasm for Mr. Pitt is unbounded, while she does not disguise her repugnance to George Grenville and Wedderburn, whom she says she cannot bear, because "*they are such enemies to America.*" So it is throughout, in every line she writes, in every word she utters; and thus was she, unconsciously, receiving that training which in the end was to fit her for an American patriot's wife.

Onward, however, step by step, the Monarch and his Ministry—he, if possible, more infatuated than they—advanced in the career of tyrannical folly. Remonstrance was vain. They could not be persuaded that it would ever become resistance. In 1769 and 1770, the crisis was almost reached. Five years of folly had done it all. In the former of these years, the lovers were re-united, Mr. Reed returning on an uncertain visit to England. He found everything, but her faithful affection, changed. Political disturbance had had its usual train of commercial disaster ; and Mr. De Berdt had not only become bankrupt, but unable to rally on such a reverse in old age, had sunk into his grave. All was ruin and confusion ; and on the 31st of May, 1770, Esther De Berdt became an American wife, the wedding being privately solemnized at St. Luke's Church, in the city of London.

In October, the young couple sailed for America, arriving at Philadelphia in November, 1770. Mr. Reed immediately changed his residence from Trenton to Philadelphia, where he continued to live. Mrs. Reed's correspondence with her brother and friends in England, during the next five years, has not been preserved. It would have been interesting, as showing the impressions made on an intelligent mind by the primitive state of society and modes of life in these wild Colonies, some eighty years ago, when Philadelphia was but a large village—when the best people lived in Front street, or on the water-side, and an Indian frontier was within an hundred miles of the Schuylkill. They are, however, all lost. The influence of Mrs. Reed's foreign connections can be traced only in the interesting correspondence between her husband and Lord Dartmouth, during the years 1774 and 1775, which has been recently given to the public, and which narrates, in the most genuine and trust-worthy form, the progress of colonial discontent in the period immediately anterior to actual revolution. In all the initiatory measures of peaceful resistance, Mr. Reed, as is well known, took a large and active share ; and in all he did, he had his young wife's ardent sympathy. The English girl had grown at once into the American matron.

Philadelphia was then the heart of the nation. It beat generously and boldly when the news of Lexington and Bunker's Hill startled the whole land. Volunteer troops were raised—money in large sums was remitted, much through Mr. Reed's direct agency, for the relief of the sufferers in New England, At last, a new and controlling incident here occurred. It was in Philadelphia that, walking in the State House yard, John Adams first suggested Washington as the National Commander-in-chief; and from Philadelphia that in June, 1775, Washington set out, accompanied by the best citizens of the liberal party, to enter on his duties.*

* As this memoir was in preparation, the writer's eye was attracted by a notice of the Philadelphia obsequies of John Q. Adams, in March, 1848. It is from the New York Courier and Enquirer :

" That part of the ceremonial which was most striking, more impressive than any thing I have ever seen, was the approach through the old State House yard to Independence Hall. I have stood by Napoleon's dramatic mausoleum in the Invalides, and mused over the more simple tomb of Nelson, lying by the side of Collingwood, in the crypt of St. Paul's ; but, no impression was made like that of yesterday. The multitude—for the crowd had grown into one—being strictly excluded from the square, filled the surrounding streets and houses, and gazed silently on the simple ceremonial before them. It was sunset, or nearly so—a calm, bright spring evening. There was no cheering, no disturbance, no display of banners, no rude sound of drum. The old trees were leafless ; and no- one's free vision was disappointed. The funeral escort proper, consisting of the clergy, comprising representatives of nearly all denominations, the committee of Congress, and the city authorities—in all, not exceeding a

Mr. Reed accompanied him, as his family supposed, and as he probably intended, only as part of an escort, for a short distance. From New York he wrote to his wife that, yielding to the General's solicitations, he had become a soldier, and joined the staff as Aid, and Military Secretary. The young mother—for she was then watching by the cradle of two infant children—neither repined nor murmured. She knew that it was no restless freak, or transient appetite for excite-

hundred, with the body and pall bearers, alone were admitted. They walked slowly up the middle path from the south gate, no sound being heard at the point from which I saw it, but the distant and gentle music of one military band near the Hall, and the deep tones of our ancient bell that rang when Independence was proclaimed. The military escort, the company of Washington Greys, whose duty it was to guard the body during the night, presented arms as the coffin went by; and as the procession approached the Hall, the clergy, and all others, uncovered themselves, and, as if awed by the genius of the place, approached reverently and solemnly. This simple and natural act of respect, or rather reverence, was most touching. It was a thing never to be forgotten. This part of the ceremonial was what I should like a foreigner to see. It was genuine and simple.

"And thoughout, remember, illusion had nothing to do with it. These were simple, actual realities, that thus stirred the heart. It was no empty memorial coffin; but here were the actual honored remains of one who was part of our history—the present, the recent, and remote past. And who could avoid thinking, if any spark of consciousness remained in the old man's heart, it might have brightened as he was borne along by the best men of Philadelphia, on this classic path, in the shadow of this building, and to the sound of this bell. The last of the days of Washington was going by, and it was traversing the very spot, where, seventy years ago, John Adams had first suggested Washington as Commander-in-chief of the army of the Revolution. It reposed last night in Independence Hall."

ment, that took away her husband; for no one was more conscious than she, how dear his cheerful home was, and what sweet companionship there was in the mother and her babes. It was not difficult to be satisfied that a high sense of duty was his controlling influence, and that hers it was "to love and be silent."

At Philadelphia she remained during Mr. Reed's first tour of duty at Cambridge; and afterwards, in 1776, when being appointed Adjutant-General, he rejoined the army at New York. In the summer of that year, she took her little family to Burlington; and in the winter, on the approach of the British invading forces, took deeper refuge at a little farm-house near Evesham, and at no great distance from the edge of the Pines.

We, contented citizens of a peaceful land, can form little conception of the horrors and desolation of those ancient times of trial. The terrors of invasion are things which now-a-days imagination can scarcely compass. But then, it was rugged reality. The unbridled passions of a mercenary soldiery, compounded not only of-the brutal element that forms the vigor of every army, but of the ferocity of Hessians, hired and paid for violence and rapine, were let loose on the land. The German troops, as if to inspire especial terror, were sent in advance, and occupied, in December, 1776, a chain of posts extending from Trenton to Mount Holly, Rhal commanding at the first, and Donop at the other. General Howe, and his main army, were rapidly advancing by the great route to the Delaware. On the other hand, the river was filled with American gondolas, whose crews, landing from time to time on the Jersey shore, by their lawlessness, and threats of retaliation, kept the pacific inhabitants in continual alarm. The American army, if it deserved the name, was literally scattered along the right bank of the Delaware ; Mr. Reed being with a small detachment of Philadelphia volunteers, under Cadwalader, at Bristol.

Family tradition has described the anxious hours passed by the sorrowing group at Evesham. It consisted of Mrs. Reed, who had recently been confined, and was in feeble health, her three children, an aged mother, and a female friend, also a soldier's wife: the only male attendant being a boy of fourteen or fifteen years of age. If the enemy were to make a sudden advance, they would be entirely cut off from the ordinary avenues of escape ; and precautions were taken to avoid this risk. The wagon was ready, to be driven by the boy we have spoken of, and the plan was matured, if they failed to get over the river at Dunk's or Cooper's Ferry, to cross lower down, near Salem, and push on to the westward settlements. The wives and children of American patriot-soldiers thought themselves safer on the perilous edge of an Indian wilderness, than in the neighborhood of the soldiers who, commanded by noblemen—by "men of honor and cavaliers," for such, according to all heraldry, were the Howes and Cornwallises, the Percies and Rawdons of that day—were sent by a gracious monarch to lay waste this land. The English campaigning of our Revolution—and no part of it more so than this—is the darkest among the dark stains that disfigure the history of the eighteenth century ; and if ever there be a ground for hereditary animosity, we have it in the fresh record of the outrages which the military arm of Great Britain committed on this soil. The transplanted sentimentalism which now-a-days calls George III. a wise and great monarch, is absolute treason to America. There was in the one Colony of New Jersey, and in a single year, blood enough shed, and misery enough produced, to outweigh all the spurious merits which his admirers can pre-tend to claim. And let such for ever be the judgment of American history.

It is worth a moment's meditation to pause and think of the sharp contrasts in our heroine's life. The short in-terval of less than six years had changed her not merely to womanhood, but to womanhood with extraordinary trials. Her youth was passed in scenes of peaceful prosperity, with no greater anxiety than for a distant lover, and with all the comforts which independence and social position could supply. She had crossed the ocean a bride, content to follow the fortunes of her young husband, though she little dreamed what they were to be. She had become a mother ; and, while watching by the cradle of her infants, had seen her household broken up by war in its worst form—the in-ternecine conflict of brothers in arms against each other —her husband called away to scenes of bloody peril, and forced, herself, to seek uncertain refuge in a wilderness. She too, let it be remembered, was a native-born Eng-

lishwoman, with all the loyal sentiments that beat by
instinct in an Englishwoman's heart—reverence for the
throne, the monarch, and for all the complex institutions
which hedge that mysterious oracular thing called the
British Constitution. "God save the king," was neither
then, nor is it now, a formal prayer on the lips of a
British maiden. Coming to America, all this was
changed. Loyalty was a badge of crime. The king's
friends were her husband's and her new country's
worst enemies. That which, in the parks of London,
or at the Horse-Guards, she had admired as the holiday
pageantry of war, had become the fearful apparatus of
savage hostility. She, an Englishwoman, was a fugitive from the brutality of English soldiers. Her destiny, her fortunes, and more than all, her thoughts,
and hopes, and wishes, were changed ; and happy
was it for her husband that they were changed completely and thoroughly, and that her faith to household
loyalty was exclusive.

Hers it was, renouncing all other allegiance—

> "In war or peace, in sickness, or in health,
>   In trouble and in danger, and distress,
>   Through time and through eternity, to love."

"I have received," she writes, in June, 1777, to her
husband, "both my friend's letters. They have contributed to raise my spirits, which, though low enough,
are better than when you parted with me. The reflection how much I pain you by my want of resolution,
and the double distress I occasion you, when I ought

to make your duty as light as possible, would tend to depress my spirits, did I not consider that the best and only amends is, to endeavor to resume my cheerfulness, and regain my usual spirits. I wish you to know, my dearest friend, that I have done this as much as possible, and beg you to free your mind from every care on this head."

But to return to the narrative—interrupted, naturally, by thoughts like these. The reverses which the British army met at Trenton and Princeton, with the details of which every one is presumed to be familiar, saved that part of New Jersey where Mrs. Reed and her family resided, from further danger; and on the retreat of the enemy, and the consequent relief of Philadelphia from further alarm, she returned to her home. She returned there with pride as well as contentment; for her husband, inexperienced soldier as he was, had earned military fame of no slight eminence. He had been in nearly every action, and always distinguished. Washington had, on all occasions, and at last in an especial manner, peculiarly honored him. The patriots of Philadelphia hailed him back among them; and the wife's smile of welcome was not less bright because she looked with pride upon her husband.

Brief, however, was the new period of repose. The English generals, deeply mortified at their discomfiture in New Jersey, resolved on a new and more elaborate attempt on Philadelphia; and in July, 1777, set sail with the most complete equipment they had yet been able to prepare, for the capes of the Chesapeake. On the land-

ing of the British army at the head of Elk, and during
the military movements that followed, Mrs. Reed was
at Norristown, and there remained, her husband having
again joined the army, till after the battle of Brandywine, when she and her children were removed first to
Burlington, and thence to Flemington. Mr. Reed's
hurried letters show the imminent danger that even
women and children ran in those days of confusion.
" It is quite uncertain," he writes on 14th September,
1777, "which way the progress of the British army
may point. Upon their usual plan of movement, they
will cross, or endeavor to cross, the Schuylkill, somewhere near my house ; in which case I shall be very
dangerously situated. If you could possibly spare Cato,
with your light wagon, to be with me to assist in getting off if there should be necessity, I shall be very
glad. I have but few things beside the women and
children ; but yet, upon a push, one wagon and two
horses would be too little." Mrs. Reed's letters show
her agonized condition, alarmed as she was, at the continual and peculiar risk her husband was running. A
little later (in February, 1778), Mrs. Reed says, in writing to a dear female friend : " This season which used
to be so long and tedious, has, to me, been swift, and
no sooner come than nearly gone. Not from the pleasures it has brought, but the fears of what is to come ;
and, indeed, on many accounts, winter has become the
only season of peace and safety. Returning spring
will, I fear, bring a return of bloodshed and destruction
to our country. That it must do so to this part of it,

seems unavoidable; and how much of the distress we may feel before we are able to move from it, I am unable to say. I sometimes fear a great deal. It has already become too dangerous for Mr. Reed to be at home more than one day at a time, and that seldom and uncertain. Indeed, I am easiest when he is from home, as his being here brings danger with it. There are so many disaffected to the cause of their country, that they lie in wait for those who are active; but I trust that the same kind presiding Power which has preserved him from the hands of his enemies, will still do it."

Nor were her fears unreasonable. The neighborhood of Philadelphia, after it fell into the hands of the enemy, was infested by gangs of armed loyalists, who threatened the safety of every patriot whom they encountered. Tempted by the hard money which the British promised them, they dared any danger, and were willing to commit any enormity. It was these very ruffians, and their wily abettors, for whom afterwards so much false sympathy was invoked. Mr. Reed and his family, though much exposed, happily escaped these dangers.

During the military operations of the Autumn of 1777, Mr. Reed was again attached as a volunteer to Washington's staff, and during the winter that followed—the worst that America's soldiers saw—he was at, or in the immediate neighborhood, of Valley Forge, as one of a committee of Congress, of which body he had some time before been chosen a member. Mrs. Reed with her mother and her little family took refuge at Flemington, in the upper part of New Jersey. She remained there

3

till after the evacuation of Philadelphia and the battle of Monmouth, in June, 1778.

While thus separated from her husband, and residing at Flemington, new domestic misfortune fell on her, in the death of one of her children by small-pox. How like an affectionate heart-stricken mother is the following passage, from a letter written at that time. Though it has no peculiar beauty of style, there is a touching genuineness which every reader—at least those who know a mother's heart under such affliction—will appreciate.

"Surely," says she, "my affliction has had its aggravation, and I cannot help reflecting on my neglect of my dear lost child. For thoughtful and attentive to my own situation, I did not take the necessary precaution to prevent that fatal disorder when it was in my power. Surely I ought to take blame to myself. I would not do it to aggravate my sorrow, but to learn a lesson of humility, and more caution and prudence in future. Would to God I could learn every lesson intended by the stroke. I think sometimes of my loss with composure, acknowledging the wisdom, right, and even the kindness of the dispensation. Again I feel it overcome me, and strike the very bottom of my heart, and tell me *the work is not yet finished.*"

Nor was it finished, though in a sense different from what she apprehended. Her children were spared, but her own short span of life was nearly run. Trial and perplexity and separation from home and husband were doing their work. Mrs. Reed returned to Philadelphia, the seat of actual warfare being for ever removed,

to apparent comfort and high social position. In the
fall of 1778, Mr. Reed was elected President, or in the
language of our day, Governor of Pennsylvania. His
administration, its difficulties and ultimate success
belong to the history of the country, and have been
elsewhere illustrated. It was from first to last a period of
intense political excitement, and Mr. Reed was the high
target at which the sharp and venomous shafts of party
virulence were chiefly shot.

The suppressed poison of loyalism mingled with the
ferocity of ordinary political animosity, and the scene
was in every respect discreditable to all concerned.
Slander of every sort was freely propagated. Personal
violence was threatened. Gentlemen went armed in
the streets of Philadelphia. Folly on one hand and
fanaticism on the other, put in jeopardy the lives of
many distinguished citizens, in October, 1779, and
Mr. Reed by his energy and discretion saved them.
There is extant a letter from his wife, written to a friend,
on the day of what is well known in Philadelphia, as
the Fort Wilson riot, dated at Germantown, which
shows her fears for her husband's safety were not less
reasonable, when he was exposed to the fury of an
excited populace, than to the legitimate hostility of an
enemy on the field of battle :

"Dear Sir :—I would not take a moment of your time
to tell you the distress and anxiety I feel, but only to beg
you to let me know in what state things are, and what is
likely to be the consequence. I write not to Mr. Reed
because I know he is not in a situation to attend to me.

I conjure you by the friendship you have for Mr. Reed, don't leave him.—E. R."

And throughout this scene of varied perplexity, when the heart of the statesman was oppressed by trouble without—disappointment, ingratitude—all that makes a politician's life so wretched, he was sure to find his home happy, his wife smiling and contented, with no visible sorrow to impair her welcome, and no murmur to break the melody of domestic joy. It sustained him to the end. This was humble, homely heroism, but it did its good work in cheering and sustaining a spirit that might otherwise have broken. Let those disparage it who have never had the solace which such companionship affords, or who never have known the bitter sorrow of its loss.

In May, 1780, Mrs. Reed's youngest son was born. It was of him, that Washington, a month later wrote, "I warmly thank you for calling the young Christian by my name," and it was he who more than thirty years afterwards, died in the service of his country,* not less gloriously because his was not a death of triumph. It was in the fall of this year, that the ladies of Philadelphia united in their remarkable and generous contribution for the relief of the suffering soldiers, by supplying them with clothing. Mrs. Reed was placed, by their united suffrage, at the head of this association. The

---

* George Washington Reed, a Commander in the U. S. Navy, died a prisoner of war in Jamaica, in 1813. He refused a parole, because unwilling to leave his crew in a pestilential climate; and himself perished.

French Secretary of Legation, M. de Marbois, in a letter that has been published, tells her she is called to the office as "the best patriot, the most zealous and active, and the most attached to the interests of her country." Notwithstanding the feeble state of her health, Mrs. Reed entered upon her duties with great animation. The work was congenial to her feelings. It was charity in its genuine form and from its purest source—the voluntary outpouring from the heart. It was not stimulated by the excitements of our day—neither fancy fairs, nor bazaars; but the American women met, and seeing the necessity that asked interposition, relieved it. They solicited money and other contributions directly, and for a precise and avowed object. They labored with their needles and sacrificed their trinkets and jewelry. The result was very remarkable. The aggregate amount of contributions in the City and County of Philadelphia, was not less than 7,500 dollars, specie; much of it, too, paid in hard money, at a time of the greatest appreciation. "All ranks of society," says President Reed's biographer, "seem to have joined in the liberal effort, from Phillis, the colored woman, with her humble seven shillings and six pence, to the Marchioness de La Fayette, who contributed one hundred guineas in specie, and the Countess de Luzerne, who gave six thousand dollars in continental paper." La Fayette's gentlemanly letter to Mrs. Reed is worth preserving.

HEAD QUARTERS, *June the 25th*, 1780.

MADAM,

In admiring the new resolution, in which the fair ones of Philadelphia have taken the lead, I am induced to feel for those American ladies, who being out of the Continent cannot participate in this patriotic measure. I know of one who, heartily wishing for a personal acquaintance with the ladies of America, would feel particularly happy to be admitted among them on the present occasion. Without presuming to break in upon the rules of your respected association, may I most humbly present myself as her ambassador to the confederate ladies, and solicit in her name that Mrs. President be pleased to accept of her offering.

With the highest respect, I have the honor to be,

Madam, your most obedient servant,

LA FAYETTE.

Mrs. Reed's correspondence with the Commander-in-chief on the subject of the mode of administering relief to the poor soldiers, has been already published,* and is very creditable to both parties. Her letters are marked by business-like intelligence and sound feminine common sense, on subjects of which as a secluded women she could have personally no previous knowledge, and Washington, as has been truly observed, "writes as judiciously on the humble topic of soldier's shirts, as on the plan of a campaign or the subsistence of an army."

All this time, it must be born in mind, it was a feeble, delicate woman, who was thus writing and laboring, her husband again away from her with the army, and her family cares and anxieties daily multiplying. She

* Life and Correspondence of President Reed

writes from her country residence on the banks of Schuylkill, as late as the 22d of August, 1780 : "I am most anxious to get to town, because here I can do little for the soldiers." But the body and the heroic spirit were alike overtasked, and in the early part of the next month, alarming disease developed itself, and soon ran its fatal course.   On the 18th of September, 1780—her aged mother, her husband and little children, the oldest ten years old, mourning around her—she breathed her last at the early age of thirty-four.   There was deep and honest sorrow in Philadelphia, when the news was circulated that Mrs. Reed was dead.   It stilled for a moment the violence of party spirit.   All classes united in a hearty tribute to her memory.

Nor is it inappropriate in closing this brief memoir, to notice a coincidence in local history; a contrast in the career and fate of two women of these times, which is strongly picturesque.

It was on the 25th of September, 1780, seven days after Mrs. Reed was carried to her honored grave, and followed thither by crowds of her own and her husband's friends, that the wife of Benedict Arnold, a native born Philadelphia woman, was stunned by the news of her husband's detected treachery and dishonor.   Let those who doubt the paramount duty of every man and every woman, too, to their country, and the sure destiny of all who are false to it, meditate on this contrast.   Mrs. Arnold had been a leader of what is called fashion, in her native city, belonging to the spurious aristocracy of a provincial town—a woman of beauty and accomplishment and rank. Her connections were all thorough and sincere loyalists, and Arnold had won his way into a circle generally exclusive and intolerant by his known disaffection, and especially his insolent opposition to the local authorities, and to Mr. Reed as the chief executive magistrate. The aristocratic beauty smiled kindly on a lover who felt the same antipathies she had been taught to cherish. While Mrs. Reed and her friends were toiling to relieve the wants of the suffering soldiers —in June, July and August, 1780, Mrs. Arnold was communing with her husband, not in plans of treason, but in all his hatreds and discontents. He probably did not trust her with the whole of the perilous stuff that was fermenting in his heart; for it was neither necessary nor safe to do so. But he knew her nature and habits of thought well enough to be sure that if success crowned his plan of treason, and if honors and rewards were earned, his wife would not frown, or reject them because they had been won by treachery. And he played his game out, boldly, resolutely, confidently. The patriot woman of Philadelphia sank into her grave, honored and lamented by those among whom so recently she had come a stranger. Her tomb, alongside of that of her husband, still stands on the soil of her country. The fugitive wife of an American traitor fled for ever from her home and native soil, and died abroad unnoticed, and by her husband's crime dishonored. She was lost in a traitor's ignominy. Such was then and such ever will be, the fate of all who betray a public and a patriot trust.

III.

~~~~~~~~

CATHARINE SCHUYLER.

THE name of Philip Schuyler adds another to the list of distinguished men indebted largely to maternal guidance. To his mother, a woman of strong and cultivated mind, he owed his early education and habits of business, with that steadfast integrity, which never faltered nor forsook him. His wife—the beloved companion of his maturer years—cherished his social virtues and added lustre to his fame. Those who shared his generous hospitality, or felt the charm of his polished manners, were ready to testify to the excellence of her whose gentle influence was always apparent. A brief notice of her is all that can here be offered.

Catharine Schuyler was the only daughter of John Van Rensselaer, called Patroon of Greenbush, a patriot in the Revolutionary struggle, and noted for his hospitality, and for his kindness and forbearance towards the tenants of his vast estates during the war. It cannot be doubted that the recent anti-rent struggles, which have almost convulsed the State of New York, can be traced to the amiable but injudicious indulgence of this great landholder and his immediate heirs.

The qualities which in some cases shone in remarka-

3*

ble acts, were constantly exercised by Mrs. Schuyler in
the domestic sphere. At the head of a large family,
her management was so perfect that the regularity with
which all went on appeared spontaneous. Her life was
devoted to the care of her children ; yet her friendships
were warm and constant, and she found time for dispensing charities to the poor. Many families in poverty
remember with gratitude the aid received from her;
sometimes in the shape of a milch cow, or other article
of use. She possessed great self-control, and as the
mistress of a household, her prudence was blended with
unvarying kindness. Her chief pleasure was in diffus-
ing happiness in her home.

The house in which the family resided, near Albany,
was built by Mrs. Schuyler, while her husband was in
England, in 1760 and 1761. It had, probably, been
commenced previously. The ancient family mansion,
large and highly ornamented in the Dutch taste, stood
on the corner of State and Washington streets, in the
city. It was taken down about the year 1800. It was
a place of resort for British officers and travellers of
note in the French war. Fourteen French gentlemen,
some of them officers who had been captured in 1758,
were here entertained as prisoners on parole. They
found it most agreeable to be in Schuyler's house, as
he could converse with them in French; and his kindness made them friends. In 1801, when Mrs. Schuyler,
and some of her family visited Montreal and Quebec,
they were received with grateful attention by the descendants of those gentlemen.

Near Saratoga, the scene of General Schuyler's triumph, he had an elegant country-seat, which was destroyed by General Burgoyne. It was one of the most picturesque incidents of the war, that the captive British general with his suite, should be received and entertained, after the surrender at Saratoga, by those whose property he had wantonly laid waste. The courtesy and kindness shown by General and Mrs. Schuyler to the late enemy, and their generous forgetfulness of their own losses, were sensibly felt and acknowledged. Madame de Riedesel says their reception was not like that of enemies, but of intimate friends. "All their actions proved, that at sight of the misfortunes of others, they quickly forgot their own." This delicacy and generosity drew from Burgoyne the observation to General Schuyler, "You are too kind to me, who have done so much injury to you." The reply was characteristic of the noble-hearted victor : "Such is the fate of war ; let us not dwell on the subject."

The Marquis de Chastellux mentions, that just previous to this visit, General Schuyler being detained at Saratoga, where he had seen the ruins of his beautiful villa, wrote thence to his wife to make every preparation for giving the best reception to Burgoyne and his suite. "The British commander was well received by Mrs. Schuyler, and lodged in the best apartment in the house. An excellent supper was served him in the evening, the honors of which were done with so much grace, that he was affected even to tears, and said, with a deep sigh, ' Indeed, this is doing too much for the man who has ravaged their lands, and burned their dwellings.' The next morning he was reminded of his misfortunes by an incident that would have amused any one else. His bed was prepared in a large room; but as he had a numerous suite, or family, several mattresses were spread on the floor for some officers to sleep near him. Schuyler's second son, a little fellow about seven years old, very arch and forward, but very amiable, was running all the morning about the house. Opening the door of the saloon, he burst out a laughing on seeing all the English collected, and shut it after him, exclaiming, ' You are all my prisoners!' This innocent cruelty rendered them more melancholy than before."

Thus were even the miseries of war softened by Mrs. Schuyler's graceful courtesy; while the military renown won by her husband's illustrious services, was associated with remembrances of disinterested kindness bestowed in requital for injury. In reverse, her resolution and courage had been proved equal to the emergency. When the continental army was retreating from Fort Edward before Burgoyne, Mrs. Schuyler went up herself, in her chariot from Albany to Saratoga, to see to the removal of her furniture. While there, she received directions from the General, to set fire, with her own hand, to his extensive fields of wheat, and to request his tenants, and others, to do the same, rather than suffer them to be reaped by the enemy. The injunction shows the soldier's confidence in her spirit, firmness, and patriotism.

Many of the women of this family appear to have been remarkable for strong intellect and clear judgment. The Mrs. Schuyler described in Mrs. Grant's memoirs, was a venerated relative of the General. He lost his admirable wife in 1803. Her departure left his last years desolate, and saddened many hearts in which yet lives the memory of her bright virtues. One of her daughters, Mrs. Alexander Hamilton, now resides in Washington. D. C., and another at Oswego.

IV.

~~~~~~~

CATHARINE GREENE.

CATHARINE LITTLEFIELD, the eldest daughter of John Littlefield and Phebe Ray, was born in New Shoreham, on Block Island, 1753. When very young, she came with her sister to reside in the family of Governor Greene, of Warwick, a lineal descendant of the founder of the family, whose wife was her aunt. The house in which they lived, twelve or fourteen miles south of Providence, is still standing. It is situated on a hill, which commands a view of the whole of Narragansett Bay, with its islands. Mount Hope, associated with King Philip, and the Indian traditions, fills the back-ground, rising slightly above the line of the horizon. It was here that Miss Littlefield's happy girlhood was passed; and it was here also that she first knew Nathanael Greene. She often went on a visit to her family at Block Island. Nathanael would come there to see her; and the time was spent by the young people in amusements, particularly in riding and dancing, of which the future general was remarkably fond, notwithstanding

his father's efforts to whip out of him such idle propen-
sities. He was not discouraged by the example of his
fair companion from any of these outbreaks of youthful gaiety; for the tradition of the country around, and
the recollections of all who knew her, testify that there
never lived a more joyous, frolicsome creature than
"Kate Littlefield." In person, she was singularly lovely.
Her figure was of the medium height, and light and
graceful at this period, though in after years she was inclined to *embonpoint*. Her eyes were gray, and her complexion fair; her features regular and animated. The
facilities for female education being very limited at that
period, Miss Littlefield enjoyed few advantages of early
cultivation. She was not particularly fond of study,
though she read the books that came in her way, and pro-
fited by what she read. She possessed, moreover, a mar-
vellous quickness of perception, and the faculty of com-
prehending a subject with surprising readiness. Thus
in conversation, she seemed to appreciate every thing
said on almost any topic ; and frequently would astonish others by the ease with which her mind took
hold of the ideas presented. She was at all times an
intelligent listener. On one occasion, when the conversation turned on botany, she looked over the books
and collection of a Swedish botanist, making remarks
from time to time which much interested him, and
showed her an observer of no common intelligence.
This extraordinary activity of mind, and tact in seizing
on points, so as to apprehend almost intuitively, distin-

guished her through life. It enabled her, without apparent mental effort, to apply the instruction conveyed in the books she read, to the practical affairs of life, and to enrich her varied conversation with the knowledge gained from them, and her observation of the world. This power of rendering available her intellectual stores, combined with a retentive memory, a lively imagination, and great fluency in speech, rendered her one of the most brilliant and entertaining of women. When to these gifts was added the charm of rare beauty, it cannot excite wonder that the possessor of such attractions should fascinate all who approached her.

How, when, or by what course of wooing, the youthful lover won the bright, volatile, coquettish maiden, cannot be ascertained ; but it is probable their attachment grew in the approving eyes of their relatives, and met with no obstacle till sealed by the matrimonial vow. The marriage took place July 20th, 1774, and the young couple removed to Coventry. Little, it is likely, did the fair Catharine dream of her future destiny as a soldier's wife ; or that the broad-brimmed hat of her young husband covered brows that should one day be wreathed with the living laurels won by genius and patriotism. We have no means of knowing with how much interest she watched the over-clouding of the political horizon, or the dire advance of the necessity that drove the Colonies to armed resistance. But when her husband's decision was made, and he stood forth a determined patriot, separating himself from the commu-

nity in which he had been born and reared, by embrac-
ing a military profession, his spirited wife did her part
to aid and encourage him. The papers of the day frequently notice her presence, among other ladies, at head-
quarters. Like Mrs. Washington, she passed the active
season of the campaign at home. Hers was a new establishment at Coventry, a village in Rhode Island,
where her husband had erected a forge, and built himself
what then passed for a princely house on the banks of
one of those small streams which form so beautiful a
feature in Rhode Island scenery. When the army before Boston was innoculated for the small pox, she gave
up her house for a hospital. She was there during the
attack on Rhode Island; and every cannon on the hard
fought day which closed that memorable enterprise,
must have awakened the echoes of those quiet hills.
When the army went into winter quarters, she always
set out to rejoin her husband, sharing cheerfully the narrow quarters and hard fare of a camp. She partook of
the privations of the dreary winter at Valley Forge, in
that "darkest hour of the Revolution;" and it appears
that, as at home, her gay spirit shed light around her
even in such scenes, softening and enlivening the gloom
which might have weighed many a bold heart into
despondency. There are extant some interesting little
notes of Kosciusko, in very imperfect English, which
show her kindness to her husband's friends, and the
pleasure she took in alleviating their sufferings.

How much her society was prized by General Greene,
and how impatiently he bore separation from her, may

be seen in his letters.* When about to start for the
South, in October, 1780, he waits for her arrival to join
him, expecting she will overtake him at camp, or in
Philadelphia; and expresses the greatest anxiety that
she should avoid the dangerous route by Peekskill.
His fears for her safety at last impel him to request her
not to encounter the risk. Mr. Hughes, who knows
the feelings of the anxious wife, detains the letters: and
afterwards, confessing the unwarrantable liberty—for
which he "deserved to appear before a court-martial"—
says: "But if I do, I will plead Mrs. General Greene."
Again he writes: "Give me leave to say that your lady,
if possible, without injury to herself, must see you. My
God! she will suffer a thousand times as much by a
disappointment, as she can by going ten times the
distance!"

Notwithstanding her ardent wish to accompany the
General, it seems that Mrs. Greene was prevented from
doing so. Mrs. Washington writes to her from Mount
Vernon, to say that General Greene was well, and
had spent the evening at Mount Vernon, on his way
to Richmond. General Weedon, in a letter to her,
announces that the General had stopped for the night
at his house in Richmond; and invites Mrs. Greene,
if she should come as far as Virginia, to quarter
under his roof. A letter from the Commander-in-chief,
written from New Windsor on the 15th of December,

---

* The letters quoted or referred to in this sketch are from the MS.
correspondence of General Greene, in the possession of his grandson,
Prof. George W. Greene, of Providence, R. I., late Consul at Rome.

encloses Mrs. Greene a letter from her husband, and offers to forward hers.

"Mrs. Washington," he says, "who is just arrived at these my quarters, joins me in most cordial wishes for your every felicity, and regrets the want of your company. Remember me to my namesake. Nat, I suppose, can handle a musket."

The "namesake" alluded to, was the eldest son, who was afterwards drowned in the Savannah River. His mother never recovered her spirits after this shock.

Mrs. Greene joined her husband in the South after the close of the active campaign of 1781, and remained with him till the end of the war, residing on the islands during the heats of summer, and the rest of the time at head-quarters. In the spring of 1783, she returned to the North where she remained till the General had completed his arrangements for removing to the South. They then established themselves at Mulberry Grove, on a plantation which had been presented to Greene by the State of Georgia.

Mrs. Greene's first impressions of southern life and manners are painted in lively colors in her letters to northern friends. The following passage is from one to Miss Flagg :—

"If you expect to be an inhabitant of this country, you must not think to sit down with your netting pins; but on the contrary, employ half your time at the toilet, one quarter to paying and receiving visits; the other quarter to scolding servants, with a hard thump every now and then over the head; or singing, dancing, reading, writing, or saying your prayers. The latter is here quite a phenomenon; but you need not tell how you employ your time."

The letters of General Greene to his wife breathe the most entire confidence and affection. His respect for her judgment and good sense is shown in the freedom with which he expresses his thoughts and unfolds his hopes and plans. He evidently looked to her for support and sympathy in all his cares and troubles. His lighter hours, even in absence, were shared with her. Sometimes his youthful gaiety breaks forth in his descriptions of adventures and persons encountered in his travels. And regard for his interests was plainly above every other thought in the mind of his wife. After his death, she writes to Mr. Wadsworth, his executor, September 19th, 1788, "I consider ——— ——— ——— debts of honor, and would starve, rather than they should not be paid."—— "I am a woman—unaccustomed to any thing but the trifling business of a family; yet my exertions may effect something. If they do not, and if I [sacrifice] my life in the cause of my children, I shall but do my duty, and follow the example of my illustrious husband."

It was while on a visit to Savannah with his wife, that General Greene was seized with the disease which in a few days closed his brilliant career. They were then preparing to return and pass the summer at the North. The weight of care that fell on Mrs. Greene in consequence of this event, would have crushed an ordinary mind; but she struggled nobly through it all.

Some years afterwards, thinking that some lands she owned on Cumberland Island offered greater advantages than Mulberry Grove, she removed there with her family; dividing her time between her household duties and the cares of an extensive hospitality; occasionally visiting the North in the summer, but continuing to look upon the South as her home. It was while she lived at Mulberry Grove, that she became instrumental in introducing to the world an invention which has covered with wealth the fields of the South.

Late in 1792, her sympathies were enlisted in behalf of a young man, a native of Massachusetts, who having come to Georgia to take the place of private teacher in a gentleman's family, had been disappointed in obtaining the situation, and found himself without friends or resources in a strange land. Mrs. Greene and her family treated him with great kindness. He was invited to make his home in her house while he pursued the study of the law, to which he had determined to devote himself. According to the account of some, his attention was attracted to the cotton plant growing in the garden, and to Mr. Miller's observation that cotton of that sort could be cultivated as a staple, provided some method could be found of cleaning it from the seed. According to others, a party of gentlemen on a visit to the family, spoke of the want of an effective machine for separating the cotton from the seed, without which, it was allowed, there could be no profitable cultivation of this more productive species. Mrs. Greene spoke of the mechanical genius of her young protegé; introduced him to the company, and showed little specimens of his skill, in tambour frames and articles for the children. Eli Whitney, for that was the name of the young student, was strongly impressed with the conversation. He examined the cotton, and communicated his plans to Mrs. Greene and Mr. Miller, who gave him warm encouragement. A basement room, into which no one else was admitted, was appropriated for his work. He labored day after day, making the necessary tools; and persevering with unwearied industry. By spring the COTTON GIN was completed, and exhibited to the wonder and delight of planters invited from different parts of Georgia to witness its successful operation.

Mr. Phineas Miller entered into an agreement with Whitney, to bear the expense of maturing the invention, and to divide the future profits. He was a man of remarkably active and cultivated mind. Mrs. Greene married him some time after the death of General Greene. She survived him several years—dying just before the close of the late war with England. Her remains rest in the family burial-ground at Cumberland Island, where but a few years afterwards, the body of one of her husband's best officers and warmest friends —the gallant Lee—was brought to moulder by her side. She left four children by her first marriage—three daughters and one son—of whom the son and second daughter are still living.

Mrs. Miller related to a lady residing in New York, the incident of Colonel Aaron Burr's requesting permission to stop at her house, when he came South,

after his fatal duel with General Hamilton. She would
not refuse the demand upon her hospitality, but his victim had been her friend; and she could not receive as a
guest, one whose hands were crimsoned with his blood.
She gave Burr permission to remain; but at the same time
ordered her carriage, and quitted her house; returning
as soon as he had taken his departure. This little
anecdote is strongly illustrative of her impulsive and
generous character. The lady who mentioned it to me
had herself experienced, in time of the illness of one dear
to her, Mrs. Miller's sympathy and active kindness; and
described her manners as gentle, frank and winning.
Her praise, were I at liberty to mention her name,
would do the highest honor to its object.

The descendants of Mrs. Greene regard her with affectionate reverence. She was a loved and honored
wife, and a tender yet judicious mother. Her discipline
was remarkably strict, and none of her children ever
thought of disobeying her. Yet she would sometimes
join with child-like merriment in their sports. A lady
now living in Providence states, that one day, after the
close of the 'war, passing General Greene's house in
Newport, she saw both him and his wife playing "puss
in the corner," with the children.

She loved a jest, and sometimes too, a hearty laugh
upon her friends. On one occasion, while living at
Newport after the close of the war, she disguised herself like an old beggar-woman, so effectually that she
was not recognized even by her brother-in-law. In this
dress she went round to the houses of her friends to ask

charity—telling a piteous tale of losses and sufferings. At one house they were at the card-table ; and one of her most intimate friends, as she ordered her off, desired the servant to look well as she went out and see that she did not steal something from the entry.   At another, the master of the house was just sitting down to supper ; and though an old acquaintance and a shrewd man, was not only deceived, but so moved by her story, that he gave her the loaf he was on the point of cutting for himself.   When she had sufficiently amused herself with this practical test of her friends' charity, she took off her disguise, and indulged her merriment at their expense ; reminding them that with the exception of the loaf, she had been turned away without any experience of their liberality.

Mrs. Greene's power of fascination, described as absolutely irresistible, may be illustrated by a little anecdote.   A lady, who is still living, had heard much of her, and resolved—as young ladies sometimes will when they hear too much about a person—that she would not like her.   One day she chanced to be on a visit at the late Colonel Ward's in New York, where she saw a lady—dressed completely in black, even to the head dress, which was drawn close under the throat—who from her seat on the sofa was holding the whole company in breathless attention to the lively anecdotes of the war, and the brilliant sketches of character, which she was drawing so skillfully and in a tone so winning, that it was impossible not to listen to her.   Still the young girl's resolution was not shaken.   She might be compelled to admire, but the liking depended on herself; and she took a seat at the opposite side of the room. How long she remained there she was never able to tell; but her first consciousness was of being seated on a stool at the old lady's feet, leaning upon her knee, and looking up in her face as confidingly as if she had been her own mother.

4

V.

~~~~~~~~~

MERCY WARREN.

THE name of Mercy Warren belongs to American history. In the influence she exercised, she was perhaps the most remarkable woman who lived at the Revolutionary period. She was the third child of Colonel James Otis, of Barnstable, in the old colony of Plymouth; and was born there, September 25th, 1728.* The Otis family came to the country in 1630 or 1640, and settled first in Hingham.

The youth of Miss Otis was passed in the retirement of her home, in a routine of domestic employments, and the duties devolving upon her as the eldest daughter in a family of high respectability. Her love of reading was early manifested; and such was her economy of time, that, never neglecting her domestic cares or the duties of hospitality, she found leisure not only to improve her mind by careful study, but for various works of female ingenuity. A card-table is preserved by one of her descendants in Quincy, as a monument of her taste and industry. The design was her own,

* This date, with that of her death, is taken from the entries in the family Bible at Plymouth.

the patterns being obtained by gathering and pressing flowers from the gardens and fields. These are copied in worsted work, and form one of the most curious and beautiful specimens to be found in the country.

At that period, the opportunities for female education were extremely limited, but perhaps the more prized on that account. Miss Otis gained nothing from schools. Her only assistant, in the intellectual culture of her earlier years, was the Rev. Jonathan Russell, the minister of the parish, from whose library she was supplied with books, and by whose counsels her tastes were in a measure formed. It was from reading, in accordance with his advice, Raleigh's "History of the World," that her attention was particularly directed to history, the branch of literature to which she afterwards devoted herself. In later years, her brother James, who was himself an excellent scholar, became her adviser and companion in literary pursuits. There existed between them a strong attachment, which nothing ever impaired. Even in the wildest moods of that insanity, with which, late in life the great patriot was afflicted, her voice had power to calm him, when all else was without effect.

These favorite employments of reading, drawing and needle work, formed the recreation of a quiet life, in the home which Miss Otis rarely quitted. A visit to Boston, at the time of her brother's graduation at Harvard College, in 1743, was the occasion of her first absence for any length of time.

When about twenty-six, she became the wife of James Warren, then a merchant of Plymouth, Massa-

chusetts. In him she found a partner of congenial mind.
Her new avocations and cares were not allowed to
impair the love of literature which had been the delight
of her youth.   It was while residing occasionally for a
few weeks with her husband and children on a farm
a few miles from the village, to which she gave the
name of "Clifford," that most of her poetical produc-
tions were written. On the other hand, attached as
she was to these pursuits, she never permitted them to
interfere with household duties, or the attention of a
devoted mother to her children. Her attainments fitted
her to give them valuable instruction ; and the lessons
of her loving spirit of wisdom were not lost.

With this fondness for historical studies, and the
companionship of such a brother and husband, it is not
strange that the active and powerful intellect of Mrs.
Warren should become engaged with interest in political
affairs.   These were now assuming an aspect that
engrossed universal attention.   Decision and action
were called for on the part of those inclined to one or
the other side.   How warmly Mrs. Warren espoused
the cause of her country—how deeply her feelings were
enlisted—appears in her letters. Her correspondence
with the great spirits of that era, if published, would
form a most valuable contribution to our historical
literature. This rich correspondence has been preserved
by her descendants ; and affords the material for the
present memoir. It includes letters, besides those from
members of her own family, from Samuel and John
Adams, Jefferson, Dickinson, Gerry, Knox and others

These men asked her opinion in political matters, and acknowledged the excellence of her judgment. Referring to some of her observations on the critical state of affairs after the war, General Knox writes :—" I should be happy, Madam, to receive your communications from time to time, particularly on the subject enlarged on in this letter. Your sentiments shall remain with me." Mrs. Warren herself thus writes to Mr. Adams, before the meeting of the first Congress :

" Though you have condescended to ask my sentiments, in conjunction with those of a gentleman qualified both by his judgment and integrity, as well as his attachment to the interest of his country, to advise at this important crisis, yet I shall not be so presumptuous as to offer any thing but my fervent wishes that the enemies of America may hereafter for ever tremble at the wisdom and firmness, the prudence and justice of the delegates deputed from our cities, as much as did the *Phocians* of old at the power of the *Amphyctions* of Greece. But if the *Locrians* should in time appear among you, I advise you to beware of choosing an ambitious Philip as your leader. Such a one might subvert the principles on which your institution is founded, abolish your order, and build up a *monarchy* on the ruins of the happy institution.*

* Letter, July 14th, 1774. All the extracts from letters in this memoir, are from the manuscript correspondence of Mrs. Warren, in the possession of her daughter-in-law, who resides at Plymouth. This lady is herself a descendant of Governor Winslow, whose family intermarried with the Warrens in the fourth and sixth generations. One of the curiosities of her parlor is an easy chair belonging to Governor

Colonial difficulties, and the signs of the times, formed subjects of communication continually between Mrs. Warren and her female friends. Mrs. Adams says to her, in 1773, "You, madam, are so sincere a lover of your country, and so hearty a mourner in all her misfortunes, that it will greatly aggravate your anxiety to hear how much she is now oppressed and insulted. To you, who have so thoroughly looked through the deeds of men, and developed the dark designs of a "Rapatio" soul, no action, however base or sordid, no measure, however cruel and villanous, will be matter of any surprise. The tea, that baneful weed, is arrived: great, and I hope effectual opposition, has been made to the landing."

The friendship that existed between these two gifted women was truly beautiful and touching. Commenced in early youth, it continued unchanged through the vicissitudes of a long and eventful life—unshaken by troubles, unchilled by cares, unalienated by misunderstanding. Their thoughts were communicated to each other with perfect freedom and openness; and they found in joy and sorrow, a solace, or an added pleasure, in each other's sympathy and affection. The sister of Abigail Adams, who married Mr. Shaw, was also warmly attached to Mrs. Warren.

Winslow, which was brought over in the Mayflower. The iron staples are still attached, by which it was fastened to the cabin floor of the Pilgrim ship; and its present covering is the dress of white brocade richly embroidered, worn by Mercy Warren on the day after her marriage. Some of the ancient china also remains; several pieces one hundred and fifty years old, are of surpassing beauty.

The celebrated Mrs. Macauley was another of her favorite correspondents, though they were not personally acquainted till that lady's visit to New England. Mrs. Warren's letters to her describe the progress of the Revolutionary spirit. That written December 29th, 1774, speaks forcibly of the aspect of things :

"America stands armed with resolution and virtue ; but she still recoils at the idea of drawing the sword against the nation from whence she derived her origin. Yet Britain, like an unnatural parent, is ready to plunge her dagger into the bosom of her affectionate offspring. But may we not yet hope for more lenient measures! You, madam, can easily delineate the characters of the new Parliament."

* * * * *

" The seeds of empire are sown in this new world : the ball rolls westward fast, and though we are daily threatened with the depredations of Britain with foreign auxiliaries, and the incursions of the savages, yet each city, from Nova Scotia to Georgia, has her Decii and her Fabii, ready to sacrifice their devoted lives to preserve inviolate, and to convey to their children the inherent rights of men, conferred on all by the God of nature, and the privileges of Englishmen claimed by Americans from the sacred sanction of compacts."

In the following year she writes :

"I hinted that the sword was half drawn from the scabbard. Since that it has been unsheathed. * * Almost every tongue is calling on the justice of heaven to punish or disperse the disturbers of the peace, liberty, and happiness of their country."

She says to John Adams:

"I have my fears. Yet, notwithstanding the complicated difficulties that rise before us, there is no receding; and I should blush if in any instance the weak passions of my sex should damp the fortitude, the patriotism, and the manly resolution of yours. May nothing ever check that glorious spirit of freedom which inspires the patriot in the cabinet, and the hero in the field, with courage to maintain their righteous cause, and to endeavor to transmit the claim to posterity, even if they must seal the rich conveyance to their children with their own blood."*.

*   *   *   *   *

"The desk, the pews, and other incumbrances are taken down in the Old South (a church long venerated in the town), to make it convenient for the accommodation of General Burgoyne's light horse; while the infamous Dr. Morrison, whose character I suppose you are acquainted with, reads prayers in the church in Brattle street to a set of banditti, who, after the rapines, robberies, and devastations of the week, dare—some of them—to lift up their sacrilegious hands, and bow before the altar of mercy.

*   *   "I will breathe one wish more; and that is for the restoration of peace—peace, I mean, on equitable terms; for pusillanimous and feeble as I am, I can-

* Letter, August 2d, 1775.

not wish to see the sword quietly put up in the scabbard, until justice is done to America."*

During the years that preceded the Revolution, and after its outbreak, Mrs. Warren's house appears to have been the resort of much company. As she herself says, "by the Plymouth fireside were many political plans originated, discussed, and digested." She reminds Mr. Adams while he is in Europe, of his words once uttered in a moment of despondency, that "the dispute between Great Britain and America will not be settled till your sons and my sons are able to assist and negotiate with the different European courts."—"A lady replied, though perhaps not from prescience, but from presentiment or presumption, that you must do it yourself; that the work must be done immediately; and that she expected from you in the intervals of business, a pleasing narration of the different customs, manners, taste, genius, and policy of nations with whom, at present, we were little acquainted. You assented a compliance if the prediction took place."

Although her home was in Plymouth, her place of residence was occasionally changed during the war. At one time she lived in the house at Milton, which Governor Hutchinson had occupied. Wherever she was, the friends of America were always welcomed to the shelter of her roof, and the hospitalities of her table. In different passages of her letters to Mr. Adams, the officers with whom she became acquainted are described. The following extract is interesting:

* Letter, October, 1775.

4*

"The Generals Washington, Lee, and Gates, with several other distinguished officers from head-quarters, dined with us (at Watertown) three days since. The first of these I think one of the most amiable and accomplished gentlemen, both in person, mind, and manners, that I have met with. The second, whom I never saw before, I think plain in his person to a degree of ugliness, careless even to unpoliteness—his garb ordinary, his voice rough, his manners rather morose; yet sensible, learned, judicious, and penetrating: a considerable traveller, agreeable in his narrations, and a zealous, indefatigable friend to the American cause; but much more from a love of freedom, and an impartial sense of the-inherent rights of mankind at large, than from any attachment or disgust to particular persons or countries. The last is a brave soldier, a high republican, a sensible companion, an honest man, of unaffected manners and easy deportment."

She speaks thus of the Count D'Estaing :

"While the errand on which the Count D'Estaing came out excites our gratitude, the dignity of his deportment commands respect; and his reserved affability, if I may so express it, heightens our esteem."

And La Fayette is praised in laconic fashion :

"Penetrating, active, sensible, and judicious, he acquits himself with the highest applause in the public eye, while the politeness of his manners, and the sociability of his temper, insure his welcome at every hospitable board."

Every page from the pen of Mrs. Warren, is remark-

able for clearness and vigor of thought. Thus her style
was not vitiated by the artificial tastes of the day ; yet
her expression is often studiously elaborated, in accordance with the prevalent fashion. This is the case in
her letters written with most care ; while in others her
ardent spirit pours out its feelings with irrepressible
energy, portraying itself in the genuine and simple language of emotion. The following passage perhaps did
not then appear studied, even in a familiar letter :

" The late convulsions are only the natural struggles
which ensue when the genius of liberty arises to assert
her rights in opposition to the ghost of tyranny. I
doubt not this fell form will ere long be driven from
our land : then may the western skies behold virtue
(which is generally the attendant of freedom) seated on
a throne of peace, where may she ever preside over the
rising Commonwealth of America."*

About this time, as it appears, was published " The
Group"—a satirical dramatic piece in two Acts, in which
many of the leading tory characters of the day were
humorously introduced. A strong political influence
has been ascribed to this and other satirical poems from
her pen. It is in allusion to this that Mrs. Adams
speaks of "a Rapatio soul"—Governor Hutchinson
being thus designated. The following description is
applied to him :

> " But mark the traitor—his high crime glossed o'er
> Conceals the tender feelings of the man,

* Letter to Mrs. Lathrop, 1775.

The social ties that bind the human heart;
He strikes a bargain with his country's foes,
And joins to wrap America in flames.
Yet with feigned pity, and satanic grin,
As if more deep to fix the keen insult,
Or make his life a farce still more complete,
He sends a groan across the broad Atlantic,
And with a phiz of crocodilian stamp,
Can weep, and wreathe, still hoping to deceive;
He cries—the gathering clouds hang thick about her,
But laughs within; then sobs—
Alas, my country!"

ACT II. SCENE I.

With the classical allusions then common, she mentions

"——— India's poisonous weed,
Long since a sacrifice to Thetis made,
A rich regale. Now all the watery dames
May snuff souchong, and sip in flowing bowls
The higher flavored choice Hysonian stream,
And leave their nectar to old Homer's gods."

It may be imagined that such bold and keen satire would produce a marked sensation, and be severely felt by the persons against whom it was aimed. The author herself seems to have had some misgivings, fearing lest her patriotic feelings should have carried her too far. Mrs. Adams thus re-assures her :

"I observe my friend is laboring under apprehension, lest the severity with which a certain *Group* was drawn, was incompatible with that benevolence which ought always to be predominant in a female character.

Though 'an eagle's talon asks an eagle's eye,' and
satire in the hands of some is a very dangerous weapon; yet when it is so happily blended with benevolence, and is awakened only by the love of virtue and
abhorrence of vice—when truth is unavoidably preserved, and ridiculous and vicious actions are alone the
subject, it is so far from blamable that it is certainly
meritorious."

Mrs. Warren employed much of her leisure with her
pen. She kept a faithful record of occurrences during
the dark days of her country's affliction, through times
that engaged the attention both of the philosopher and
the politician. She did this with the design of transmitting to posterity a faithful portraiture of the most
distinguished characters of the day.

Her intention was fulfilled in her history of the war.
Her poetical compositions, afterwards collected and de-
dicated to General Washington, were the amusement
of solitude, when many of her friends were actively
engaged in the field or cabinet. Some of them contain allusions to bodily sufferings, her health being far
from robust. The tragedies, "The Sack of Rome,"
and "The Ladies of Castile," are more remarkable for
patriotic sentiment than dramatic merit. The verse is
smooth and flowing, and the language poetical, but
often wanting in the simplicity essential to true pathos.
An interest deeper than that of the story is awakened
by the application of many passages to the circumstances of the times. The truth of the following lines
must have been dolefully felt :

" 'Mongst all the ills that hover o'er mankind,
    Unfeigned, or fabled in the poet's page,
    The blackest scroll the sister furies hold
    For red-eyed wrath, or malice to fill up,
    Is incomplete to sum up human woe ;
    Till civil discord, still a darker fiend,
    Stalks forth unmasked from his infernal den,
    With mad Alecto's torch in his right hand,
    To light the flame, and rend the soul of nature."

Both these tragedies were read with interest, and much praised in after years. Alexander Hamilton writes to the author, July 1st, 1791 :

" It is certain that in the " Ladies of Castile," the sex will find a new occasion of triumph. Not being a poet myself, I am in the less danger of feeling mortification at the idea that in the career of dramatic composition at least, female genius in the United States has out-stripped the male."

The criticism of John Adams—who writes from London, Dec. 25th, 1787, is equally favorable.

" The " Sack of Rome" has so much spirit in itself, that for the honor of America, I should wish to see it acted on the stage in London, before crowded audiences. The dedication of it does so much honor to me, that I should be proud to see it in print, even if it could not be acted. It requires almost as much interest and intrigue to get a play acted, as to be a member of Parliament."

At another time he says of her Poems :   " The Poems are not all of them new to me, by whom some of them have been read and esteemed some years ago.   How-

ever foolishly some European writers may have sported
with American reputation for genius, literature and
science, I know not where they will find a female
poet of their own to prefer to the ingenious author of
these compositions."*

"A Poetical Reverie" was published before the
breaking out of the war. It gives a poetical view of
the future greatness of America, and the punishment
of her oppressors. "The Squabble of the Sea Nymphs,"
celebrates the pouring of the tea into the sea, and is
something in the Rape of the Lock style. The lines to
a friend, who on the American determination to sus-
pend all commerce with Great Britain, except for the
necessaries of life, requested a poetical list of the articles
the ladies might comprise under that head, have some
fine satire. The reader will not object to the following
specimen :

> " An inventory clear
> Of all she needs, Lamira offers here ;
> Nor does she fear a rigid Cato's frown
> When she lays by the rich embroidered gown,
> And modestly compounds for just enough,—
> Perhaps some dozens of more slighty stuff :
> With lawns and lutestrings—blond and mechlin laces,
> Fringes and jewels, fans and tweezer cases ;
> Gay cloaks and hats, of every shape and size,
> Scarfs, cardinals, and ribbons of all dyes ;
> With ruffles stamped, and aprons of tambour,
> Tippets and handkerchiefs, at least three score :
> With finest muslins that fair India boasts,

* MS. Letter to Mrs. Warren, Dec. 26th, 1790.

And the choice herbage from Chinesan coasts;
(But while the fragrant hyson leaf regales,
Who'll wear the home-spun produce of the vales?
For if 'twould save the nation from the curse
Of standing troops—or name a plague still worse,
Few can this choice delicious draught give up,
Though all Medea's poisons fill the cup.)
Add feathers, furs, rich satins, and ducapes,
And head-dresses in pyramidal shapes;*
Side-boards of plate, and porcelain profuse,
With fifty dittos that the ladies use;
If my poor treacherous memory has missed,
Ingenious T——l shall complete the list.
So weak Lamira, and her wants so few,
Who can refuse? they're but the sex's due.

    "In youth, indeed, an antiquated page
Taught us the threatenings of a Hebrew sage
'Gainst wimples, mantles, curls and crisping pins,
But rank not these among our modern sins;
For when our manners are well understood,
What in the scale is stomacher or hood?

    'Tis true, we love the courtly mien and air,
The pride of dress, and all the debonair:
Yet Clara quits the more dressed negligé,
And substitutes the careless polancé;
Until some fair one from Britannia's court

* It is mentioned in Sanderson's Biography of the Signers of Independence, that the Whig ladies of Philadelphia having adopted the tory fashion of high head-dresses, after the evacuation of the city by the British, some Whigs dressed a negress in the full costume of a loyalist lady, took her to a place of resort, where the fashionables displayed their towering top-knots, seating her in a conspicuous place,— and afterwards paraded her through the city. Nothing, however, could stop the progress of the fashion, which for a season became general in America.

> Some jaunty dress, or newer taste import ;
> This sweet temptation could not be withstood,
> Though for the purchase paid her father's blood ;
> Though loss of freedom were the costly price,
> Or flaming comets sweep the angry skies ;
> Or earthquakes rattle, or volcanoes roar ;
> Indulge this trifle, and she asks no more ;
> Can the stern patriot Clara's suit deny ?
> Tis beauty asks, and reason must comply."

The powers of Mrs. Warren were devoted to nobler objects than chastising the follies of the day. She gave her tenderest sympathies to the sufferings of her friends, and poured the balm of consolation into many a wounded heart. The letters of Mrs. Adams show how much she leaned, amidst her heavy trials, on this faithful support. Nor was her kindness limited to the circle of her acquaintance. Every sufferer from this cruel war had a claim her heart acknowledged, and her benevolence went forth on its gentle mission among strangers. She addressed a letter of condolence to the widow of the brave Montgomery, Jan. 20th, 1776, in which the consolatory suggestions are those of a patriot and a Christian.

"While you are deriving comfort," she says, "from the highest source, it may still further brighten the clouded moment to reflect that the number of your friends is not confined to the narrow limits of a province, but by the happy union of the American Colonies, (suffering equally by the rigor of oppression,) the affections of the inhabitants are cemented ; and the urn of the companion of your heart will be sprinkled with the tears of thousands who revere the commander at the gates of Quebec, though not personally acquainted with General Montgomery."

Montgomery, as is known, married Janet Livingston, a sister of Chancellor Robert R. Livingston. Her life was a secluded one, and affords few materials for biography; but her letters expressive of her feelings have a deep interest. Mrs. Warren says with truth— writing to her Nov. 25th, 1777 :—

"The sensibility of soul, the pathos of grief so strongly marked in your letters, have convinced me that the brave Montgomery had a partner worthy of his character."

The following is an extract from her letter in reply to Mrs. Warren :—

"My dear Madam,

"The sympathy that is expressed in every feature of your letter, claims from me the warmest acknowledgments; and the professions of friendship from one who so generously feels and melts at the woes of a stranger, not only soothe but flatter me.

"It is very kind of you, madam, to seek for alleviating consolations in a calamity (though of so much glory). I thank God I feel part of their force, and it is owing to such affectionate friends as you, that have lightened the load of misery.

"As a wife I must ever mourn the loss of the husband, friend and lover; of a thousand virtues, of all domestic bliss; the idol of my warmest affections, and in one word, my every dream of happiness. But with America

I weep the still greater loss of the firm soldier and the friend to freedom. Let me repeat his last words when we parted: '*You shall never blush for your Montgomery.*'

"Nobly has he kept his word; but how are my sorrows heightened! Methinks I am like the poor widow in the Gospel, who having given her mite, sits down quite destitute. Yet would I endeavor to look forward to the goal with hope; and though the path is no longer strewed with flowers, trust to the sustaining hand of friendship to lead me safely through, and in assisting me to rise superior to my misfortunes, make me content to drag out the remainder of life, till the Being who has deprived me of husband and father, will kindly close the melancholy scene, and once more unite me to them in a world of peace, where the tyrant shall no more wantonly shed the blood of his innocent subjects, and where vice and virtue will receive their reward."

All the letters of Mrs. Montgomery preserved in the correspondence of Mrs. Warren, dwell on her irreparable loss, breathing a tender sorrow, mingled with an ardent spirit of patriotism. She writes, Nov. 20th, 1780:

"I have been interrupted. Another alarm of the enemy's being in full march for Saratoga, and the poor harrassed militia are again called upon. My impatient spirit pants for peace. When shall the unfortunate individual have the gloomy satisfaction of weeping alone for his own particular losses! In this luckless state, woes follow woes—every moment is big with something fatal. We hold our lives and fortunes on the most

precarious tenure.   Had Arnold's plan taken place, we
could not have escaped from a fate dreadful in thought;
for these polished Britons have proved themselves fertile
in inventions to procrastinate [protract] misery."

When going with her nephew to visit her husband's
family in Dublin, her patriotic feeling is still fervent.
"When I return," she says, "I hope to find my dear
country, for which I have *bled*, the envy of her enemies
and the glory of her patriots."

The friendships formed by Mrs. Warren were not
short-lived.   The letters addressed to her evince the
warmth of attachment she inspired; and her own true
heart never swerved from its faith.   The interchange
of sentiments was continued for years; and when interrupted, resumed with the same affectionate ardor as
soon as the obstacles were removed.   Mrs. Washington
was one of her favorite correspondents.   On her visit
to head-quarters in Cambridge, Mrs. Warren invited
her to her house, and paid her many attentions.   Her
letter from Valley Forge, describing their accommodations, and others have been elsewhere published.   The
Commander-in-chief joined in his wife's feelings of
regard.

Another of Mrs. Warren's intimate friends, was
Hannah Winthrop, the wife of Dr. Winthrop, of Cambridge.   Her letters discover a mind of no common order.
They corresponded sometimes under the signatures
of Honoria and Philomela, the last name being bestowed
on Mrs. Warren for her powers of song.   The poetical
signature assumed by Mrs. Warren was "Marcia,"

afterwards given at her request to a beloved grand-daughter. But as the subjects became momentous on which the two wrote, the fanciful appellations were dropped. Some portions of Mrs. Winthrop's letters are so characteristic, that extracts will be interesting. She writes, in Jan. 1773, "I think one of the most extraordinary political manœuvres this century has produced, is the ministerial mandate to the Newportians for transporting them a thousand leagues for trial. Oh, America! you have reason to tremble and arouse, if we of this side of the Atlantic are not able to say to this Royal Vengeance—hitherto shalt thou come and no further; here shall thy proud waves be stayed! I should rejoice to see the Plymouthean spirit prevail, which discovers such noble disinterested virtue, and such a sacred regard to rights purchased at the expense of every thing valuable by those persevering, self-denying patriarchs, who, if permitted to be spectators of these terrestrial scenes, must view those of their sons who set so little value upon the dear bought purchases, with displeasure. Many are waiting impatiently the meeting of our assembly. * * I hope Colonel Warren will not fail of favoring his country with his presence at that important crisis, when every eye will be upon our political fathers."

Again, Jan. 1st, 1774, her patriotic spirit breaks out. "Yonder, the destruction of the detestable weed, made so by cruel exaction, engages our attention. The virtuous and noble resolution of America's sons, in defiance of threatened desolation and misery from arbitrary despots, demands our highest regard. May they yet be endowed with all that firmness necessary to carry them through all their difficulties, till they come off conquerors. We hope to see good accounts of the tea cast away on the Cape. The union of the Colonies, the firm and sedate resolution of the people, is an omen for good unto us. And be it known unto Britain, even American daughters are politicians and patriots, and will aid the good work with their female efforts." * * * *

"— Nor can she ever forget, nor will old time ever erase—the horrors of that midnight cry, preceding the bloody massacre at Lexington, when we were roused from the benign slumbers of the season, by beat of drum and ringing of bells, with the dire alarm that a thousand of the troops of George the Third had gone forth to murder the peaceful inhabitants of the surrounding villages. A few hours, with the dawning day, convinced us the bloody purpose was executing; the platoon firing assuring us the rising sun must witness the bloody carnage. Not knowing what the event would be at Cambridge, at the return of these bloody ruffians, and seeing another brigade dispatched to the assistance of the former, looking with the ferocity of barbarians, it seemed necessary to retire to some place of safety, till the calamity was passed. My partner had been confined a fortnight by sickness. After dinner we set out, not knowing whither we went. We were directed to a place called Fresh-pond, about a mile from the town; but what a distressed house did we find it, filled with women whose husbands had gone forth to meet

the assailants, seventy or eighty of these (with numberless infant children,) weeping and agonizing for the fate
of their husbands.   In addition to this scene of distress,
we were for sometime in sight of the battle; the glittering instruments of death proclaiming by an incessant
[fire] that much blood must be shed; that many widowed
and orphaned ones [must] be left as monuments of British
barbarity.   Another uncomfortable night we passed;
some nodding in their chairs, some resting their weary
limbs on the floor.   The welcome harbingers of day
gave notice of its dawning light.   [It] brings no news.
It is unsafe to return to Cambridge, as the enemy were
advancing up the river, and fixing on the town to stay
in.

   "Thus with precipitancy we were driven to the
town of Anderson, following some of our acquaintance—
five of us to be conveyed with one poor tired horse and
chaise ; thus we began our pilgrimage, alternately
walking and riding, the roads filled with frighted
women and children ; some in carts with their tattered
furniture, others on foot fleeing into the woods.   But
what added greatly to the horrors of the scene, was our
passing through the bloody field at Monotong, which
was strewed with the mangled bodies.   We met one
affectionate father with a cart, looking for his murdered
son, and picking up his neighbors who had fallen in
battle, in order for their burial."

   "July 8th, 1775.—Our barrack, or wigwam, or whatever name you may please to give it when you see it,
ornamented with broken chairs and unlegged tables,

with shattered etceteras, is entirely at your service. Methinks I need not repeat the pleasure I shall have in administering comfort to my friends."

She writes in the following August, after the conflagration of Charlestown—" The laying a whole town in ashes, after repeated promises that if they would protect their troops in their return from Concord, it should be the last place that should suffer harm! How did they give shelter to the wounded expiring soldiers! Their houses, their beds, were prepared to receive them; the women readily engaged in pouring balm into their wounds, making broths and cordials to support their exhausted spirits, for at that time the softer sex had not been inured to trickling blood and gaping wounds. Some of the unhappy victims died. They gave up the ghost blessing the hands that gave relief; and now in return for this kindness, they take the first opportunity to make five hundred householders miserable; involving many a poor widow and orphan in one common ruin. Be astonished, O heavens, at this, and let the inhabitants of America tremble to fall into the hands of such a merciless foe."

The following extract, the last that will be given from Mrs. Winthrop's letters, describes the entry into Cambridge of the captive army of Burgoyne. The letter bears date November 11th, 1777:

" It is not a great while since I wrote my dear friend, on my disappointment in not paying her a visit. Now methinks I hear her wondering how it is with her Cambridge friends, who are at this time delayed with British

and Hessian—what shall I call them? who are prancing and patrolling in every corner of the town, ornamented with their glittering side-arms—weapons of destruction. A short detail of our situation may perhaps amuse
you. You will be able to form a judgment of our unhappy circumstances. Last Thursday, which was a
very stormy day, a large number of British troops came
softly through the town *via* Watertown to Prospect
Hill. On Friday we heard the Hessians were to make
a procession in the same route. We thought we should
have nothing to do but view them as they passed. To
be sure the sight was truly astonishing. I never had
the least idea that the creation produced such a sordid
set of creatures in human figure—poor, dirty, emaciated
men. Great numbers of women, who seemed to be
the beasts of burden, having bushel-baskets on their
backs, by which they were bent double. The contents
seemed to be pots and kettles, various sorts of furniture, children peeping through gridirons and other utensils—some very young infants, who were born on the
road—the women barefoot, clothed in dirty rags. Such
effluvia filled the air while they were passing, that
had they not been smoking all the time, I should have
been apprehensive of being contaminated. After a
noble-looking advanced-guard, General Burgoyne headed this terrible group on horseback. The other generals also clothed in blue cloaks—Hessians, Waldeckers,
Anspackers, Brunswickers, etc., etc., followed on. The
Hessian generals gave us a polite bow as they passed.
Not so the British. Their baggage-wagons [were] drawn

5

by poor, half-starved horses.   But to bring up the rear, another fine, noble-looking guard of American brawny victorious yeomanry, who assisted in bringing these sons of slavery to terms.   Some of our wagons drawn by fat oxen, driven by joyous-looking Yankees, closed the cavalcade.   The generals and other officers, went to Bradish's, where they quarter at present.   The privates trudged through thick and thin to the hills, where we thought they were to be confined.   But what was our surprise, when in the morning we beheld an inundation of those disagreeable objects filling our streets ? How mortifying is it !—they in a manner demanding our houses and colleges for their genteel accommodation.   Did the brave General Gates ever mean this ? Did our legislature ever intend the military should prevail above the civil ?   Is there not a degree of unkindness in loading poor Cambridge, almost ruined before this great army seemed to be let loose upon us !   What will be the consequence, time will discover.   Some polite ones say we ought not to look on them as prisoners—that they are persons of distinguished rank. Perhaps, too, we must not view them in the light of enemies.   I fear this distinction will be soon lost.   Surprising that our general, or any of our colonels, should insist on the first university in America being disbanded for their more genteel accommodation ; and we, poor oppressed people, seek an asylum in the woods against a piercing winter! Where is the stern virtue of a ————, who opposed such infractions, in former days ?   Who is there to plead our cause ?   Pity—pity it is our Assembly had not settled these matters before their adjournment. It will be vastly more difficult to abridge them after such an unbounded license. Perhaps you may see some of them at Plymouth. For my part, I think insults, famine, and a train of evils present themselves to view. General Burgoyne dined on Saturday in Boston with General ———. He rode through the town properly attended, down Court street and through the main street; and on his return walked on foot to Charlestown Ferry, followed by a great number of spectators as ever attended a Pope; and generously observed to an officer with him, the decent and modest behavior of the inhabitants as he passed; saying, if he had been conducting prisoners through the city of London, not all the Guards of Majesty could have prevented insults. He likewise acknowledges Lincoln and Arnold to be great generals. It is said we shall have not less than seven thousand persons to feed in Cambridge and its environs, more than its inhabitants. Two hundred and fifty cords of wood will not serve them a week. Think then how we must be distressed. Wood has risen to £5 10s. per cord, and but a little to be purchased. I never thought I could lie down to sleep surrounded by these enemies; but we strangely become inured to those things which appear difficult when distant."

* * * * *

"If you like anecdotes, I will give you one more:

"When General Phillips was travelling back of Albany, where it is very rocky and barren, he expressed his astonishment that they should ever cross the Atlantic, and go through such difficulty to conquer so unfavorable a country, which would not be worth keeping when conquered. When they came upon the fertile banks of Connecticut River, General Whipple said to him, " This is the country which we are fighting for." " Ah," replied the General, " this is a country worth a ten years' war."

Her indignation does not seem to have subsided at once. In February she says :

" Methinks I hear Mrs. Warren wondering how they do at head-quarters at Cambridge. Perhaps her wonder may increase when I tell her the British officers live in the most luxurious manner possible, rioting on the fat of the land, and talking at large with the self-importance of lords of the soil."

To return to Mrs. Warren. From her retirement, in which she was constantly visited by her friends, she continued to watch the progress of the struggle, and to treasure her observations for the historical work she had in contemplation. Early in 1777 she writes to her friend, Mrs. Macaulay :

" The approaching spring appears big with the fate of empires, and the wheels of revolution move in swift progression. They may smite the diadem from the brow, and shake some tyrant from his throne before he is aware. The flatterers of majesty may be more attended to than the prophetic voice that augurs evil ; yet when the *mene tekel* is inscribed on the walls of the palace, it cannot be blotted out by the hand of the prince who humbles not himself, though he sees the works that have been done in the days of his fathers."

After the close of the war, Mrs. Macaulay visited this country, and met with a reception due to the celebrity her works had gained. Her principles endeared her to the Americans, who were willing to bestow lasting honor on such as had distinguished themselves by the sword or the pen in defence of their opinions. Mrs. Warren says of her, writing to Mr. Adams, " She is a lady of most extraordinary talents, of commanding genius, and brilliancy of thought. This, in my opinion, often outruns her capacity of expression."

Mrs. Warren's correspondence with Mr. Adams continued while he remained abroad. From time to time she demands of him an account of the busy and important scenes in which he is engaged ; and when she fails to receive intelligence, playfully accuses the watery nymphs of Neptune's court of having robbed the woodland dames of America. This was in allusion to the practice during the war, of sinking all packages in case of capture. " Otherwise," she says, " a folio from the court of France would, ere this, have reached Braintree, and one small octavo at least have found its way to Plymouth." The statesman was under an engagement to make observations for the use of more than one woman on the western side of the Atlantic. In a letter to him, dated October, 1778, she thus mentions Franklin :

" Are you, sir, as much in the good graces of the Parisian ladies, as your venerable colleague, Dr. F——?

We often hear he is not more an adept in politics than a favorite of the ladies. He has too many compliments of gratulation and esteem from each quarter of the globe, to make it of any consequence whether I offer my little tribute of respect or not. Yet I would tell him as a friend to mankind, as a daughter of America, and a lover of every exalted character, that no one more sincerely wishes the continuance of his health and usefulness ; and so disinterested is my regard, that I do not wish him to leave the soft caresses of the court of France ; for his unpolished countrywomen will be more apt to gaze at and admire the virtues of the philosopher, than to embrace the patriotic sage."

A soul like Mrs. Warren's must have been continually saddened by grief and pity, in the view not only of the miseries of war, but the depravity prevalent as one of its consequences. Yet while she mourned the crimes and follies of many to whom her country looked for succor, she followed with ardent admiration the career of those incorruptible patriots who kept their faith unshaken by misfortune or temptation. Her anxieties and hopes were freely communicated to her friends, whose answers show the intense interest felt in every movement. Miss Catharine Livingston, the sister of Mrs. Montgomery, writes in April, 1781 :

"The news from the southward is by no means so favorable as the sanguine among us expected. Arnold, it is feared, will get off safely as well as Cornwallis. I think the British understand retreat better than we do pursuit. It has been an observation, this war, whenever the expectations of the multitude were raised to almost a certainty of success, the event has turned directly opposite to their views. This I believe we may extend to private, as well as public concerns."

A letter from Mrs. Montgomery, the year previous, so agreeably describes Mrs. Jay, that an extract must be given :

" You speak of my dear friend Mrs. Jay. We have heard from her at Hispaniola, where she was obliged to put in after the storm, in which she had like to have been taken. When she arrives at Paris, I expect to hear from her ; if in the descriptive way, it shall be entirely at your service. She is one of the most worthy women I know—has a great fund of knowledge, and makes use of most charming language ; added to this she is very handsome, which will secure her a welcome with the unthinking, whilst her understanding will gain her the hearts of the most worthy. Her manners will do honor to our countrywomen ; and I really believe will please even at the splendid court of Madrid.

*   *   *   *   *

" The starting tear, and the heaving sigh, interrupt my thread. Strange that self will for ever discover itself! I find I am to learn much before I become a philosopher ; but in every instance of my life I hope you, my dear madam, will ever find me your most sincere friend and humble servant,

" J. MONTGOMERY."

Mrs. Warren wrote many letters to her sons at college, containing sound advice, of which she preserved copies, labelling the packages for the use of her grand-children. Space can be afforded for but a single pas-sage from one of these parental missives :

"I am persuaded you will never counteract those native dictates that lead you to struggle for distinction by cherishing that ambition that dignifies the rational creature. May you extend your views beyond the narrow limits of time, that you may rank not only with those models of virtue and heroism that have been so much your admiration from your earliest youth, but may be able to stand with confidence before HIM who dis-criminates character not according to the weak decisions of man, but by the unerring scale of eternal truth."

Rochefoucault, in his Travels in the United States, speaks of Mrs. Warren's extensive and varied reading. She was then seventy; and he says, " truly interesting; for, lively in conversation, she has lost neither the activ-ity of her mind, nor the graces of her person." Her history of the Revolution was written, but not published till some years afterwards. This work exhibits her as a writer in advance of the age. Its sound judgment and careful research, with its clear and vigorous style, give it a high and lasting value. Her portraiture of Mr. Adams gave offence to the great statesman, which for a time threatened to interrupt the affectionate rela-tions between the two families. But after a sharp cor-respondence, it was amicably settled; and as a token of reconciliation, Mrs. Adams sent her friend a ring containing her own and her husband's hair. This is now in the possession of one of Mrs. Warren's descendants.

For many years before her death Mrs. Warren was afflicted with the failure of her sight; but she submitted to the trial with pious resignation, continuing to receive with cheerfulness the company that frequented her house, and to correspond with her friends by means of a secretary. A passage from a letter to one of her sons, written in 1799, amidst the convulsions that agitated Europe, may serve to show that she still occasionally indulged in the elaborate style so much in vogue:

" The *ices of the Poles* seem to be dissolved to swell the tide of popularity on which swim the idols of the day; but when they have had their day, the tide will retire to its level, and perhaps leave the floating lumber on the strand with other perishable articles, not thought worth the hazard of attempting their recovery."

Towards the close of her protracted life, her influence did not diminish; for her mental superiority was still unimpaired and acknowledged. Seldom has one woman in any age, acquired such an ascendency over the strongest, by the mere force of a powerful intellect. She is said to have supplied political parties with their arguments; and she was the first of her sex in America who taught the reading world in matters of state policy and history.

By her own relatives and connections she was reverenced and beloved in a degree that affords the best

5*

testimony to her elevated character, and the faithfulness with which she had discharged her duty towards them. The influence commanded by her talents was enhanced by her virtues, and by the deep religious feeling which governed her throughout life. Her descendants are still taught to cherish her memory with reverent affection.

The portrait from which the engraving is taken, was painted by Copley. A lady who visited Mrs. Warren in 1807, describes her as at that time erect in person, and in conversation full of intelligence and eloquence. Her dress was a steel-colored silk gown, with short sleeves and very long waist; the black silk skirt being covered in front with a white lawn apron. She wore a lawn mob-cap, and gloves covering the arm to the elbows, cut off at the fingers.

In her last illness, her constant fear was that she might lose her mental faculties as death approached. She prayed to be spared this; and her prayer was granted. With an expression of thankfulness upon her lips—that reason was clear, and the vision of her spirit unclouded—she passed to the rest that awaits the faithful Christian, October 19th, 1814, in the eighty-seventh year of her age.

VI.

~~~~~~

LUCIA KNOX.

WHEN MAJOR HENRY KNOX, then a resident of Boston, was parading the company to the command of which he had just been elected, he was seen, among many who admired the young officer, by Miss Lucia Flucker, the daughter of the Secretary of the Province of Massachusetts. His noble form and martial appearance naturally attracted the attention of the young lady; and on a personal acquaintance, a mutual sentiment of regard grew up and ripened into love. Interruption to its course was threatened by the growing troubles of the times. Thomas Flucker, the father of Lucia, who had long held office under the British government, adhered to the royal side amidst popular discontent. The maiden had adopted her lover's views and feelings. In the gathering storm, the time came when her decision was to be made. It was made with a true woman's faith and self-devotion; and she pledged herself to the fortunes of a soldier's wife. The separation from her family that became necessary, was a painful trial, but submitted to with firmness and resolution. Mr. Flucker and his family removed from the country soon after the battle of Lexington; and Mrs. Knox, with her husband, joined the American army at Cambridge. From this time she adhered to her determination to encounter the perils and hardships incident to a military life. Neither her courage nor her powers of endurance failed. When Boston was occupied by the British, she escaped with her husband; and in their precipitate retreat, it is said that she concealed the sword he wore through the war, by having it quilted within the lining of her cloak.

In various journals we find the presence of Mrs. Knox noticed in camp. Chastellux describes the hut on a small farm where she lived with her children, a short distance from head-quarters at Verplanck's Point. Whenever her health permitted, she followed the army; and it is represented that her presence and cheerful manners did much to diffuse contentment and enliven dreary scenes. The soldiers could not murmur at privations which she endured without complaint. Sad it is, that no record remains of the ministrations of women in thus softening war's grim features. The good they did, however, was at the time acknowledged with respectful gratitude. There is reason to believe that General Knox often deferred to his wife's judgment, regarding her as a superior being; and it is said that her influence and superiority were owned by Washington himself. Her mind was undoubtedly of a high order, and her character a remarkable one. She appears to have possessed an ascendency over all with whom she associated. After the close of the struggle, while General Knox held the office of Secretary of War, his wife's position was next to that of Mrs. Washington, whom she advised in matters of ceremony. Mrs. Knox had a taste for the management and show of public life, and was a leader of the ton in the social circles at the seat of government. When the General retired from the political arena, she accompanied him to his—or rather her estates in Maine. She had inherited a share of the domain on Penobscot River and Bay which belonged to her mother's father, General Waldo, the proprietor of the Waldo patent in Maine. The property had been confirmed by government to her and General Knox after the peace.

Their residence was at Thómaston, in a splendid mansion at the head of St. George's River, furnished with taste and elegance. Here the soldier enjoyed the honors he had won, and spent his time in the indulgence of his literary tastes, and the companionship of his friends. His hospitality was unbounded, and numerous visitors frequented his house.* The influence of "Madam Knox," as she was called, on all within the circle of her acquaintance, was decided ; and she shared the lot of all remarkable persons, in having ene-

---

* Sullivan, in his " Familiar Letters on Public Characters," speaks of the hospitality of Knox at his superb mansion. It was not unusual for him in summer, when visited by great numbers of his friends, to kill an ox and twenty sheep every Monday morning, and to have a hundred beds made up daily in the house. He kept for his own use and that of his friends, twenty saddle horses and several pairs of carriage horses in his stables. This expensive style of living encroached greatly on his means.

mies as well as friends.   Tradition speaks much of her;
but little of what is said is sufficiently well authenticated
to relate.   With rare powers of conversation, a memory stored with interesting incidents, and much knowledge of the world, she was, when she pleased, one of
the most entertaining of women; yet she sometimes
awed without charming, or gave offence by an air of
independence, or the boldness of her manners.   Her
thoughts were expressed without reserve to those with
whom she conversed, and sometimes without due regard
to the sensibilities of others.   She is said to have possessed a great talent for management, and to have
been fond of match-making.   The military life of which
she had partaken, and her association with those in
command, perhaps imparted a tone to her character and
deportment.   In person she is described as being tall
and large; and in manner lofty and dignified.   She
preferred the society of men to that of her own sex;
and according to accounts given by those who remember her, mingled little with females, and had few inti-
mates among them.   Mrs. Hull was her frequent companion in Boston, and reported to be of a spirit congenial
to her own.   Both appear to have been what is called
" independent women."   It is said that in the decline
of life Mrs. Knox expressed, with deep feeling, her
regret that her interest in political men and measures
had engrossed her mind to the exclusion of aspirations
and associations more befitting a woman's sphere;
and asserted that were her life to be lived over again,
she " would be more of a wife, more of a mother, more

of a woman." She had ten children, only three of
whom lived beyond infancy. She lived at her place
after the death of General Knox, continuing active in
her charities, and in the exercise of hospitality, during
her almost eighteen years of widowhood. She died in
1824.

THE manuscript correspondence of General Gates,
now in the library of the New York Historical Society,
còntains many letters addressed to Mrs. Gates, and
some written by her. Although these give no detail of
her personal history, they throw light upon some points
in her character, showing that she was an efficient help-
mate as well as an intelligent companion to her husband
in all affairs that came properly under her supervision.
She was undoubtedly well skilled in the art of managing
the concerns of the household and farm, and acquainted
with their details. Her interest in public affairs is
however, not the less manifest. Colonel Wilkinson
announces to her the news of the victory at Saratoga;
and continual allusions in the correspondence show
that she closely observed the progress of events. Her
letter to the Count D'Estaing in acknowledgment of
the compliments paid her husband, may serve to show
that she could write both with ease and grace.

DANBURY, *Oct.*, 1778.

SIR:

The terms in which your Excellency has expressed
your esteem for General Gates are so personally obliging,

that I am afraid I am rather more grieved than pure patriotism permits, that I cannot at this time send you his portrait. It is in Virginia.

If I can have it in time before you leave these parts, I need not assure you, Sir, that my partiality to the General will be such powerful inducement to my transmitting it to the painter you have directed to copy it, that you may depend on the gratification of what your kindness to the General has made you wish for.

With all the gratitude which the honor you feel inclined to confer on General Gates entitles you to from his family, and with the respect your personal merit commands from all, I have the honor to be,

Sir, your Excellency's most humble
and most obedient servant.*

The maiden name of Mrs. Gates was Phillips. She was the daughter of a British officer. She and the General resided several years on their estate in Berkeley County, Virginia. They afterwards removed to New York, and fixed their abode at the country seat near the city which received the name of Rosehill. Here General Gates appears to have enjoyed a happy retirement, cheered by visits from his friends, for whom "my Mary" had always a cordial welcome.

* From the original MS.

VII.

~~~~~~~~

MARY DRAPER.

WHEN the news reached Connecticut that blood had been shed, Putnam, who was at work in the field, left his plough in the furrow, and started for Cambridge without delaying to change his apparel. Stark was sawing pine logs without a coat; he shut down the gate of his mill, and commenced the journey to Boston in his shirt-sleeves.* The same spirit prevailed far and near. The volunteers waited not to be supplied with arms, but seizing on whatever rude weapons were at hand, hastened away to fight for home and liberty. The women, lacking not their share of patriotic zeal, were active in preparations to encourage, assist, and sustain them. Among many whose persevering exertions were ready and efficient, Mrs. Draper is still remembered with admiration by those who knew her.† She was the wife of Captain Draper, of Dedham, Massachusetts, and lived on a farm. Her house, which was

* Sabine.

† The facts were communicated by a lady who was well acquainted with Mrs. Draper, and has often heard her relate particulars of the war.

always a home for the destitute while occupied by her, is yet standing, and is owned by one of her descendants. It was her abode to the age of one hundred years.

Mrs. Draper felt the deepest sympathy for the hardships inevitably encountered by the newly raised troops, and considered the limited means she possessed not as her own property, but belonging to her distressed country. When the first call to arms sounded throughout the land, she exhorted her husband to lose no time in hastening to the scene of action ; and with her own hands bound knapsack and blanket on the shoulders of her only son, a stripling of sixteen, bidding him depart and do his duty. To the entreaties of her daughter that her young brother might remain at home to be their protector, she answered that every arm able to aid the cause belonged to the country. "He is wanted and must go. You and I, Kate, have also service to do. Food must be prepared for the hungry ; for before to-morrow night, hundreds, I hope thousands, will be on their way to join the continental forces. Some who have travelled far will need refreshment, and you and I, with Molly, must feed as many as we can."

This undertaking, though of no small labor, was presently commenced. Captain Draper was a thriving farmer ; his granaries were well filled, and his wife's dairy was her special care and pride. All the resources at her command were in requisition to contribute to her benevolent purpose. Assisted by her daughter and the domestic, she spent the whole day and night, and

the succeding day, in baking brown bread. The ovens
of that day were not the small ones now in use, but
were suited for such an occasion, each holding bread
sufficient to supply a neighborhood. By good fortune
two of these monster ovens appertained to the establishment, as is frequently the case in New England. These
were soon in full blast, and the kneading trough was
plied by hands that shrank not from the task. At that
time of hurry and confusion, none could stop long
enough to dine. The people were under the influence
of strong excitement, and all were in such haste to join
the army, that they stayed only to relieve the cravings
of hunger, though from want of food, and fatigue, many
were almost exhausted. With the help of a disabled
veteran of the French war, who had for years resided in
her family, Mrs. Draper had soon her stores in readiness.
A long form was erected by the road-side ; large pans
of bread and cheese were placed upon it, and replenished
as often as was necessary; while old John brought
cider in pails from the cellar, which, poured into tubs,
was served out by two lads who volunteered their
services. Thus were the weary patriots refreshed on
their way. Mrs. Draper presided at the entertainment;
and when her own stock of provisions began to fail,
applied to her neighbors for aid. By their contributions
her hospitable board was supplied, till in a few days
the necessity for extraordinary exertion had in a
measure passed, and order and discipline took the place
of popular tumult. When each soldier carried his

rations, the calls on private benevolence were less
frequent and imperative.

But ere long came the startling intelligence, after the
battle of Bunker Hill, that a scarcity of ammunition
had been experienced.   General Washington called
upon the inhabitants to send to head-quarters every
ounce of lead or pewter at their disposal, saying that
any quantity, however small, would be gratefully
received.

This appeal could not be disregarded.   It is difficult
at this day to estimate the value of pewter as an ornamental as well as indispensable convenience. The more
precious metals had not then found their way to the
tables of New Englanders; and throughout the country, services of pewter, scoured to the brightness of
silver, covered the board, even in the mansions of the
wealthy. Few withheld their portion in that hour of
the country's need; and noble were the sacrifices made
in presenting their willing offerings. Mrs. Draper was
rich in a large stock of pewter, which she valued as
the ornament of her house. Much of it was precious
to her as the gift of a departed mother. But the call
reached her heart, and she delayed not obedience, thank-
ful that she was able to contribute so largely to the re-
quirements of her suffering country. Her husband
before joining the army had purchased a mould for
casting bullets, to supply himself and son with this
article of warfare. Mrs. Draper was not satisfied with
merely giving the material required, when she could

possibly do more ; and her platters, pans, and dishes were soon in process of transformation into balls.

The approach of winter brought fears that the re-sources of the country would hardly yield supplies for the pressing wants of the army.   Mrs. Draper was one of the most active in efforts to meet the exigencies of the times ; and hesitated at no sacrifice of personal convenience to increase her contributions.   The supply of domestic cloth designed for her family was in a short time converted by her labor, assisted by that of her daughter and maid, into coats for the soldiers : the sheets and blankets with which her presses were stored, were fashioned into shirts ; and even the flannel already made up for herself and daughter, was altered into men's habiliments.   Such was the aid rendered by women whose deeds of disinterested generosity were never known beyond their own immediate neighborhood !

ANOTHER anecdote may here be mentioned, illustrative of the spirit that was abroad.   On the morning after the battle of Lexington, a company of nearly a hundred halted before the house of Colonel Pond of West Dedham.   They had marched all night, and were covered with dust, and faint from fatigue and want of food. Their haste was urgent, and the mistress of the house whose hospitality they claimed, was unprepared for the entertainment of so large a party.   Her husband was absent with the army, and she had only one female assistant and a hired man.   But the willing heart can do wonders.   In a few minutes she had a large brass kettle holding ten pails full, over the fire, filled with water and Indian meal for hasty pudding.   In the barn-yard were ten cows ready to contribute their share to the morning meal.   Near the farm-house was a store well supplied with brown earthen dishes, and pewter spoons tied in dozens for sale.   The military guests volunteered their aid.   Some milked the cows, others stirred the pudding; while the two domestics collected all the milk in the neighborhood.   Thus, in the short space of an hour, by the energetic efforts of one kind-hearted woman, a hundred weary, hungry soldiers were provided with refreshment.   They ate, and marched on to the place of their destination; receiving encour-agement, it cannot be doubted, from this simple mani-festation of good-will, which was not soon forgotten.

VIII.

~~~~~~

FREDERICA DE RIEDESEL.

GENERAL WILKINSON, who was personally acquainted with Madame de Riedesel, published fragments of her journal in his Memoirs. He calls her "the amiable, accomplished, and dignified baroness."—"I have more than once," he says, "seen her charming blue eyes bedewed with tears, at the recital of her sufferings." The regard she inspired, however, was not due entirely to admiration of her loveliness; for others in the American ranks, as well as in Europe, were deeply interested in her account of her adventures.

Frederica Charlotte Louisa, the daughter of Massow, the Prussian Minister of State, was born in Brandenburgh, in 1746. Her father was Intendant General of the allied army at Minden, where, at the age of seventeen, she married Lieutenant Colonel Baron de Riedesel. In the war of the Revolution, he was appointed to the command of the Brunswick forces in the British service in America, and his wife followed him in 1777, with her three young children. Her journal, and letters addressed to her mother, describe her travels with the camp through various parts of the country,

and the occurrences she witnessed. These papers, intended only for a circle of the writer's friends, were
first published by her son-in-law in Germany in 1801,
shortly after the death of General Riedesel. Portions
having been copied into periodicals, and read with interest, the whole was translated, and presented to the
American public. It forms an appropriate appendix
to the history of the period, with its graphic pictures of
scenes in the war and the state of society, and its
notices of distinguished men. But it is still more valuable as exhibiting an example of female energy, fortitude, and conjugal devotion. The moral is the more
striking as drawn from the experience of a woman of
rank, subjected to dangers and privations from which
the soldier might have shrunk. The readiness with
which she hastened to cross the ocean that she might
bear her husband company through toils or want, or
suffering, or death, the courage with which she encountered perils, and the cheerful resignation displayed under
trials felt the more severely for the sake of those she
loved, present a touching picture of fidelity and tenderness. After she has joined her husband in Canada,
and is again separated from him, she thinks only of joy
at being permitted at last to follow the army. Obliged to pass the night on a lonely island, where the only
shelter is a half-finished house, and the only couch a
cluster of bushes over which the traveller's cloaks
are spread, she utters no murmur, nor complains of
the scarcity of food. "A soldier," she says, "put a pot
to the fire. I asked him what it contained. 'Some

potatoes,' quoth he, 'which I brought with me.' I threw a longing glance at them; but as they were few, it would have been cruel to deprive him of them. At last my desire to have some for my children overcame my diffidence; and he gave me half his little provision (about twelve potatoes), and took at the same time from his pocket two or three ends of candles, which I accepted with pleasure; for my children were afraid to remain in the dark. A dollar which I gave him made him as happy as his liberality had made me."

With her three children, the Baroness proceeded to meet her husband at Fort Edward. When the army broke up the encampment, she would not remain behind. Her spirits rose at the observation of General Burgoyne on the passage across the Hudson—" Britons never retrograde." The action at Freeman's Farm took place in her hearing, and some of the wounded were brought to the house where she was. Among them was a young English officer, an only son, whose sufferings excited her deepest sympathy, and whose last moans she heard. A calash was ordered for her further progress with the army. They marched through extensive forests, and a beautiful district, deserted by the inhabitants, who were gone to re-inforce General Gates.

The Diary gives a touching account of the scenes passed through at the memorable conclusion of Burgoyne's campaign, with the battles of Saratoga. "On the seventh of October," she says, " our misfortunes began." Generals Burgoyne, Phillips, and Frazer, with

6

the Baron, were to dine with her on that day. She
had observed in the morning an unusual movement in
the camp; and had seen a number of armed Indians in
their war dresses, who answered "War! war!" to her
inquiries whither they were going. As the dinner hour
approached, an increased tumult, the firing, and the yell-
ing of the savages, announced the approaching battle.
The roar of artillery became louder and more incessant.
At four o'clock, instead of the guests invited, General
Frazer was brought in mortally wounded. The table,
already prepared for dinner, was removed to make room
for his bed. The Baroness, terrified by the noise of the
conflict raging without, expected every moment to see
her husband also led in pale and helpless. Towards
night he came to the house, dined in haste, and desired
his wife to pack up her camp furniture, and be ready
for removal at an instant's warning. His dejected
countenance told the disastrous result. Lady Ackland,
whose tent was adjoining, was presently informed that
her husband was wounded, and a prisoner! Thus
through the long hours till day, the kind ministries of
the Baroness were demanded by many sufferers. "I
divided the night," she says, "between her I wished to
comfort, and my children who were asleep, but who I
feared might disturb the poor dying General. Several
times he begged my pardon for the trouble he thought
he gave me. About three o'clock I was informed he
could not live much longer; and as I did not wish to
be present at his last struggle, I wrapped my children

in blankets, and retired into the room below. At eight in the morning he expired."

All day the cannonade continued, while the melancholy spectacle of the dead was before their eyes. The women attended the wounded soldiers who were brought in, like ministering angels. In the afternoon the Baroness saw the house that had been built for her in flames.

Frazer's last request had been that he should be buried at six in the evening, in the great redoubt on the hill; and the retreat was delayed for this purpose. The generals, with their retinues, followed the honored corpse to the spot, in the midst of a heavy fire from the Americans; for General Gates knew not that it was a funeral procession. The women stood in full view of this impressive and awful scene, so eloquently described by Burgoyne himself:

"The incessant cannonade during the solemnity; the steady attitude and unaltered voice with which the the chaplain officiated, though frequently covered with dust which the shot threw up on all sides of him; the mute but expressive mixture of sensibility and indignation upon every countenance; these objects will remain to the last of life upon the mind of every man who was present."

The deepening shadows of evening closed around the group thus rendering the last service to one of their number, while each might anticipate his own death in the next report of artillery. A subject was presented

for the pencil of a master. An appropriate side-piece
to the picture might represent the group of anxious
females who shared the peril, regardless of themselves.
" Many cannon-balls," says Madame de Riedesel, " flew
close by me ; but I had my eyes directed towards the
mountain where my husband was standing amidst the
fire of the enemy · and of course I did not think of my
own danger."

That night the army commenced its retreat, leaving
the sick and wounded ; a flag of truce waving over the
hospital thus abandoned to the mercy of the foe. The
rain fell in torrents all day of the 9th, and it was dark
when they reached Saratoga. The Baroness suffered
cruel suspense as to the fate of her husband. She had
taken charge of some valuables belonging to the officers,
and having no place to change her drenched apparel,
lay down with her children upon some straw by the
fire. Her provisions were shared the next day with the
officers; and being insufficient to satisfy their hunger,
she made an appeal to the Adjutant-General in their
behalf. Again the alarm of battle, and reports of muskets and cannon, drove them to seek shelter in a house,
which was fired at under the impression that the generals were there. It was occupied by women and crippled
soldiers. They were obliged at last to descend into the
cellar, where the Baroness laid herself in a corner,
supporting her children's heads on her knees. The
night was passed in the utmost terror and anguish; and
with the morning the terrible cannonade commenced
anew. So it continued for several days. But in the

midst of the dreadful scenes, when the Baron spoke of sending his family to the American camp, the heroic wife declared that nothing would be so painful to her as to owe safety to those with whom he was fighting. He then consented that she should continue to follow the army. "However," she says—"the apprehension that he might have marched away, repeatedly entered my mind; and I crept up the staircase more than once to dispel my fears. When I saw our soldiers near their watchfires, I became more calm, and could even have slept."

"The want of water continuing to distress us, we could not but be extremely glad to find a soldier's wife so spirited as to fetch some from the river, an occupation from which the boldest might have shrunk, as the Americans shot every one who approached it. They told us afterwards that they spared her on account of her sex.

"I endeavored to dispel my melancholy by continually attending to the wounded. I made them tea and coffee, and often shared my dinner with them. One day a Canadian officer came creeping into our cellar, and was hardly able to say that he was dying with hunger. I felt happy to offer him my dinner, by eating which he recovered his health, and I gained his friendship."

At length the danger was over.

> " A gallant army formed their last array
> Upon that field, in silence and deep gloom,
> And at their conquerors' feet'
> Laid their war weapons down.

"Sullen and stern—disarmed but not dishonored;
Brave men—but brave in vain—they yielded there;—
   The soldier's trial task
   Is not alone ' to die.' "

On the seventeenth, the capitulation was carried into effect. The generals waited upon Gates, and the troops surrendered themselves prisoners of war. "At last," writes the fair Riedesel, "my husband's groom brought me a message to join him with the children. I once more seated myself in my dear calash; and while driving through the American camp, was gratified to observe that nobody looked at us with disrespect; but on the contrary, greeted us, and seemed touched at the sight of a captive mother with three children. I must candidly confess that I did not present myself, though so situated, with much courage to the enemy. When I drew near the tents, a fine-looking man advanced towards me, helped the children from the calash, and kissed and caressed them. He then offered me his arm, and tears trembled in his eyes. "You tremble, madam," said he; "do not be alarmed, I beg of you." "Sir," cried I—"a countenance so expressive of benevolence, and the kindness you have evinced towards my children, are sufficient to dispel all apprehension." He then ushered me into the tent of General Gates, whom I found engaged in friendly conversation with Generals Burgoyne and Phillips. General Burgoyne said to me— "You can now be quiet and free from all apprehension of danger." I replied that I should indeed be reprehensible, if I felt any anxiety, when our general was on such friendly terms with General Gates.

" All the Generals remained to dine with the American commander. The gentleman who had received me with so much kindness, came and said to me: " You may find it embarrassing to be the only lady in so large a company of gentlemen. Will you come with your children to my tent, and partake of a frugal dinner, offered with the best will?" " You show me so much kindness," replied I, " I cannot but believe that you are a husband and a father." He informed me that he was General Schuyler. The dinner was of excellent smoked tongues, beefstakes, potatoes, fresh butter, and bread. Never did a meal give me so much pleasure. I was easy after many months of anxiety, and I read the same happy change in the countenances of those around me. That my husband was out of danger, was a still greater cause of joy. After our dinner, General Schuyler begged me to pay him a visit at his house near Albany, where he expected that General Burgoyne would also be his guest. I sent to ask my husband's directions, who advised me to accept the invitation. We were two days' journey from Albany, and as it was now five o'clock in the afternoon, he wished me to endeavor to reach, on that day, a place distant about three hours' ride. General Schuyler carried his civilities so far as to solicit a well-bred French officer to accompany me on that first part of my journey. As soon as he saw me safely established in the house where I was to remain, he went back to the General.

"We reached Albany, where we had so often wished ourselves; but did not enter that city, as we had hoped, with a victorious army. Our reception, however, from General Schuyler, and his wife and daughters, was not like the reception of enemies, but of the most intimate friends. They loaded us with kindness; and they behaved in the same manner towards General Burgoyne, though he had without any necessity ordered their splendid establishment to be burnt. All their actions proved that at the sight of the misfortunes of others, they quickly forgot their own. Burgoyne was so much affected by this generous deportment, that he said to Schuyler: "You are too kind to me—who have done you so much injury." "Such is the fate of war," he replied; "let us not dwell on this subject." We remained three days with that excellent family, and they seemed to regret our departure."

General Riedesel, who brooded continually on the late disastrous events, and upon his captivity, was not able to bear his troubles with the spirit and cheerfulness of his wife. He became moody and irritable; and his health was much impaired in consequence of having passed many nights in the damp air. "One day," says the Baroness, "when he was much indisposed, the American sentinels at our doors were very noisy in their merriment and drinking; and grew more so when my husband sent a message desiring them to be quiet; but as soon as I went myself, and told them the General was sick,

they were immediately silent.   This proves that the
Americans also respect our sex."

The prisoners at length reached Boston ; and after a
stay of three weeks, were transported to Cambridge,
where Madame de Riedesel and her family were lodged
in one of the best houses of the place.*   None of the
officers were permitted to enter Boston ; but Madame
de Riedesel went to visit Mrs. Carter, the daughter of
General Schuyler, and dined with her several times.
Boston she describes as a fine city ; but the inhabitants
as "outrageously patriotic."   The captives met in some
instances with very different treatment from that
which they had before encountered ; and the worst, she
says, from persons of her own sex.   They gazed at
her with indignation, and testified contempt when she
passed near them.   Mrs. Carter resembled her parents
in mildness and goodness of heart ; but the Baroness has
no admiration for her husband—"this wicked Mr. Carter,
who, in consequence of General Howe's having burnt
several villages and small towns, suggested to his
countrymen to cut off our generals' heads, to pickle
them, and to put them in small barrels ; and as often as
the English should again burn a village—to send them
one of these barrels."   She here adds some sad stories
of American cruelty towards the loyalists.

On the third of June, 1778, Madame de Riedesel

* On one of the windows of this house the name "Riedesel," written
on the glass with a diamond, is still to be seen.   In front are several
beautiful lime-trees, and the view is a lovely one.   The house near it,
which Washington occupied as his head-quarters, is now the residence
of the poet Longfellow.

6*

gave a ball and supper to celebrate her husband's birth-
day. The British officers were invited, with Mr. and
Mrs. Carter, and General Burgoyne, of whom the fair
hostess records that he sent an excuse after he had
made them wait till eight o'clock. "He had always
some excuse," observes she—"for not visiting us, until
he was about departing for England, when he came
and made me many apologies; to which I made no
other reply than that I should be extremely sorry if he
had put himself to any inconvenience for our sake."
The dance and supper were so brilliant, and so numer-
ously attended, and the toasts drunk with such enthusiasm, that the house was surrounded with people, who
began to suspect a conspiracy. The Baroness here
notices the American method of telegraphing by lighting
torches on surrounding heights, when they wish to call
troops together. When General Howe attempted to
rescue the troops detained in Boston, the inhabitants
planted their torches, and a crowd of people without
shoes or stockings—their rifles on their shoulders,
flocked together; so that the landing would have been
attended with extreme difficulty. Towards the approach of winter the prisoners received orders to set
out for Virginia. The ingenuity of Madame de Riedesel
devised means of preserving the colors of the German
regiments, which the Americans believed they had
burned. A mattress was made under her direction,
into which the honorable badges were introduced.
Captain O'Connel, under pretence of some commission,
took the mattress to New York; and the Baroness

received it again at Halifax, on their voyage from New York to Canada, and had it placed in her cabin.

A rascal on no small scale was the cook of Madame la Baronne. She had given him money for the daily expenditure—but he had paid nobody; and while preparations for the journey were going on, bills were presented to the amount of a thousand dollars. The cook was arrested; but escaping, went into the service of General Gates, who finding him too expensive, he entered into the employment of General La Fayette. The Marquis used to say, "that he was a cook only fit for a king."

The Baroness had the accommodation of an English coach in commencing her journey to Virginia, November, 1778. The provisions followed in the baggage wagon; but as that moved more slowly, they were often without food, and were obliged to make a halt every fourth day. At Hartford, General La Fayette was invited to dine by the Baron, somewhat to the perplexity of his wife, who feared she would have difficulty in preparing her provisions so as to suit one who appreciated a good dinner. The Marquis is mentioned with great respect; but Madame de Riedesel thinks the suspicions of the Americans were excited by hearing them speak French.

"We reached one day a pretty little town; but our wagon remaining behind, we were very hungry. Seeing much fresh meat in the house where we stopped, I begged the landlady to sell me some. "I have," quoth she, "several sorts of meat; beef, mutton and lamb." I said, "let me have some; I will pay you liberally." But snapping her fingers, she replied; "You shall not have a morsel of it; why have you left your country to slay and rob us of our property? Now that you are our prisoners, it is our turn to vex you." "But," rejoined I, "see those poor children; they are dying of hunger." She remained still unmoved; but when at length my youngest child, Caroline, who was then about two years and a half old, went to her, seized her hands, and said in English: "Good woman, I am indeed very hungry," she could no longer resist; and carrying the child to her room, she gave her an egg. "But," persisted the dear little one, "I have two sisters." Affected by this remark, the hostess gave her three eggs, saying, "I am loth to be so weak, but I cannot refuse the child." By-and-by she softened, and offered me bread and butter. I made tea: and saw that the hostess looked at our tea-pot with a longing eye; for the Americans are very fond of that beverage; yet they had stoutly resolved not to drink any more, the tax on tea, as is well known, having been the immediate cause of the contest with Great Britain. I offered her, however, a cup, and presented her with a paper case full of tea. This drove away all clouds between us. She begged me to go with her into the kitchen, and there I found her husband eating a piece of pork. The woman went into the cellar to bring me a basket of potatoes. When she returned into the kitchen, the husband offered her some of his dainty food; she tasted it, and returned to him what remained. I was disagreeably struck with this partnership; but the man probably thought I was envious of it, on account of the hunger I had manifested; and presented me with the little both had left. I feared by refusing, to offend them, and lose the potatoes. I therefore accepted the morsel, and having kept up the appearance as if I ate, threw it secretly into the fire. We were now in perfect amity; with the potatoes and some butter I made a good supper, and we had to ourselves three neat rooms, with very good beds."

On the banks of the Hudson, in a skipper's house, they were not so fortunate in finding good accommodations—being given the remnants of breakfast after the hostess, children, and servants had finished their meal. The woman was a staunch republican, and could not bring herself to any courtesies towards the enemies of her country. They fared a little better after crossing the river. When the aids-de-camp who accompanied them to the house where they were to lodge, wished to warm themselves in the kitchen, the host followed, and taking them by their arms, said, " Is it not enough that I give you shelter, ye wretched royalists?" His wife, however, was more amiable; and his coarseness gradually softened, till they became good friends.

They stopped one night on the road, at the house of a Colonel Howe, to whom the Baroness meant to pay a compliment by asking him if he was a relative of the general of that name. "Heaven forbid!" replied he, in great anger; "he is not worthy of that honor." Madame de Riedesel is amusingly indignant at the sanguinary temper of this gentleman's daughter, who was very pretty and only fourteen years of age. "Sitting with her near the fire, she said on a sudden, staring at the blaze, 'Oh! if I had here the king of England, with how much pleasure I could roast and eat him!' I looked at her with indignation, and said, 'I am almost ashamed to belong to a sex capable of indulging such fancies!' I shall never forget that detestable girl."

Passing through a wild, grand, and picturesque country, they at length arrived in Virginia. At a day's distance from the place of destination, their little stock of provisions gave out. At noon they reached a house, and begged for some dinner; but all assistance was denied them, with many imprecations upon the royalists. "Seizing some maize, I begged our hostess to give me some of it to make a little bread. She replied that she needed it for her black people. 'They work for us,' she added, 'and you come to kill us.' Captain Edmonstone offered to pay her one or two guineas for a little wheat. But she answered, 'You shall not have it even for hundreds of guineas; and it will be so much the better if you all die!' The captain became so enraged at these words, that he was about to take the maize; but I prevented him from doing it, thinking we should soon meet with more charitable people. But in this I was much mistaken; for we did not see even a solitary hut. The roads were execrable, and the horses could hardly move. My children, starving from hunger, grew pale, and for the first time lost their spirits. Captain Edmonstone, deeply affected at this, went about asking some-

thing for the children; and received at last from one of
the wagoners who transported our baggage, a piece of
stale bread, of three ounces weight, upon which many
a tooth had already exercised its strength. Yet to my
children it was at this time a delicious morsel. I broke
it, and was about giving the first piece to the youngest,
but she said, ' No, mamma; my sisters are more in
want of it than I am.' The two eldest girls, with no
less generosity, thought that little Caroline was to have
the first piece. I then distributed to each her small
portion. Tears ran down my cheeks; and had I ever
refused to the poor a piece of bread, I should have
thought retributive justice had overtaken me. Captain
Edmonstone, who was much affected, presented the
generous wagoner who had given us his last morsel,
with a guinea; and when we were arrived at our place
of destination, we provided him, besides, with bread for
a part of his journey homewards."

The place of their destination was Colle, in Virginia,
where General Riedesel, who had advanced with the
troops, already expected them with impatient anxiety.
This was about the middle of February, 1779. They
had passed, in the journey, through the States of Connecticut, New York, New Jersey, Pennsylvania, and
Maryland; and in about three months had travelled
six hundred and twenty-eight miles. They hired a
house belonging to an Italian who was about leaving
the country. The troops were at Charlottesville, three
hours' ride distant—the road thither running through a
fine wood.

The life of Madame de Riedesel and her family in
Virginia was not an unhappy one, though they suffered
from the heat during the summer.   The General was
brought home one day with a *coup de soleil*, which for
years afterwards affected his health.   His physician and
acquaintances advised him to go to Frederic Springs.
It was there that he and his wife became acquainted
with General Washington's family, and with some other
amiable persons attached to the American cause.

While at Frederic Springs, General Riedesel received the news that he and General Phillips, with their
aids-de-camp, were expected in New York, where
they were to be exchanged for American prisoners.
He returned to Colle, to place the troops during his
absence, under the care of Colonel Specht.   In August,
1779, the Baroness left the Springs to join her husband
in Pennsylvania, stopping near Baltimore to pay a visit
to one of the ladies with whom, though of opposite
political opinions, she had formed a friendship at the
Springs.   This visit was a charming episode in the
troubled life of Madame de Riedesel.   She remembered
long after, with gratitude, the hospitality and kindness
received.   " The loyalists," she says, " received us with
frank hospitality, from political sympathy ; and those of
opposite principles gave us a friendly welcome, merely
from habit ; for in that country it would be considered a crime to behave otherwise towards strangers."

At Elizabethtown they met with many friends to
their cause.   They were exulting in the anticipation

of an exchange, and restoration to freedom, when an officer arrived, commissioned by Washington to deliver to General Phillips a letter containing an order to return to Virginia—Congress having rejected the proposal of a cartel. The disappointment was excessive, but unavoidable ; and after a day's halt, they commenced their journey back. On reaching Bethlehem, the two Generals, Riedesel and Phillips, obtained permission to remain there till the difficulties respecting the cartel should be removed. Their bill, after six weeks' lodging for the party, with the care of their horses, amounted to thirty-two thousand dollars in paper money, corresponding to about four hundred guineas in specie. A traveller who bought silver coin, gave them eighty dollars in paper money for every dollar in silver, and thus enabled them to leave the place, when at last permitted to go to New York.

Arrived at New York, a soldier went before the travellers " from the gate of the city," to show the way to their lodging. This proved to be the house of the Governor, General Tryon, where the Baroness made herself at home with her children and attendants, under the belief that they had been conducted to a hotel. She received visits here from General Patterson, the Commandant of the city ; and also from Generals Cornwallis and Clinton ; and had a romantic introduction to her host, who did not announce his name at the first visit, nor till she had expressed a wish to become personally acquainted with him.

Madame de Riedesel went from the city to Genera.

Clinton's country-seat, a mile distant, where her children were innoculated for the small-pox. When the danger of infection was over, they returned and spent the winter in New York. The charming country-seat was again their residence in the summer of 1780. The situation was uncommonly beautiful; around the house were meadows and orchards, with the Hudson at their feet; and they had abundance of delicious fruit. General Clinton visited them frequently, and the last time was accompanied by Major André, the day before he set out on his fatal expedition.

The breaking out of a malignant fever, which made dreadful ravages in the city and neighborhood, disturbed their pleasure. In the house no less than twenty were laboring under the disease. The Baron himself was dangerously ill; and the cares and nursing devolved on his wife, who was worn out with anxiety. "We were one day," she says, "in anxious expectation of our physician from New York, my husband's symptoms having become of late more and more threatening. He was continually in a lethargic stupor, and when I presented him the sago water, which the physician had ordered for him, he turned round, desiring me to let him die quietly. He thought his end must be near. The physician having entered the room at that moment, I urgently begged him to tell me the truth, and to let me know if there was any hope of my husband's recovery. He had scarcely said 'Yes,' when my children, on hearing this merciful word, sprang from under a table where they had lain concealed in dreadful expectation of the doctor's sentence, threw themselves at his feet, and kissed his hands with rapturous feelings of gratitude. Nobody could have witnessed the scene without sharing my deep emotion." *   * "Out of thirty persons of whom our family consisted, ten only escaped the disease. It is astonishing how much the frail human creature can endure; and I am amazed that I survived such hard trials. My happy temperament permitted me even to be gay and cheerful, whenever my hopes were encouraged. The best health is often undermined by such sufferings; still I rejoice to think I had it in my power to be useful to those who are dearest to me; and that without my exertions, I might have lost those who now contribute so much to my felicity. At length all my patients were cured."

In the autumn Generals Phillips and Riedesel were exchanged; although the rest of the army who surrendered at Saratoga still remained prisoners. General Clinton wished to replace the Baron in active service, and appointed him Lieutenant General, investing him with the command at Long Island. A second dangerous attack of fever so impaired his health, that the physicians thought he could never recover as long as he resided in that climate. But he would not leave the army, nor ask a furlough.

In the following spring, the Baroness was established on Long Island. Her husband's health mended slowly; and his thoughts being often fixed on the remnant of his late regiments, which had remained in Canada, General Clinton at length consented that he should pay them a visit. Being about to depart in July, Madame de Riedesel sent the residue of their wood—about thirty cords—to some poor families, and took but a few articles of furniture, returning the rest to the commissary of the army. They at last embarked for Canada, and reached Quebec after a journey of about two months, in September, 1781.

Madame de Riedesel gives a pleasing description of her life in Canada, which seems to have been very agreeable. She had an opportunity of observing the habits of the Indians, some of whom were under her husband's command. Before she joined him on her first arrival in Canada, one of the savages, having heard that M. de Riedesel was ill, that he was married, and felt uneasy on account of the delay in his wife's arrival, came with his own wife, and said to the General; "I love my wife—but I love thee also; in proof of which I give her to thee." The Indian seemed distressed and almost offended at the refusal of his gift. It is somewhat remarkable that this man was by birth a German, who had been taken prisoner by the savages when about fifteen years of age.

In the summer of 1783, the General having received news of the death of his father, became impatient to return to Europe. They made all necessary arrangements for the voyage, and after the troops had embarked, were accompanied by many of their friends to the vessel.

General and Madame de Riedesel were graciously received by the king and queen of Great Britain when they reached London. Their return to Germany was welcomed by their old friends and acquaintance; and the fair traveller rejoiced on seeing her husband once more "standing in the midst of his soldiers, and a multitude of parents, wives, children, brothers and sisters, who either rejoiced at meeting again their relatives who had been so long absent, or mourned over the loss of those who had been long missed and expected."

It is to be presumed that the after life of one who possessed a spirit so generous and cheerful, was happy. The record of her sojourn in America impresses the reader with feelings of admiration and esteem for her. Such details have a value beyond that of a mere narration of facts; they illustrate character, and add the warm coloring of life to the outlines of history. They afford light by which we can more clearly read the great lessons in the story of battle and victory. In the midst of our enthusiasm for the achievement of Saratoga, we do not lose pity for the disasters that accompanied the triumph. We see courtesy and humanity prevailing in the midst of the strife, and honor both the opposing principles of loyalty and patriotism. "If the figures of the picture are at first fierce and repulsive—the figures of brethren armed against brethren, of mercenary Germans and frantic savages, Canadian rangers and American plough- men, all bristling together with the horrid front of war —what a charm of contrast is presented, when among these stern and forbidding groups is beheld the form of a Christian woman moving to and fro, disarming the heart of every emotion but reverence, softening the misfortunes of defeat, and checking the elation of victory!"

After the death of General Riedesel, in 1800, the Baroness fixed her residence at Berlin, where she died, on the 29th of March, 1808. She established here an asylum for military orphans, and an alms-house for the poor in Brunswick.

She was long remembered, with her interesting family, in Virginia, as well as in other parts of the continent. She is described as full in figure, and possessing no small share of beauty. Some of her foreign habits rendered her rather conspicuous; such as riding in boots, and in what was then called, "the European fashion;" and she was sometimes charged with carelessness in her attire. She was visited by many families in the neighborhood of Charlottesville.

IX.

DOROTHY HANCOCK.

MRS. HANCOCK was one of those who, at Cambridge, extended courtesies to the ladies of Burgoyne's army, when under the convention of surrender. She was the daughter of Edmund Quincy, of Massachusetts, and was born in 1750. At the age of twenty-four she was married to one of the greatest men of the age. The honor that encircled the name of John Hancock, received added lustre from the fair partner of his fortunes. Moving in the best circles of society, and a leader in taste and fashion, she filled her illustrious station with dignity, and dispensed with grace the hospitalities of her house. There might be seen at her table all classes; the grave clergy, the veteran and the gay—and the gifted in song, or anecdote, or wit. The social customs of the day savored of profusion. It was a practice in families of respectability, to have a tankard of punch made in the morning, of which visitors during the day were invited to partake. Dinners and suppers were frequently interchanged: and the tables were loaded with provision. The dinner hour was at one or two o'clock; and three was the latest for formal

occasions.   The evening amusement was usually a game
at cards; and dancing was much in vogue.   There
were concerts; but theatrical amusements were pro-
hibited.   Much attention was paid to dress; and coats
various in color were worn.

Mrs. Hancock was not only admirable in the pleasing
duties of mistress of her household, but in hours of
disease and pain soothed her husband and calmed his
sensitive and irritable temper.   She had her share, too,
in the terrors and dangers of the war.   When the
British made their attack at Lexington and Concord,
she was at the latter place with Mr. Hancock, and fled
with him to Woburn.   Many a scene of Revolutionary
days, in which she was herself an actor or a spectator,
she was accustomed to depict in after years.   She would
often describe the appearance and manners of the
British officers who had been quartered in Boston,
dwelling particularly on the military virtue of Earl
Percy, who slept in a tent among his soldiers encamped
on the Common in the winter of 1774–5, and whose
voice could be heard at the dawn of day, drilling his
troops.

During the life of her husband, Mrs. Hancock was
of necessity much in the gay world, in which she occupied a position so distinguished.   After his death she
married Captain Scott, with whom she passed a less
brilliant, yet not a less happy life.   Her later years
were spent in seclusion.   She was still, however, surrounded by friends who were instructed and charmed
by her superior mind, and cheerful conversation.   She

went but little into society, and whenever she appeared, was received with great attention.   La Fayette, on his visit to this country, called upon her, and many spoke of the interesting interview witnessed between "the once youthful chevalier and the splendid belle."

She died in her seventy-eighth year.   Several anecdotes are told of her sprightliness, good sense, and benevolence, but unfortunately cannot be obtained in a form sufficiently authentic for this sketch.

~~~~~~~~~~~~

SARAH HULL, the wife of Major William Hull, was one of those women who followed their husbands to the camp, resolved to partake their dangers and privations.   She was with the army at Saratoga, and joined the other American ladies in kind and soothing attentions to the fair captives after the surrender.   She was the daughter of Judge Fuller, of Newton, Massachusetts, and was born about 1755.   At the close of the war she returned home ; and when her gallant husband was appointed general of the county militia, did the honors of his marquée, and received guests of distinction with a grace, dignity, and affability that attracted general admiration.   For several years General Hull held the office of Governor of Michigan Territory. In her eminent station, Mrs. Hull displayed so much good sense, with more brilliant accomplishments, that she improved the state of society in her neighborhood, without provoking envy by her superiority.   The influence of a strong intellect, with cultivated taste and

7

refinement, presided in her circle. Those who visited the wild country about them found a generous welcome at her hospitable mansion, and departed with admiring recollections of her and her daughters.

But it was in the cloud of misfortune that the energy of Mrs. Hull's character was most clearly shown. Governor Hull having been appointed Major General in the war of 1812, met with disasters which compelled his surrender, and subjected him to suspicions of treason. His protracted trial and his defence belong to history. His wife sustained these evils with a trustful serenity, hoping that the day would yet come when all doubts should be cleared away, and her husband restored to public confidence. The loss of her son in battle was borne with the same Christian fortitude. Her quiet, calm demeanor exhibited no trace of the suffering that had wrung her heart. She lived to see her hopes realized in the General's complete vindication ; and died in 1826, in less than a year from his decease.

X.

———∼∼∼∼———

HARRIET ACKLAND.

THE story of female heroism, fidelity, and piety, with
which the name of Lady Harriet Ackland is associated,
is familiar to the readers of American history. To the
fairer page where such examples of virtue are recorded,
we delight to turn from the details of military achievement. The presence that shed radiance on the sunny
days of hope and success, relieved and brightened the
season of disaster. Her offices of mediation softened
the bitterness of political animosity. The benevolent
and conciliating efforts are known by which this heroine
endeavored to settle differences that arose between the
captive British soldiers and their conquerors, at the
time the troops were quartered at Cambridge after the
surrender.

Lady Harriet was the wife of Major Ackland, an
officer in Burgoyne's army. She accompanied him to
Canada in 1776, and in the disastrous campaign of the
following year, from Canada to Saratoga. Beautiful
and admired as she was, and accustomed to all the
luxuries and refinements incident to rank and fortune,
her delicate frame ill calculated to sustain the various

hardships to be undergone, she yet shrank not from her husband's perils and privations in traversing the dreary wilderness. When he lay ill at Chambly, in a miserable hut, her attention was assiduous, in defiance of fatigue and discomfort. When he was wounded at Hubbardton, she hastened from Montreal, where she had been at first persuaded to remain, and crossed Lake Champlain, resolved to leave him no more. Her vehicle of conveyance on the march of the army, was part of the time a small two-wheeled tumbril, drawn by a single horse, over roads almost impassable. The women followed in the rear of the artillery and baggage; but heard all the uproar in encounters with the enemy.

On the advance of the army to Fort Edward, the tent in which Lady Ackland lodged took fire, the light being pushed over by a pet Newfoundland dog; and she and her husband made their escape with the utmost difficulty. But no hazards dissuaded the wife from her purpose. She was not only the ministering angel of him she loved so devotedly, but won the admiration of the army by her amiable deportment; continually making little presents to the officers belonging to his corps, whenever she had any thing among her stores worth acceptance; and receiving in return every kind attention which could mitigate the hardships she had daily to encounter.*

In the decisive action of the seventh of October, Lady Ackland was again in the tumult of battle. Dur-

* Burgoyne's Campaign; Thacher's Military Journal; and other authorities.

ing the heat of the conflict, tortured by anxiety, she took refuge among the wounded and dying. Her husband, commanding the grenadiers, was in the most exposed part of the battle, and she awaited his fate in awful suspense. The Baroness Riedesel, and the wives of two other field officers, were her companions in apprehension. One of the officers was brought in wounded, and the death of the other was announced. In the midst of the heart-rending scenes that followed, intelligence came that the British army was defeated, and that Major Ackland was desperately wounded and a prisoner.

The unhappy lady, sustained by the counsels of her friend the Baroness, determined to join her husband in the American camp. She sent a message to General Burgoyne, through his aid-de-camp, Lord Petersham, to ask permission to depart. The British commander was astonished at this application. He was ready to believe patience and fortitude most brightly displayed in the female character; but he could hardly understand the courage of a woman, who after suffering so long the agitation of suspense, exhausted by want of rest and want of food, was ready to brave the darkness of night and the drenching rain for many hours, and to deliver herself to the enemy, uncertain into what hands she might fall! "The assistance I was able to give," he says, "was small indeed. I had not even a cup of wine to offer her. All I could furnish was an open boat, and a few lines written on dirty and wet paper to General Gates, recommending her to his protection."

How picturesque is the grouping of scenes we have at this point, and how do woman's strength of character and ardent affection shine amid the surrounding gloom! The army on its retreat—the sick and wounded abandoned to the mercy of the victors—the state of confusion following disasters so fatal to British power—the defeated general appealing in behalf of the suffering wife, by his tribute, written in haste and agitation, to her grace and excellence, and his expression of compassion for her hard fortune—and her own forgetfulness of danger. in hastening to her husband's aid!

She obtained from the wife of a soldier the refreshment of a little spirits and water, and set out in an open boat, accompanied by the British chaplain Brudenell, her own waiting-maid, and her husband's valet, who had been severely wounded in the search for his master when first missing from the field of battle. They went down the river during a violent storm of rain and wind, and arrived at the American out-posts in the night, having suffered much from wet and cold. The sentinel of the advance-guard heard the sound of oars, and hailed the boat. What must have been his surprise to hear that a woman had braved the storm on such an errand! He sent for Major Dearborn, the officer of the guard, before he would permit the passengers to land. Major Dearborn invited Lady Ackland to his guard-house, offered her a cup of tea, and every accommodation in his power, and gave her the welcome intelligence of her husband's safety. In the morning she. experienced the kindness of General Gates, who treated

her with the tenderness of a parent, bestowing every
attention which her sex and circumstances required.
She was conveyed, under a suitable escort, to the
quarters of General Poor on the heights, to her wounded
husband; and there remained till he was taken to Albany. Her resolution, and devotion to him, touched
the feelings of the Americans, and won the admiration
of all who heard her story.

It is related that Major Ackland showed his sense of
the generous treatment he had received, by doing all in
his power, while in New York on parole, to alleviate
the condition of American prisoners of distinction.
After his return to England, he lost his life in defence
of American honor. At a dinner of military gentlemen, a Lieutenant Lloyd threw out sneering remarks
upon the alleged cowardice of the American troops.
This was an indirect aspersion on the bravery of the
unfortunate officers who had been taken captive with
Burgoyne's army, and was felt and resented by Major
Ackland. High words ensued, and a duel was the consequence, in which Ackland fell at the first fire. The
shock of his death deprived Lady Harriet of reason,
and she remained two years in that sad condition.
After her recovery she quitted the gay world, and gave
her hand to the Rev. Mr. Brudenell, who had accompanied her on that gloomy night to the camp of General Gates. She survived him many years, and died at
an advanced age.

THE narrative of that celebrated campaign contains an anecdote of female compassion which, though not connected with the subject of this notice, may be properly mentioned here.

"Colonel Cochran having been sent to Canada as a spy, his mission was suspected, and a large bounty offered for his head. While there he was taken sick, and knowing that he was suspected, concealed himself for a few days in a brush heap, within about two miles of the American lines, unable to make his escape, or even to walk. Having suffered much from his sickness and want of nourishment, and having discovered a log cabin at considerable distance from the spot where he was concealed, the only one in sight, he crept to it on his hands and knees, for the purpose of soliciting assistance. On his approach to the rear of the cabin, he heard three men in earnest conversation; and it happened that he was the subject of their discourse. Having heard of the heavy bounty offered for the Colonel, and having seen a man in the vicinity a few days before, answering the description of him, they were forming their plans, and expressing their determination to find his whereabouts, and take him for the sake of the bounty. One of the men was the owner of the cabin. His wife was also present; and the others were his brother and brother-in-law. Soon after this conversation, the three men departed in pursuit. He crept into the cabin, and frankly told the woman, who seemed favorably impressed towards him on account of his

almost helpless condition, that he had overheard the
conversation ; that *he* was the man of whom they were
in search ; and that he should throw himself entirely
upon her mercy, trusting to her fidelity for protection.
This she very kindly promised him to the utmost of
her ability. Having received some restoratives, which
seemed to give relief, and taken suitable nourishment, he lay down on a bed in the room for the
purpose of taking some repose. After the men had
been absent about three hours, they returned ; when she
concealed him in a closet by the side of the fire-place,
and shut the door, taking good care while the men
were in the house, to keep near it, that if any thing
should be wanted from within, she might be ready to
get it herself. During the time the men were in the
cabin, they expressed much confidence in the belief
that the Colonel was concealed somewhere in the
vicinity, and named many places in which they intended to look for him. Having taken some food, and
otherwise prepared themselves, the men departed to
renew their search.

"Soon after they retired, the woman, not considering the Colonel's present situation safe, proposed that
he should conceal himself at some distance from the
cabin, where she might secretly bring him food, and
render such other assistance as he needed. She accordingly directed him to take post on a certain hill about
half a mile distant, where he might be able to discover
any person's approach, and to flee, if he was able,
should it become necessary. He manifested an incli-

7*

nation to resume his former position in the brush heap, which was in the midst of a patch of ground that had been cut over for a fallow; but she told him her husband intended to burn it the next day, and in that case he would certainly be discovered, or perish in the confla-gration. He then submitted entirely to her directions; and crept along to the hill in the best way he could. He remained sometime in this place of concealment, undiscovered by any one except this faithful Rahab of the forest, who like a good Samaritan, poured in the oil and wine, until his strength was in a measure restored, and he was enabled to return to his country and his home.

"Some years after the close of the war, and while the Colonel lived at Ticonderoga, he accidentally met with this kind-hearted woman, whose name I have not been able to ascertain, and rewarded her handsomely for her fidelity."

XI.

~~~~~~~~~

HANNAH ERWIN ISRAEL.

ABOUT the close of the year 1777, while the commander-in-chief of the British forces was in possession of Philadelphia, a foot passenger might have been seen on the road leading from Wilmington to that city. He was a young man of tall figure and powerful frame, giving evidence of great muscular strength, to which a walk of over thirty miles, under ordinary circumstances, would be a trifle. But the features of the traveller were darkened by anxiety and apprehension; and it was more the overtasking of the mind than the body which occasioned the weariness and lassitude under which he was plainly laboring. His dress was that of a simple citizen, and he was enveloped in a large cloak, affording ample protection against the severity of the weather, as well as serving to conceal sundry parcels of provisions, and a bag of money, with which he was laden. It was long after dark before he reached the ferry; but renewed hope and confidence filled his heart as he approached the termination of his journey.

Sir William Howe, it will be remembered, had entered the capital towards the end of September, after much manœuvring and several battles—Washington having made ineffectual efforts to prevent the accomplishment of his object. He was received with a welcome, apparently cordial, by the timid or interested citizens. His first care was to reduce the fortifications on the Delaware, and remove the obstructions prepared by the Americans to prevent the British fleet from ascending the river. While Fort Mifflin at Mud Island, and Fort Mercer at Red Bank, were occupied by their garrisons, he could have no communication with his fleet, and was in danger of being speedily compelled to evacuate the city. Count Donop, detached with the Hessian troops to take possession of the fort at Red Bank, was repulsed and mortally wounded. The invader's fortune, however, triumphed; and the Americans were finally driven from their posts. Their water force was compelled to retire from the fire of the batteries; and the British at length gained free communication, by way of the Delaware, between their army and the shipping. Thus the reverses in New Jersey and Pennsylvania had cast a gloom over the country, which could not be altogether dispelled even by the brilliant victories of Saratoga and the capture of Burgoyne and his army. The condition of the American army, when it retired into winter quarters at Valley Forge, was deplorable enough to change hope into despair, and presented truly a spectacle unparalleled in history. "Absolute destitution held high court; and never was the chivalric heroism of patriotic suffering more tangibly manifested than by that patriot-band within those frail log huts that barely covered them from the falling snow, or sheltered them from the keen wintry blasts." This privation of necessary food and clothing during one of the most rigorous winters ever experienced in the country—this misery—the detail of which is too familiar to need repetition, was endured by the continental soldiers at the same time that the English in the metropolis were revelling in unrestrained luxury and indulgence.* Many whig families, meanwhile, who remained in Philadelphia, plundered and insulted by the soldiers, wanted the comforts of life, and received assistance clandestinely from their friends at a distance.

To return to our narrative. When the traveller arrived at the ferry, he was promptly hailed by the sentinel, with " Who goes there?"

" A friend," was the reply.

" The countersign!"

The countersign for the night was promptly given.

---

* Marshall's MS. Journal says,—December 28th, 1777, " Our affairs wear a very gloomy aspect. Great part of our army gone into winter quarters; those in camp wanting breeches, shoes, stockings [and] blankets, and by accounts brought yesterday, were in want of flour." * * * " Our enemies revelling in balls, attended with every degree of luxury and excess in the city; rioting and wantonly using our houses, utensils and furniture; all this [and] a numberless number of other abuses, we endure from that handful of banditti, to the amount of six or seven thousand men, headed by that monster of rapine, General Howe."

" Pass, friend !" said the soldier ; and the other went on quickly.

Israel Israel was a native of Pennsylvania. He had left America at twenty-one, for the island of Barbadoes; and by nine or ten years of patient industry had amassed considerable property. He returned rich to his native country ; but in a few months after his marriage the war broke out, and his whole fortune was lost or sacrificed by agents. He had resolved, with his brother, at the commencement of the struggle, to take up arms in the cause of freedom. But the necessity was imperative that one should remain for the protection of the helpless females of the family ; and their entreaties not to be left exposed to a merciless enemy without a brother's aid, at last prevailed. Israel and Joseph drew lots to determine which should become a soldier. The lot fell upon the younger and unmarried one. At this period the residence of Israel was on a small farm near Wilmington, Delaware. His mother had removed with her family to Philadelphia, her house at Newcastle being thought too much exposed in the vicissitudes of war. After the occupation of the capital by the British, they endured severe hardships, sometimes suffering the want of actual necessaries. Israel watched over their welfare with incessant anxiety.

The knowledge that his beloved ones were in want of supplies, and that his presence was needed, determined him to enter the city at this time, notwithstanding the personal hazard it involved. One of his tory neighbors, who professed the deepest sympathy for his feelings, procured for him the countersign for the night. He had thus been enabled to elude the vigilance of the sentinel.

When arrived at his mother's dwelling, Mr. Israel found that it was in the possession of several soldiers, quartered upon the family. Among them was a savage-looking Hessian, with aspect of itself quite enough to terrify timid women. But all annoyances, and the fatigues of his long walk, were forgotten in the joyful meeting. A still more pleasing surprise was reserved for him; his young brother, Joseph, was that very hour on a secret visit to the family. For some hours of the evening the household circle was once more complete.

But such happiness, in those times of peril, was doomed to be short-lived. At eleven o'clock, while the family were seated at supper, the tramp of horses was heard without; and the rough voices of soldiers clamored at the door. Within, all was confusion; and the terrified women entreated the brothers to fly. They followed the younger with frantic haste up the stairs, where he left his uniform, and made his escape from the roof of the house. The knocking and shouting continued below; Israel descended, accompanied by the pale and trembling females, and himself opened the door. The intruders rushed in. At their head was the Hessian sergeant, who instantly seized the young man's arm, exclaiming, "We have caught him at last—the rebel rascal!"

Mr. Israel's presence of mind never forsook him

under the most appalling circumstances. He was sensible of the imminence of his own danger, and that his brother's safety could be secured only by delay. He shook off the grasp of the officer, and calmly demanded what was meant, and *who* it was that accused him of being a rebel.

"There he is!" replied the Hessian, pointing to Cæsar, a slave Mr. Israel had brought from the West Indies, and given his mother for a guard.

The master fixed upon the negro his stern and penetrating look so steadfastly, that Cæsar trembled and hung his head. "*Dare* you, Cæsar, call me rebel?" he exclaimed. "Gentlemen"—the muscles of his mouth worked into a sneer as he pronounced the word—"there is some mistake here. My brother Joe is the person meant, I presume. Let me fetch the uniform; and then you can judge for yourselves. Cæsar, come with me."

So saying, and taking the black by the arm with a vice-like grasp, he led him up stairs. "Not one word, you rascal," was whispered in his ear, "or I kill you upon the spot." The negro drew his breath hard and convulsively, but dared not speak. The uniform was produced and exhibited; and Israel made efforts to put it on before his captors. The person whom it fitted being short and slight in figure, its ludicrous disproportion to the towering height and robust form of the elder brother, convinced the soldiers of their mistake; and the sergeant made awkward apologies, shaking the hand of the man he had so lately called a rebel, assuring him he had no doubt he was an honest and loyal subject; and that he would take care his fidelity should be mentioned in the proper quarter.

"And now," he said, "as your supper is ready, we will sit down." He seated himself beside his host, whose resentment at the familiarity was tempered by the thought that his brother was saved by the well-timed deceit. The ladies also were compelled to take their places, and to listen in silence to the coarse remarks of their unwelcome guest. With rude protestations of good will, and promises of patronage, he mingled boastful details of his exploits in slaughtering "the rebels," that caused his auditors to shudder with horror. Mr. Israel used to relate afterwards that he grasped the knife he was using, and raised it to strike down the savage; but that his mother's look of agonized entreaty withheld the blow. The Hessian continued his recital, accompanied by many bitter oaths.

"That Paoli affair," cried he, "was capital! I was with General Grey in that attack. It was just after midnight when we forced the outposts, and not a noise was heard so loud as the dropping of a musket. How the fellows turned out of their encampment when they heard us! What a running about—barefoot and half clothed—and in the light of their own fires! These showed us where to chase them, while they could not see us. We killed three hundred of the rebels with the bayonet; I stuck them myself like so many pigs—one after another—till the blood ran out of the touchhole of my musket."

The details of the Hessian were interrupted by Mr. Israel's starting to his feet, with face pale with rage, convulsed lips, and clenched hands. The catastrophe that might have ensued was prevented by a faint shriek from his young sister, who fell into his arms in a swoon. The sergeant's horrible boastings thus silenced, and the ‘whole room in confusion, he bade the family good night, saying he was on duty, and presently quitted the house.

The parting of those who had just gone through so agitating a scene was now to take place. Cæsar was sternly questioned, and reprimanded for his perfidy; but the black excused himself by pleading that he had been compelled to do as he had done. For the future, with streaming eyes, he promised the strictest fidelity; and to his credit be it said, remained steadfast in the performance of this promise.

Having bidden adieu to his family, Mr. Israel set forth on his journey homeward. He arrived only to be made a prisoner. The loyalist who had given him the countersign, had betrayed the secret of his expedition. He and his wife's brother were immediately seized and carried on board the frigate Roebuck, lying in the Delaware, a few miles from the then borough of Wilmington—and directly opposite his farm—in order to be tried as *spies.*

Being one of the "Committee of Safety," the position of Mr. Israel, under such an accusation, was extremely critical. On board the ship he was treated with the utmost severity. His watch, silver shoe-buckles, and various articles of clothing were taken from him; his bed was a coil of ropes on deck, without covering from the bitter cold of the night air; and to all appearances his fate was already decided. The testimony of his tory neighbors was strong against him. Several were ready to swear to the fact, that while the loyal population of the country had willingly furnished their share of the provisions needed by the ships of war, *he* had been heard to say repeatedly, that he "*would sooner drive his cattle as a present to General Washington, than receive thousands of dollars in British gold for them.*"

On being informed of this speech, the commander gave orders that a detachment of soldiers should proceed to drive the rebel's cattle, then grazing in a meadow in full view, down to the river, and slaughter them in the face of the prisoners.

What, meanwhile, must have been the feelings of the young wife—herself about to become a mother—when her husband and brother were led away in her very sight? The farm was a mile or more from the river; but there was nothing to intercept the view—the ground from the meadow sloping down to the water. Mrs. Israel was at this period about nineteen years of age; and is described as of middle height, and slight but symmetrical figure; of fair complexion, with clear blue eyes and dark hair; her manners modest and retiring. She was devoted to her family and her domestic concerns. It needed the trying scenes by which she was surrounded, to develop the heroism which, in times more peaceful, might have been unmarked by those who knew her most intimately.

From her position on the look-out, she saw the soldiers land from the ships, shoulder arms, and advance towards the meadow. In an instant. she divined their purpose; and her resolution was taken. With a boy eight years old, whom she bade follow her at his utmost speed, she started off, determined to baffle the enemy, and save the cattle at the peril of her life. Down went the bars, and followed by the little boy, she ran to drive the herd to the opening.

The soldiers called out repeatedly to her to desist, and threatened, if she did not, to fire upon her.

" Fire away!" cried the heroic woman. They fired! The balls flew thickly around her. The frightened cattle ran in every direction over the field.

" This way!" she called to the boy, nothing daunted; "this way, Joe! Head them there! Stop them, Joe! Do not let one escape!"

And *not one* did escape! The bullets fired by the cowardly British soldiers continued to whistle around her person. The little boy, paralyzed by terror, fell to the ground. She seized him by the arm, lifted him over the fence, and herself drove the cattle into the barn-yard. The assailants, baffled by the courage of a woman, and probably not daring, for fear of the neighbors, to invade the farm-houses, retraced their steps, and returned disappointed to the ship.

All this scene passed in sight of the officers of the "Roebuck" and the two prisoners. The agony of suspense and fear endured by the husband and brother, when they saw the danger to which the wife exposed herself, may be better imagined than described. It may also be conceived how much they exulted in her triumph.

The trial was held on board the ship. The tory witnesses were examined in due form; and it was but too evident that the lives of the prisoners were in great danger. A kind-hearted sailor sought an opportunity of speaking in private with Mr. Israel, and asked him if he were a freemason. The answer was in the affirmative. The sailor then informed him that a lodge was held on shipboard, and the officers, who belonged to it, were to meet that night.

The prisoners were called up before their judges, and permitted to answer to the accusations against them. Mr. Israel, in bold but respectful language, related his story; and acknowledged his secret visit to Philadelphia, not in the character of a spy, but to carry relief to his suffering parent and her family. He also acknowledged having said, as was testified, that "he would rather give his cattle to Washington, or destroy the whole herd than sell them for British gold." This trait of magnanimity might not have been so appreciated by the enemies of his country, as to operate in his favor, but that—watching his opportunity, he made to the commanding officer the secret sign of masonic brotherhood. The effect was instantly observable. The officer's stern countenance softened; his change of opinion and that of the other judges, became evident; and after some further examination, the court was broken up. The informants, and those who had borne testimony against the prisoners, hung their heads in shame at the severe rebuke of the court, for their cowardly conduct in betraying, and preferring charges against an honorable man, bound on a mission of love and duty to his aged mother. The acquitted prisoners were dismissed, loaded with presents of pins, handkerchiefs, and other articles not to be purchased at that time, for the intrepid wife; and were sent on shore in a splendid barge, as a mark of special honor from the officer in command.

Such was the adventure in which the courage and patriotism of the subject of this notice was displayed. The records of the Grand Lodge of Pennsylvania, of which Mr. Israel was Grand Master for many years, bear testimony to his having been saved from an ignominious death *by masonry.* Mrs. Israel's family name was Erwin; her ancestors were Quakers who came with Penn, her parents native Americans; and she herself was born in Wilmington, Delaware. Her first meeting with her husband was romantic enough. Mr. Israel had sailed in a sloop, or packet, from Philadelphia, to visit New Castle, where his mother and family resided. He observed on deck an extremely pretty girl, hardly seventeen years of age, and very neatly and tastefully dressed, with the finest turned foot and ankle in the world. All who went on such voyages were then obliged to furnish themselves with provisions; and his attention was drawn by the young girl's kindly distribution of her little stock, handing it about from one to another, till but little was left for her own portion. In passing him, she modestly hesitated a moment, and then offered him a share. This led to conversation; he learned that she was the daughter of highly respectable parents, and resided in Wilmington. Love at first sight was as common in those days as now. After seeing his mother, he visited Wilmington; became better acquainted, offered himself and was accepted; and on his marriage, rented the farm above mentioned, and commenced life anew. It may be proper to mention here—that the *castle* from which the town of New Castle took its name, was in very early days the property and residence of his ancestors. Subsequently he became the purchaser of the old castle; and removed the tiles that covered it, with the vane that graced it, to his country-seat, where part of them, several hundred years old, are still to be seen.

Mr. Israel died in 1821, at the age of seventy-eight. The death of his wife took place at his country-seat near Philadelphia, at the age of fifty-six. She was the mother of thirteen children, many of whom died young. But two are now living—and reside in Philadelphia. One of them is the accomplished lady—herself the wife of a gallant officer thirty-five years engaged in the service of his country—from whom I received these particulars.

To this glance at the condition of some of the citizens of Philadelphia at that time, may be added a description, from a lady's letter to her friend, of the first entrance of the British army into the city.

"We had for a neighbor, and an intimate acquaintance, a very amiable English gentleman, who had been in the British army, and had left the service on marrying a rich and excellent lady of Philadelphia, some years before. He endeavored to give my mother confidence that the inhabitants would not be ill-treated. He advised that we should be all well-dressed, and that we should keep our houses closed. The army marched in, and took possession of the town in the morning. We were up stairs, and saw them pass to the State House. They looked well—clean and well-clad; and the contrast between them and our poor barefooted and ragged troops was very great, and caused a feeling of despair. It was a solemn and impressive day; but I saw no exultation in the enemy, nor indeed in those who were reckoned favorable to their success. Early in the afternoon Lord Cornwallis's suite arrived, and took possession of my mother's dwelling. But my mother was appalled by the numerous train in her house, and shrank from having such inmates; for a guard was mounted at the door, and the yard filled with soldiers and baggage of every description; and I well remember what we thought of the haughty looks of Lord Rawdon and the other aid-de-camp, as they traversed the apartments. My mother desired to speak with Lord Cornwallis, and he attended her in the front parlor. She told him of her situation, and how impossible it would be for her to stay in her own house with such a train as composed his lordship's establishment. He behaved with great politeness to her; said he should be sorry to give trouble, and would have other quarters looked out for him. They withdrew that very afternoon, and we felt glad of the exemption. But it did not last long; for directly the quartermasters were employed in billeting the troops, and we had to find room for two officers of artillery; and afterwards, in addition, for two gentlemen, secretaries of Lord Howe."

"General Howe, during the time he stayed in Philadelphia, seized and kept for his own use Mary Pemberton's coach and horses, in which he used to ride about the town."

"My wife," says Marshall in his manuscript diary, February 14th, 1778, "looks upon every Philadelphian who comes to see us as a person suffering in a righteous cause, and entitled to partake of our hospitality." Tradition has preserved, in several families, anecdotes illustrative of the strait to which even women and children were then reduced. One of Mary Redmond may be mentioned. She was the daughter of a patriot somewhat distinguished among his neighbors in Philadelphia. Many of her relatives were loyalists; and she was playfully called among them "the little black-eyed rebel." She was accustomed to assist several women whose husbands were in the American army, to procure intelligence. The despatches were usually sent from their friends by a boy, who carried them stitched in the back of his coat. He came into the city bringing provisions to market. One morning, when there was some reason to fear he was suspected, and his movements watched by the enemy, Mary undertook to get the papers in safety

8

from him.   She went, as usual, to the market, and in a
pretended game of romps, threw her shawl over the
boy's head, and thus secured the prize.   She hastened
with the papers to her anxious friends, who read them
by stealth, after the windows had been carefully closed.
When the news came of Burgoyne's surrender, and the
whig women were secretly rejoicing, the sprightly girl,
not daring to give vent openly to her exultation, put her
head up the chimney and gave a shout for Gates.

XII.

───∿∿∿───

LYDIA DARRAH.*

ON the second day of December, 1777, late in the afternoon, an officer in the British uniform ascended the steps of a house in Second street, Philadelphia, immediately opposite the quarters occupied by General Howe, who, at that time, had full possession of the city. The house was plain and neat in its exterior, and well known to be tenanted by William and Lydia Darrah, members of the Society of Friends. It was the place chosen by the superior officers of the army for private conference, whenever it was necessary to hold consultations on subjects of importance ; and selected, perhaps, on account of the unobtrusive character of its inmates, whose religion inculcated meekness and forbearance, and forbade them to practise the arts of war.

The officer, who seemed quite familiar with the man-

---

* Sometimes spelled *Darrach.* This anecdote is given in the first number of the American Quarterly Review, and is said to be taken from Lydia's own narration. It is mentioned or alluded to by several other authorities, and in letters written at the time. The story is familiar to many persons in Philadelphia, who heard it from their parents; so that there appears no reason to doubt its authenticity.

sion, knocked at the door.   It was opened; and in the neatly-furnished parlor he met the mistress, who spoke to him, calling him by name.   It was the adjutant-general; and he appeared in haste to give an order. This was to desire that the back-room above stairs might be prepared for the reception that evening of himself and his friends, who were to meet there and remain late.   "And be sure, Lydia," he concluded, "that your family are all in bed at an early hour.   I shall expect you to attend to this request.   When our guests are ready to leave the house, I will myself give you notice, that you may let us out, and extinguish the fire and candles."

Having delivered this order with an emphatic manner which showed that he relied much on the prudence and discretion of the person he addressed, the adjutant-general departed.   Lydia betook herself to getting all things in readiness.   But the words she had heard, especially the injunction to retire early, rang in her ears; and she could not divest herself of the indefinable feeling that something of importance was in agitation. While her hands were busy in the duties that devolved upon her, her mind was no less actively at work.   The evening closed in, and the officers came to the place of meeting.   Lydia had ordered all her family to bed, and herself admitted the guests, after which she retired to her own apartment, and threw herself, without undressing, upon the bed.

But sleep refused to visit her eyelids.   Her vague apprehensions gradually assumed more definite shape.

She became more and more uneasy, till her nervous restlessness amounted to absolute terror. Unable longer to resist the impulse—not of curiosity, but surely of a far higher feeling—she slid from the bed, and taking off her shoes, passed noiselessly from her chamber and along the entry. Approaching cautiously the apartment in which the officers were assembled, she applied her ear to the key-hole. For a few moments she could distinguish but a word or two amid the murmur of voices; yet what she did hear but stimulated her eager desire to learn the important secret of the conclave.

At length there was profound silence, and a voice was heard reading a paper aloud. It was an order for the troops to quit the city on the night of the fourth, and march out to a secret attack upon the American army, then encamped at White Marsh.

Lydia had heard enough. She retreated softly to her own room, and laid herself quietly on the bed. In the deep stillness that reigned through the house, she could hear the beating of her own heart—the heart now throbbing with emotions to which no speech could give utterance. It seemed to her that but a few moments had elapsed, when there was a knocking at her door. She knew well what the signal meant, but took no heed. It was repeated, and more loudly; still she gave no answer. Again, and yet more loudly, the knocks were repeated; and then she rose quickly, and opened the door.

It was the adjutant-general, who came to inform her they were ready to depart. Lydia let them out, fastened the house, and extinguished the lights and fire. Again she returned to her chamber, and to bed ; but repose was a stranger for the rest of the night. Her mind was more disquieted than ever. She thought of the danger that threatened the lives of thousands of her countrymen, and of the ruin that impended over the whole land. Something must be done, and that immediately, to avert this wide-spread destruction. Should she awaken her husband and inform him ? That would be to place him in special jeopardy, by rendering him a partaker of her secret ; and he might, too, be less wary and prudent than herself. No ; come what might, she would encounter the risk alone. After a petition for heavenly guidance, her resolution was formed ; and she waited with composure, though sleep was impossible, till the dawn of day. Then she waked her husband, and informed him flour was wanted for the use of the household, and that it was necessary she should go to Frankford to procure it. This was no uncommon occurrence ; and her declining the attendance of the maid-servant excited little surprise. Taking the bag with her, she walked through the snow; having stopped first at head-quarters, obtained access to General Howe, and secured his written permission to pass the British lines.

The feelings of a wife and mother—one whose religion was that of love, and whose life was but a quiet round of domestic duties—bound on an enterprise so hazardous, and uncertain whether her life might not be the forfeit, may be better imagined than described.

Lydia reached Frankford, distant four or five miles, and deposited her bag at the mill. Now commenced the dangers of her undertaking; for she pressed forward with all haste towards the outposts of the American army. Her determination was to apprise General Washington of the danger.

She was met on her way by an American officer, who had been selected by General Washington to gain information respecting the movements of the enemy. According to some authorities, this was Lieutenant-Colonel Craig, of the light horse. He immediately recognized her, and inquired whither she was going. In reply, she prayed him to alight and walk with her; which he did, ordering his men to keep in sight. To him she disclosed the secret, after having obtained from him a solemn promise not to betray her individually, since the British might take vengeance on her and her family.

The officer thanked her for her timely warning, and directed her to go to a house near at hand, where she might get something to eat. But Lydia preferred returning at once; and did so, while the officer made all haste to the commander-in-chief. Preparations were immediately made to give the enemy a fitting reception.

With a heart lightened and filled with thankfulness, the intrepid woman pursued her way homeward, carrying the bag of flour which had served as the ostensible object of her journey. None suspected the grave, demure Quakeress of having snatched from the English their anticipated victory. Her demeanor was, as usual, quiet, orderly, and subdued, and she attended to the duties of her family with her wonted composure. But her heart beat, as late on the appointed night, she watched from her window the departure of the army— on what secret expedition bound, she knew too well! She listened breathlessly to the sound of their footsteps and the trampling of horses, till it died away in the distance, and silence reigned through the city.

Time never appeared to pass so slowly as during the interval which elapsed between the marching out and the return of the British troops. When at last the distant roll of the drum proclaimed their approach; when the sounds came nearer and nearer, and Lydia, who was watching at the window, saw the troops pass in martial order, the agony of anxiety she felt was too much for her strength, and she retreated from her post, not daring to ask a question, or manifest the least curiosity as to the event.

A sudden and loud knocking at her door was not calculated to lessen her apprehensions. She felt that the safety of her family depended on her self-possession at this critical moment. The visitor was the adjutant-general, who summoned her to his apartment. With a pale cheek, but composed, for she placed her trust in a higher Power, Lydia obeyed the summons.

The officer's face was clouded, and his expression stern. He locked the door with an air of mystery when Lydia entered, and motioned her to a seat. After a moment of silence, he said—

"Were any of your family up, Lydia, on the night when I received company in this house?"

"No." was the unhesitating reply. "They all retired at eight o'clock."

"It is very strange"—said the officer, and mused a few minutes. "You, I know, Lydia, were asleep; for I knocked at your door three times before you heard me —yet it is certain that we were betrayed. I am altogether at a loss to conceive who could have given the information of our intended attack to General Washington! On arriving near his encampment we found his cannon mounted, his troops under arms, and so prepared at every point to receive us, that we have been compelled to march back without injuring our enemy, like a parcel of fools."

It is not known whether the officer ever discovered to whom he was indebted for the disappointment.

But the pious quakeress blessed God for her preservation, and rejoiced that it was not necessary for her to utter an untruth in her own defence. And all who admire examples of courage and patriotism, especially those who enjoy the fruits of them, must honor the name of Lydia Darrah.

XIII.

~~~~~~

REBECCA FRANKS.

"The celebrated Miss Franks"—so distinguished for intelligence and high accomplishment, in Revolutionary times, could not properly be passed over in a series of notices of remarkable women of that period. In the brilliant position she occupied in fashionable society, she exerted, as may well be believed, no slight influence; for wit and beauty are potent champions in any cause for which they choose to arm themselves. That her talents were generally employed on the side of humanity and justice,—that the pointed shafts of her wit, which spared neither friend nor foe, were aimed to chastise presumption and folly—we may infer from the amiable disposition which it is recorded she possessed. Admired in fashionable circles, and courted for the charms of her conversation, she must have found many opportunities of exercising her feminine privilege of softening asperities and alleviating suffering—as well as of humbling the arrogance of those whom military success rendered regardless of the feelings of others. Though a decided loyalist, her satire did not spare those whose opinions she favored. It is related of her, that at a splendid ball given by the officers of the British army to the ladies of New York, she ventured one of those jests frequently uttered, which must have been severely felt in the faint prospect that existed of a successful termination to the war. During an interval of dancing, Sir Henry Clinton, previously engaged in conversation with Miss Franks, called out to the musicians, "Give us 'Britons, strike home.'" "The commander-in-chief," exclaimed she, "has made a mistake; he meant to say, 'Britons—*go home.*'"

The keenness of her irony, and her readiness at repartee, were not less promptly shown in sharp tilting with the American officers. At the festival of the Mischianza, where even whig ladies were present, Miss Franks had appeared as one of the princesses. She remained in Philadelphia after its evacuation by the British troops. Lieutenant-Colonel Jack Steward of Maryland, dressed in a fine suit of scarlet, took an early occasion to pay his compliments; and gallantly said—"I have adopted your colors, my princess, the better to secure a courteous reception. Deign to smile on a true knight." To this covert taunt Miss Franks made no reply: but turning to the company who surrounded her, exclaimed—"How the ass glories in the lion's skin!" The same officer met with another equally severe rebuff, while playing with the same weapons. The conversation of the company was interrupted by a loud clamor from the street, which caused them to hasten to the windows. High head-dresses were then the reigning fashion among the English belles. A female appeared in the street, surrounded by a crowd of idlers, ragged in her apparel, and barefoot; but adorned with a towering head-dress in the extreme of the mode. Miss Franks readily perceived the intent of this pageant; and on the lieutenant-colonel's observing that the woman was equipped in the English fashion, replied, "Not altogether, colonel; for though the style of her head is British, her shoes and stockings are in the genuine continental fashion!"*

Many anecdotes of her quick and brilliant wit are extant in the memory of individuals, and many sarcastic speeches attributed to her have been repeated. It is represented that her information was extensive, and that few were qualified to enter the lists with her. General Charles Lee, in the humorous letter he address-ed to her—*a jeu d'esprit* she is said to have received with serious anger—calls her "a lady who has had every human and divine advantage."

Rebecca Franks was the daughter and youngest child of David Franks, a Jewish merchant, who emigrated to this country about a century since. He married an Englishwoman before coming to America, and had three sons and two daughters. The eldest daughter married Andrew Hamilton, brother to the well-known proprietor of " The Woodlands." After the termination of the war, Rebecca married General Henry Johnson, a British officer of great merit, and accompanied him

* Garden.

to England. He distinguished himself by some act of
gallantry in one of the outbreaks of rebellion in Ireland,
and received the honor of knighthood. Their residence
was at Bath, where their only surviving son still lives.
The other son was killed at the battle of Waterloo.

The lady who furnished the above details, informed
me that her brother was entertained in 1810, at Lady
Johnson's house in Bath, where she was living in elegant style, and exercising with characteristic grace the
duties of hospitality, and the virtues that adorn social life.
He described her person as of the middle height, rather
inclining to embonpoint ; and her expression of countenance as very agreeable, with fine eyes. Her manners were frank and cheerful, and she appeared happy
in contributing to the happiness of others. Sir Henry
was at that time living.

It is said that Lady Johnson, not long after this
period, expressed to a young American officer her peni-
tence for her former toryism, and her pride and pleasure
in the victories of her countrymen on the Niagara frontier, in the war of 1812. It has been remarked that favorable sentiments towards the Americans are general among
loyalists residing in England ; while, on the other hand,
the political animosity of Revolutionary times is still extant in the British American Colonies. A loyal spinster
of four-score residing in one of these, when on a visit to
one of her friends, some two years since, saw on the walls,
among several portraits of distinguished men, a print
of " the traitor Washington." She was so much troubled at the sight, that her friend, to appease her, ordered

it to be taken down and put away during her visit. A story is told also of a gentleman high in office in the same colony, on whom an agent of the " New York Albion" called to deliver the portrait of Washington which the publisher that year presented to his subscribers. The gentleman, highly insulted, ordered the astonished agent to take " the —— thing" out of his sight, and to strike his name instantly from the list.

Miss Franks, it has been mentioned, was one of the princesses of the Mischianza. This Italian word, signifying a medley or mixture, was applied to an entertainment, or series of entertainments, given by the British officers in Philadelphia as a parting compliment to Sir William Howe, just before his relinquishment of command to Sir Henry Clinton, and departure to England. Some of his enemies called it his triumph on leaving America unconquered. A description of this singular fête may be interesting to many readers; I therefore abridge one written, it is said, by Major André for an English Lady's Magazine.

I have seen a *fac simile* of the tickets issued, in a volume of American Historical and Literary curiosities. The names are in a shield, on which is a view of the sea with the setting sun, and on a wreath the words " *Luceo discedens, aucto splendore resurgam.*"   At the top is General Howe's crest, with the words " *Vive vale.*" Around the shield runs a vignette; and various military trophies fill up the back-ground.

The entertainment was given on the 18th of May, 1778.   It commenced with a grand regatta, in three divisions. In the first was the Ferret galley, on board of which were several general officers and ladies. In the centre, the Hussar galley bore Sir William and Lord Howe, Sir Henry Clinton, their suite, and many ladies. The Cornwallis galley brought up the rear—General Knyphhausen and suite, three British generals, and ladies, being on board. On each quarter of these galleys, and forming their division, were five flat boats lined with green cloth, and filled with ladies and gentlemen. In front were three flat boats, with bands of music. Six barges rowed about each flank, to keep off the swarm of boats in the river. The galleys were dressed in colors and streamers ; the ships lying at anchor were magnificently decorated ; and the transport ships with colors flying, which extended in a line the whole length of the city, were crowded, as well as the wharves, with spectators. The rendezvous was at Knight's wharf, at the northern extremity of the city. The company embarked at half-past four, the three divisions moving slowly down to the music. Arrived opposite Market wharf, at a signal all rested on their oars, and the music played "God save the king," answered by three cheers from the vessels. The landing was at the Old Fort, a little south of the town, and in front of the building prepared for the company—a few hundred yards from the water. This regatta was gazed at from the wharves and warehouses by all the uninvited population of the city.

When the general's barge pushed for shore, a salute of seventeen guns was fired from his Majesty's ship

Roebuck; and after an interval, seventeen from the Vigilant. The procession advanced through an avenue formed by two files of grenadiers, each supported by a line of light-horse. The avenue led to a spacious lawn, lined with troops, and prepared for the exhibition of a tilt and tournament. The music, and managers with favors of white and blue ribbons in their breasts, led the way, followed by the generals and the rest of the company.

In front, the building pounded the view through a vista formed by two triumphal arches in a line with the landing place. Two pavilions, with rows of benches rising one above another, received the ladies, while the gentlemen ranged themselves on each side. On the front seat of each pavilion were seven young ladies as princesses, in Turkish habits, and wearing in their turbans the favors meant for the knights who contended. The sound of trumpets was heard in the distance; and a band of knights in ancient habits of white and red silk, mounted on gray horses caparisoned in the same colors, attended by squires on foot, heralds and trumpeters, entered the lists. Lord Cathcart was chief of these knights; and appeared in honor of Miss Auchmuty. One of his esquires bore his lance, another his shield; and two black slaves in blue and white silk, with silver clasps on their bare necks and arms, held his stirrups. The band made the circuit of the square, saluting the ladies, and then ranged themselves in a line with the pavilion in which were the ladies of their device. Their herald, after a flourish of trumpets, proclaimed a chal-

lenge; asserting the superiority of the ladies of the
Blended Rose, in wit, beauty and accomplishment, and
offering to prove it by deeds of arms according to the
ancient laws of chivalry. At the third repetition of the
challenge, another herald and trumpeters advanced
from the other side of the square, dressed in black and
orange, and proclaimed defiance to the challengers, in
the name of the knights of the Burning Mountain.
Captain Watson, the chief, appeared in honor of Miss
Franks; his device—a heart with a wreath of flowers;
his motto—Love and Glory. This band also rode
round the lists, and drew up in front of the White
Knights. The gauntlet was thrown down and lifted;
the encounter took place. After the fourth encounter,
the two chiefs, spurring to the centre, fought singly, till
the marshal of the field rushed between, and declared
that the ladies of the Blended Rose and the Burning
Mountain were satisfied with the proofs of love and valor
already given, and commanded their knights to desist.
The bands then filed off in different directions, saluting
the ladies as they approached the pavilions.

The company then passed in procession through
triumphal arches built in the Tuscan order, to a garden
in front of the building; and thence ascended to a
spacious hall painted in imitation of Sienna marble.
In this hall and apartment adjoining, were tea and
refreshments; and the knights, kneeling, received their
favors from the ladies. On entering the room appropriated for the faro table, a cornucopia was seen filled with
fruit and flowers; another appeared in going out, shrunk,

reversed and empty.   The next advance was to a ball-room painted in pale blue, pannelled with gold, with dropping festoons of flowers; the surbase pink, with drapery festooned in blue.   Eighty-five mirrors, decked with flowers and ribbons, reflected the light from thirty-four branches of wax lights.   On the same floor were four drawing-rooms with sideboards of refreshments, also decorated and lighted up.   The dancing continued till ten; the windows were then thrown open, and the fire-works commenced with a magnificent bouquet of rockets.

At twelve, large folding doors, which had hitherto been concealed, were suddenly thrown open, discovering a splendid and spacious saloon, richly painted, and brilliantly illuminated; the mirrors and branches decorated, as also the supper table; which was set out—according to Major André's account—with four hundred and thirty covers, and twelve hundred dishes.   When supper was ended, the herald and trumpeters of the Blended Rose entered the saloon, and proclaimed the health of the king and royal family—followed by that of the knights and ladies; each toast being accompanied by a flourish of music.   The company then returned to the ball-room; and the dancing continued till four o'clock.

This was the most splendid entertainment ever given by officers to their general.   The next day the mirrors and lustres borrowed from the citizens were sent home, with their ornaments.   The pageant of a night was over; Sir William Howe departed.   The folly and extravagance displayed were apparent not only to the

foes of Britain. It is said that an old Scotch officer of
artillery, when asked if he would be surprised at an
attack from General Washington during the festivities
of the day, replied—"If Mr. Washington possess the
wisdom and sound policy I have ever attributed to him,
he will not meddle with us at such a time. The excesses
of the present hour are to him equivalent to a victory."

It is interesting to contrast the situation of the two
hostile armies at this time; and to follow the destiny of
the revellers. When the alliance was concluded between
France and America, it was determined in Great
Britain immediately to evacuate Philadelphia, and con-
centrate the royal forces in the city and harbor of
New York. In one month knights and army marched
from the city they had occupied. Major André, represented as the charm of the company, who had aided in
painting the decorations, and illustrated the pageant by
his pen, went forth to mingle in graver scenes. General
Wayne writes, on the twelfth of July : "Tell those
Philadelphia ladies who attended Howe's assemblies
and levees, that the heavenly, sweet, pretty redcoats—
the accomplished gentlemen of the guards and grenadiers, have been humbled on the plains of Monmouth.
The knights of the Blended Roses, and of the Burning
Mount—have resigned their laurels to rebel officers,
who will lay them at the feet of *those* virtuous daughters
of America who cheerfully gave up ease and affluence
in a city, for liberty and peace of mind in a cottage."

But the empire of beauty was not to be overthrown
by political changes. The belles who had graced the

fête found the reproach cast on them by indignant patriots speedily forgotten. When the Americans, on their return to the capital, gave a ball to their own and the French officers, and it was debated whether the ladies of the Mischianza should be honored with invitations, the question was soon decided by the reflection that it would be impossible to make up an agreeable company without them.

XIV.

―――∿∿∿∿―――

ELIZABETH FERGUSON.

THE old building called the Carpenter Mansion, the site of which is now occupied by the Arcade in Philadelphia, was the residence of Doctor Thomas Graeme, the father of Mrs. Ferguson. He was a native of Scotland; distinguished as a physician in the city; and for some time was colonial collector of the port. He married Anne, the daughter of Sir William Keith, then Governor of Pennsylvania.

More than thirty years before the Revolution, when these premises were occupied by Governor Thomas, the fruit-trees, garden, and shrubbery often allured the townsfolk to extend their walks thither. The youth of that day were frequently indebted to the kindness of the Governor's lady, who invited them to help themselves from a long range of cherry-trees; and when May day came, the young girls were treated to bouquets and wreaths from the gardens. After the death of Dr. Graeme, in 1772, the property passed successively into different hands. In time of the war, the house was appropriated for the use of the sick American soldiery, who died there in hundreds, of the camp

fever. The sufferers were supplied with nourishmer
by the ladies of Philadelphia; and General Washington
himself sent them a cask of Madeira, which he had
received as a present from Robert Morris. The mansion was the scene, moreover, of a most touching spectacle, on one occasion, when the mother of a youth from
the country came to seek her son among the dead in
the hospital. While mourning over him as lost to her
for ever, she discerned signs of life, and ere long he was
restored to consciousness in her arms.*

While occupied by Dr. Graeme, the house was long
rendered attractive and celebrated, not only by his exu-
berant hospitality, but by the talents and accomplishments of his youngest daughter. She was the centre
of the literary coteries of that day, who were accustomed to meet at her father's residence. Even in early
life she discovered a mind richly endowed with intellectual gifts. These were cultivated with care by her
excellent and accomplished mother. She was born in
1739. In her youth she passed much time in study;
for which, and the cultivation of her poetical talents,
opportunities were afforded in the pleasant retreat where
her parents spent their summers—Graeme Park, in
Montgomery county, twenty miles from Philadelphia.
It is said that the translation of Telemachus into English verse—the manuscript volumes of which are in the
Philadelphia Library—was undertaken by Elizabeth
Graeme, as a relief and diversion of her mind from the
suffering occasioned by a disappointment in love. After

* See Watson's Annals of Philadelphia.

this, the failure of her health induced her father to send
her to Europe.   Her mother, who had long been declining, wished her much to go, and for a reason as singular as it is touching.*   She believed the time of her
death to be at hand; and felt that the presence of her
beloved daughter prevented that exclusive fixing of her
thoughts and affections upon heavenly things, which in
her last hours she desired.   This distrust of the heart is
not an uncommon feeling.   Archbishop Lightfoot wished to die separated from his home and family.   A
mother, some years ago, in her last moments said to her
daughter, who sat weeping at her bedside, " Leave me,
my child; I cannot die while you are in the room."
Something of the same feeling is shown in an extract
from one of Mrs. Graeme's letters, written to be delivered after her death: " My trust," she says, " is in my
heavenly Father's mercies, procured and promised by the
all-sufficient merits of my blessed Saviour; so that whatever time it may be before you see this, or whatever
weakness I may be under on my death-bed, be assured
this is my faith—*this* is my hope from my youth up
until now."

Mrs. Graeme died, as she expected, during the absence of her daughter; but left two farewell letters to
be delivered on her return.   These contained advice
respecting her future life in the relations of wife and

---

* See Hazard's Pennsylvania Register, vol. iii., p. 394, for a memoir
of Mrs. Ferguson, first published in the Port-Folio, from which are
derived these particulars of her personal history.   Some of her letters
appeared in the Port-Folio.

mistress of a household ; and the most ardent expressions of maternal affection.   Elizabeth remained a year in England, under the guardianship of the Rev. Dr. Richard Peters, of Philadelphia, whose position enabled him to introduce her into the best society.   She was sought for in literary circles, attracted the attention of distinguished persons by her mental accomplishments, and was particularly noticed by the British monarch. The celebrated Dr. Fothergill, whom she consulted as a physician, was during his life her friend and correspondent.

Her return to Philadelphia was welcomed by a numerous circle of friends, who came to condole with her upon her mother's death, and to testify their affectionate remembrance of herself.   The stores of information gained during her visit to Great Britain, where she had been " all eye, all ear, and all grasp," were dispensed for the information and entertainment of those she loved.   She now occupied the place of her mother in her father's family, managing the house and presiding in the entertainment of his visitors.   During several years of their winter residence in the city, Saturday evenings were appropriated for the reception of their friends, and strangers who visited Philadelphia with introductions to the family of Dr. Graeme.   The mansion was, in fact, the head-quarters of literature and refinement ; and the hospitality of its owner rendered it an agreeable resort.   Miss Graeme was the presiding genius.   Her brilliant intellect, her extensive and varied knowledge, her vivid fancy, and cultivated taste, offered attractions which were enhanced by the charm of her graceful manners.

It was at one of these evening assemblies that she first saw Hugh Henry Ferguson, a young gentleman lately arrived in the country from Scotland. They were pleased with each other at the first interview, being congenial in literary tastes, and a love of retirement. The marriage took place in a few months, notwithstanding that Ferguson was ten years younger than Miss Graeme. Not long after this event her father died, having bequeathed to his daughter the country-seat in Montgomery county, on which she and her husband continued to reside.

The happiness anticipated by Mrs. Ferguson in country seclusion and her books, was of brief duration. The discontents were increasing between Great Britain and America, which resulted in the war of Independence. It was necessary for Mr. Ferguson to take part with one or the other; and he decided according to the prejudices natural to his birth, by espousing the royal cause. From this time a separation took place between him and Mrs. Ferguson.

Her connection with certain political transactions exposed her for a time to much censure and mortification. But there is no reason to doubt the sincerity of her declarations with regard to the motives that influenced her conduct. Many of her unobtrusive charities testify to her sympathy with her suffering countrymen. She not only visited the cottages in her neighborhood with supplies of clothing, provisions, or medicines for the inmates, but while General Howe had possession of Philadelphia, she sent a quantity of linen into the city, spun with her own hands, and directed it to be made into shirts for the benefit of the American prisoners taken at the battle of Germantown.

Another instance of her benevolence is characteristic. On hearing, in one of her visits to the city, that a merchant had become reduced, and having been imprisoned for debt, was suffering from want of the comforts of life, she sent him a bed, and afterwards visited him in prison, and put twenty dollars into his hands. She refused to inform him who was his benefactor; but it was discovered by his description of her person and dress. At this time her annual income, it is said, was reduced to a very limited sum. Many other secret acts of charity, performed at the expense of her personal and habitual comforts were remembered by her friends, and many instances of her sensibility and tender sympathy with all who suffered.

Her husband being engaged in the British service, she was favored by the loyalists, while treated with respect at the same time by the other party as an American lady who occupied a high social position.* It was natural that she should be in some measure influenced by attachment to the old order of things, and respect for the civil institutions she had been accustomed to venerate; while her desire for the good of her

---

* The reader is referred to the LIFE AND CORRESPONDENCE OF PRESIDENT REED, by his grandson, William B. Reed. Vol. i., 381. Mrs. Ferguson's letters are there quoted, with her narrative, at length.

countrymen led to ardent wishes that the desolations and miseries she witnessed might cease. It is said she often wept over newspapers containing details of suffering. The sensibility that could not bear to look on the woes even of the brute creation, must have been severely tried by the daily horrors of civil war. It is not surprising, therefore, that she should be eager to seize any opportunity that offered, of being instrumental in ending them.

Immediately after the British took possession of Philadelphia, Mrs. Ferguson was the bearer of a letter from the Rev. Mr. Duché to General Washington, which greatly displeased him, causing him to express to her his disapprobation of the intercourse she seemed to have held with the writer, and his expectation that it should be discontinued. At a later period she came again to Philadelphia, under a pass granted her by the Commander-in-chief, for the purpose of taking leave of her husband. She was at the house of her friend Charles Stedman, which chanced to be the place appointed for the residence of Governor Johnstone, one of the commissioners sent under parliamentary authority to settle the differences between Great Britain and America. She was in company with him three times; the conversation being general on the first two occasions. His declarations, she says, were so warm in favor of American interests, that she looked upon him as really a friend to her country. He wished, since he could not himself be permitted to pass the lines, to find some person who would step forward and act a mediatorial part, by suggesting something to stop the effusion of blood likely to ensue if the war were carried on. Mrs. Ferguson said repeatedly, that she believed the sentiment of the people to be in favor of Independence. "I am certain," were her words in the last conversation on the subject —"that nothing short of Independence will be accepted." Yet it does not appear that her own views were averse to a re-union of the two countries.

Governor Johnstone then expressed a particular anxiety for the influence of General Reed; and requested Mrs. Ferguson, "if she should see him," to convey the idea, that provided he could, "comformably to his conscience and views of things," exert his influence to settle the dispute, "he might command ten thousand guineas, and the best post in the government." In reply to Mrs. Ferguson's question, if Mr. Reed would not look upon such a mode of obtaining his influence as a bribe, Johnstone immediately disclaimed any such idea ; said such a method of proceeding was common in all negotiations ; and that one might honorably make it a man's interest to step forth in such a cause. She on her part expressed her conviction that if Mr. Reed thought it right to give up the point of Independence, he would say so without fee or reward ; and if he were of a different opinion, no pecuniary emolument would lead him to give a contrary vote. Mr. Johnstone did not see the matter in this light.

A day or two after this communication was suggested, Mrs. Ferguson sent by a confidential messenger a note to General Reed, at head-quarters, requesting an

hour's conversation previous to her going to Lancaster
on business, and desiring him to fix a place where she
could meet him without the necessity of passing through
the camp.   She stated that the business on which she
wished to confer with him could not be committed to
writing.

The note was received on the 21st of June, after General Reed's arrival in the city, which had been evacu-
ated three days before by the British.   He sent word
by the bearer that he would wait upon Mrs. Ferguson
the same evening.   At this interview, the conversation
treating of Governor Johnstone's desire of settling
matters upon an amicable footing, and his favorable
sentiments towards Mr. Reed, General Reed mentioned
that he had received a letter from him at Valley Forge.
Mrs. Ferguson then repeated, in all its particulars, the
conversation that had passed at the house of Mr. Stedman.   Her repetition of the proposition of Governor
Johnstone brought from General Reed the prompt and
noble reply: "I AM NOT WORTH PURCHASING; BUT SUCH
AS I AM, THE KING OF GREAT BRITAIN IS NOT RICH
ENOUGH TO DO IT."

General Reed laid before Congress both the written
and verbal communications of Governor Johnstone;
withholding, however, the name of the lady, from motives of delicacy, and reluctance to draw down popular
indignation upon her.   An account of the transaction
was also published in the papers of the day.   It was
useless to attempt concealment of her name; suspicion
was at once directed to her; and her name was called

for by a resolution of the Executive Council of Pennsylvania.* Congress issued a declaration condemning the daring and atrocious attempts made to corrupt their integrity, and declaring it incompatible with their honor to hold any manner of correspondence with the said George Johnstone. As may be imagined, disagreeable consequences ensued, which were severely felt by Mrs. Ferguson. As soon as she saw the article in Towne's Evening Post, which reached her at Graeme Park, July 26th, 1778, she addressed a letter of remonstrance to General Reed, bitterly complaining of having been exhibited in the newspapers as a mere emissary of the commissioners. "I own I find it hard," she says, "knowing the uncorruptness of my heart, to be held out to the public as a tool to the commissioners. But the impression is now made, and it is too late to recall it. How far, at this critical juncture of time, this affair may injure my property, is uncertain; that, I assure you, is but a secondary thought."†

It appears evident that Mrs. Ferguson did not act this part in any expectation of deriving advantage for herself. Her associations and connections being chiefly with the royalists, it was natural that her opinions

* " The attempt through the wife of a loyalist to bribe a member of Congress to aid in uniting the Colonies to the mother country, proved of incalculable service in recalling the doubting and irresolute whigs to a sense of duty. The story, and the noble reply, were repeated from mouth to mouth; and from the hour it was known, the whigs had won—the tories lost—the future empire."—*Sabine's American Loyalists.*

† Letter published in the Remembrancer, vol. vi.

should be influenced by theirs; but her desire for the good of the country was undoubtedly disinterested. After the return of Governor Johnstone to England, he ventured to deny the charge preferred in the resolutions of Congress, by a letter published in Rivington's Gazette ; and in a speech in November in the House of Commons, boldly asserted the falsehood of the statement made by General Reed.   His denial no sooner reached America, than Mrs. Ferguson, anxious that justice should be done to all parties, published her narrative of the transaction, confirmed by her oath.   The excellence of the motives which had actuated her in consenting to act as Johnstone's confidential agent, is sufficiently apparent in the spirit she now exhibited.

" Among the many mortifying insinuations that have been hinted on the subject, none has so sensibly affected me, as an intimation that some thought I acted a part, in consequence of certain expectations of a post, or some preferment from Mr. Johnstone, to be conferred on the person dearest to me on earth.   On that head I shall say no more, but leave it to any person of common sense to determine, if I had any views of that kind, whether I should, in so full and solemn a manner, call in question what Mr. Johnstone has asserted in the House of Commons.   A proceeding of this kind must totally exclude all avenues of favor from that quarter, were there ever any expected, which I solemnly declare never was the case.   If this account should ever have the honor to be glanced over by the eye of Governor Johnstone, I know not in what medium he may view it.

It is possible that the multiplicity of ideas, which may be supposed to pass through the brain of a politician in the course of a few months, may have jostled the whole transaction out of his memory.   Should this be the case, insignificant and contemptible as I may appear to him, I believe there are two or three people in Britain who will venture to tell him, in all his plenitude of power, that they believe I would not set my hand to an untruth."

Mrs. Ferguson's poetical talent has been mentioned. Her verses were said to possess vigor and measure, but to lack melody, while her prose writings indicated both genius and knowledge.   She was well read in polemical divinity, and a firm believer in the doctrines of revelation.   She is said to have transcribed the whole Bible, to impress its contents more deeply upon her mind ; hence the facility with which she would select appropriate passages to illustrate or adorn the subjects of her writings or conversation.

She had no children, but adopted the son and daughter of one of her sisters, who on her death-bed committed them to her care.   The nephew, an accomplished scholar and gentleman, was till his death a lieutenant in the British army.

The talents and attainments of Mrs. Ferguson, her virtues, elevated and invigorated by Christian faith, her independence and integrity of character, and her benevolent feeling for others—endeared her name to a large circle of friends.   Yet her life appears to have been one darkened by sorrow.   In her later years, the

reduction of her income diminished her means of usefulness; but she would not permit any privations to which
she found it necessary to submit, to be a source of un-
happiness.

She died at the house of a friend near Graeme Park,
on the twenty-third of February, 1801, in the sixty-
second year of her age.

XV.

~~~~~~~~~~

MARY PHILIPSE.

In 1756, Colonel George Washington, then commander-in-chief of the Virginia forces, had some difficulties concerning rank with an officer holding a royal
commission. He found it necessary to communicate
with General Shirley, the commander-in-chief of His
Majesty's armies in America; and for this purpose left
his head-quarters at Winchester, and travelled to
Boston on horse-back, attended by his aids-de-camp.
On his way, he stopped in some of the principal cities.
The military fame he had gained, and the story of his
remarkable escape at Braddock's defeat, excited general
curiosity to see the brave young hero; and great attention was paid to him. While in New York, says his
biographer, Mr. Sparks, "he was entertained at the
house of Mr. Beverley Robinson, between whom and
himself an intimacy of friendship subsisted, which
indeed continued without change, till severed by their
opposite fortunes twenty years afterwards in the Revolution. It happened that Miss Mary Philipse, a sister

MARY MORRIS.

of Mrs. Robinson, and a young lady of rare accomplishments, was an inmate in the family. The charms of
this lady made a deep impression upon the heart of the
Virginia Colonel. He went to Boston, returned, and
was again welcomed to the hospitality of Mrs. Robinson.
He lingered there till duty called him away ; but he was
careful to entrust his secret to a confidential friend,
whose letters kept him informed of every important
event. In a few months intelligence came that a rival
was in the field, and that the consequences could not be
answered for, if he delayed to renew his visits to New
York."

Washington could not at this time leave his post,
however deeply his feelings may have been interested
in securing the favor of the fair object of his admiration.
The fact that his friend thought fit to communicate
thus repeatedly with him upon the subject, does not
favor the supposition that his regard was merely a
passing fancy, or that the bustle of camp-life, or the
scenes of war, had effaced her image from his heart.
Mr. Sparks assures me that the letters referred to, which
were from a gentleman connected with the Robinson
family, though playful in their tone, were evidently
written under the belief that an attachment existed on
Washington's part, and that his happiness was concerned. How far the demonstrations of this attachment had
gone, it is now impossible to ascertain ; nor whether
Miss Philipse had discouraged the Colonel's attentions
so decidedly as to preclude all hope. The probability

is, however, that he despaired of success. He never saw her again till after her marriage with Captain Roger Morris, the rival of whom he had been warned.

Mary Philipse was the daughter of the Hon. Frederick Philipse, Speaker of the Assembly. He was lord of the old manor of Philipsborough, and owned an immense landed estate on the Hudson. Mary was born at the Manor Hall, on the third of July, 1730. No particulars relating to her early life can be given by her relatives; but the tradition is, that she was beautiful, fascinating, and accomplished. A lady now living in New York, who knew her after she became Mrs. Morris, and had visited her at her residence near the city, tells me that she was one of the most elegant women she had ever seen; and that her manners, uniting dignity with affability, charmed every one who knew her. The rumor of Washington's former attachment was then current, and universally believed. Her house was the resort of many visitors at all seasons. She removed to New York after her marriage, in 1758, with Roger Morris, who was a captain in the British army in the French war, and one of Braddock's aids-de-camp. A part of the Philipse estate came by right of his wife into his possession, and was taken from him by confiscation, in punishment for his loyalism. Mrs. Morris was included in the attainder, that the whole interest might pass under the act.* The rights of her children,

* The authentic facts relating to Captain Morris and Colonel Robinson, and to their wives, have been preserved by Mr. Sabine in his "American Loyalists." He visited the relatives of the family in New Brunswick.

however, as time showed, were not affected ; and the reversionary interest was sold by them to John Jacob Astor.

The descendants of Mrs. Robinson, the sister of Mary Morris, speak of her with warm praise, as one who possessed high qualities of mind, and great excellence of character. To one of these, a gentleman high in office in New Brunswick, the author of the 'Loyalists' once remarked in conversation, that there was some difference to his aunt, between being the wife of the Commander-in-chief—the first President of the United States, and the wife of an exile and an outlaw —herself attainted of treason. The tables were turned upon him by the reply, that Mrs. Morris had been remarkable for fascinating all who approached her, and moulding every body to her will ; and that had she married Washington, it could not be certain that she would not have kept him to his allegiance. "Indeed, Washington would not, could not have been a traitor with such a wife as Aunt Morris." Without dwelling on the possibilities of such a contingency, one can hardly think, without some degree of national shame, that a lady whom we have every reason to believe had been the object of Washington's love, "should be attainted of treason for clinging to the fortunes of her husband."

Mrs. Morris died in England in 1825, at the advanced age of ninety-six. The portrait of her is engraved from an original painting taken after her marriage, and now in the possession of her namesake and grandniece, Mrs. Governeur, who resides at "Highland Grange," Philipstown, in the Highlands. It is stated in the History of Westchester County, that Miss Mary Philipse was the original of the lovely character of Frances, in Mr. Cooper's novel of "The Spy:" this is incorrect.

~~~~~~~~~~~~~~~~

SUSANNAH, the sister of Mary Philipse, was the wife of Beverley Robinson of New York. There is some ground for the belief that she actually exercised over her husband's mind some portion of the influence said to have been possessed by her sister; for it appears that he was at first disinclined to take any active part in the contest between the Colonies and Great Britain. He was so much opposed to the measures of the ministry, that he would not use imported merchandise; but was at length prevailed on by his friends to enter the royal service. As before-mentioned, he and Washington were intimate friends before they were separated by difference of political opinion. "The Robinson house," which had been confiscated with the lands, was occupied by Arnold as his head-quarters, and by Washington at the time of Arnold's treason.

When Colonel Robinson gave up the quiet enjoyment of country life, his wife took her share of the outlawry that awaited him; she, as well as her sister, being included in the act of confiscation. After their removal to England, they lived in retirement. She died near Bath, at the age of ninety-four, in 1822. Her descendants in New Brunswick preserve, among other relics of the olden time, a silver tea-urn, of rich and massive workmanship, said to be the first of such articles used in America.

XVI.

~~~~~~

SARAH REEVE GIBBES.

THE failure of the British commissioners to conclude an amicable adjustment of differences between the two countries—and the ill success of the effort to gain their ends by private intrigue and bribery—annihilated the hopes of those who had desired the acceptance by Congress of terms of accommodation. War was now the only prospect ; the reduction of the Colonies to obedience by force of arms, or the establishment of national Independence by a protracted struggle. The movements and expeditions which succeeded the battle of Monmouth—the incursion of the Indians and tories under Colonel John Butler and Brandt, for the destruction of the settlement in the lovely valley of Wyoming —the terrible tragedy of July, with the retaliatory expeditions against the Indians—and the repetition of the barbarities of Wyoming at Cherry Valley, in November—were the prominent events that took place in the middle and northern sections of the country during the remainder of 1778. The scene of important action was now changed to the South. In November, Count D'Estaing, with the French fleet, sailed for the West

Indies, to attack the British dependencies in that quarter. General Sir Henry Clinton, on his part, despatched Colonel Campbell from New York, on an expedition against Georgia, the feeblest of the southern provinces. His troops landed late in December near Savannah, which was then defended by the American general, Robert Howe. His small force being enfeebled by sickness, defeat was the consequence of an attack; and the remnant of the American army retreated into South Carolina. The British having obtained possession of the capital of Georgia, the plan of reducing that State and South Carolina was vigorously prosecuted in 1779, while the armies of Washington and Clinton were employed in the northern section of the Union. Soon after the fall of Savannah, General Prevost, with troops from East Florida, took possession of the only remaining military post in Georgia; and joining his forces to those of Colonel Campbell, assumed the chief command of the royal army at the South. The loyalists who came along the western frontier of Carolina to join his standard, committed great devastations and cruelties on their way. General Lincoln, who commanded the continental forces in the southern department, sent a detachment under General Ashe across the Savannah, to repress the incursions of the enemy, and confine them to the low country near the sea coast. The surprise and defeat of this detachment by Prevost, completed the subjugation of Georgia. But in April General Lincoln entered the field anew, and leaving Moultrie to watch Prevost's movements, commenced his march up the left bank of the Savannah, and crossed into Georgia near Augusta, with the intention of advancing on the capital. Prevost attacked Moultrie and Pulaski, compelling them to retreat; and then hurried to place himself before Charleston. From this position, however, he was obliged to withdraw on Lincoln's approach. He proceeded to the island of St. John's, separated from the mainland by an inlet called Stono River; and leaving a division at Stono Ferry, retired with a part of his force towards Savannah. On the 20th June, Lincoln attacked the division at Stono Ferry, but was repulsed. The British soon after established a post at Beaufort, and the main body of the army retired to Savannah. For some months the hot and sickly season prevented further action on either side.

The siege of Savannah under D'Estaing and Lincoln took place early in October, 1779. The Americans were repulsed, the gallant Pulaski receiving his death-wound; and the enterprise was abandoned. The French fleet departed from the coast; and General Lincoln retreated into South Carolina. A cloud of despondency hung over the close of this year. The flattering hopes inspired by the alliance with France had not been realized. The continental army reduced in numbers and wretchedly clothed—the treasury empty—the paper currency rapidly diminishing in value—distress was brought on all classes, and the prospect seemed more than ever dark and discouraging. On the other hand, Britain displayed new resources, and made renewed exertions, notwithstanding the formidable combination against her. Sir Henry Clinton determined to make the South his most important field of operations for the future, and planned the campaign of 1780 on an extensive scale. He arrived in Georgia late in January, and early in the succeeding month left Savannah for the siege of Charleston, then defended by General Lincoln. The fleet of Arbuthnot was anchored in the harbor, and the British overran the country on the left side of the Cooper river. The surrender of Charleston on the twelfth of May, seemed to secure the recovery of the southern section of the Union; and Clinton immediately set about re-establishing the royal government.

The foregoing brief glance at the course of events during the two years succeeding the evacuation of Philadelphia, is necessary to prepare the reader for the southern sketches that follow.

A few hundred yards from a fine landing on Stono River, upon John's Island, about two hours' sail from Charleston, stands a large, square, ancient-looking mansion, strongly built of brick, with a portico fronting the river. On the side towards the road, the wide piazza overlooks a lawn; and a venerable live oak, with aspen, sycamore, and other trees, shade it from the sun. On either side of the house, about twenty yards distant, stands a smaller two story building, connected with the main building by a neat open fence. In one of these

is the kitchen and out-offices; the other was formerly
the school-house and tutor's dwelling. Beyond are the
barns, the overseer's house, and the negro huts apper-
taining to a plantation. The garden in old times was
very large and well-cultivated, being laid out in wide
walks, and extending from the mansion to the river.
The "river walk," on the verge of a bluff eight or ten
feet in height, followed the bending of the water, and
was bordered with orange-trees. Tall hedges of the
ever-green wild orange-tree divided the flower from the
vegetable garden, and screened from view the family
burial-ground. The beautifully laid out grounds, and
shaded walks, gave this place a most inviting aspect,
rendering it such an abode as its name of "Peaceful
Retreat" indicated.

At the period of the Revolution this mansion was
well known throughout the country as the seat of hospitality and elegant taste. Its owner, Robert Gibbes,
was a man of cultivated mind and refined manners—
one of those gentlemen of the old school, of whom South
Carolina has justly made her boast. Early in life he
became a martyr to the gout, by which painful disease
his hands and feet were so contracted and crippled that
he was deprived of their use. The only exercise he
was able to take, was in a chair on wheels, in which he
was placed every day, and by the assistance of a servant, moved about the house, and through the garden.
The circuit through these walks and along the river,
formed his favorite amusement. Unable, by reason of
his misfortune, to take an active part in the war, his

feelings were nevertheless warmly enlisted on the republican side; and his house was ever open for the reception and entertainment of the friends of liberty. He had married Miss Sarah Reeve, she being at the time about eighteen years of age. Notwithstanding her youth, she had given evidence that she possessed a mind of no common order. The young couple had a house in Charleston, but spent the greater part of their time at their country-seat and plantation upon John's Island.   Here Mrs. Gibbes devoted herself with earnestness to the various duties before her; for in consequence of her husband's infirmities, the management of an extensive estate, with the writing on business it required —devolved entirely upon her. In addition to a large family of her own, she had the care of the seven orphan children of Mrs. Fenwick, the sister of Mr. Gibbes, who at her death had left them and their estate to his guardianship. Two other children—one her nephew, Robert Barnwell—were added to her charge. The multiplied cares involved in meeting all these responsibilities, with the superintendence of household concerns, required a rare degree of energy and activity ; yet the mistress of this well ordered establishment had always a ready and cordial welcome for her friends, dispensing the hospitalities of "Peaceful Retreat," with a grace and cheerful politeness that rendered it a most agreeable resort.

It was doubtless the fame of the luxurious living at this delightful country-seat—which attracted the attention of the British during the invasion of Prevost, while the royal army kept possession of the seaboard. A battalion of British and Hessians, determined to quarter themselves in so desirable a spot, arrived at the landing at the dead of night, and marching up in silence, surrounded the house. The day had not yet begun to dawn, when an aged and faithful servant tapped softly at the door of Mrs. Gibbes' apartment. The whisper— "Mistress, the redcoats are all around the house," was the first intimation given of their danger. "Tell no one, Cæsar, but keep all quiet," she replied promptly; and her preparations were instantly commenced to receive the intruders. Having dressed herself quickly, she went up stairs, waked several ladies who were guests in the house, and requested them to rise and dress with all possible haste. In the mean time the domestics were directed to prepare the children, of whom, with her own eight and those under her care, there were sixteen; the eldest being only fifteen years old. These were speedily dressed and seated in the spacious hall. Mrs. Gibbes then assisted her husband, as was always her custom—to rise and dress, and had him placed in his rolling chair. All these arrangements were made without the least confusion, and so silently, that the British had no idea any one was yet awake within the house. The object of Mrs. Gibbes was to prevent violence on the enemy's part, by showing them at once that the mansion was inhabited only by those who were unable to defend themselves. The impressive manner in which this was done produced its effect. The invaders had no knowledge that the inmates were aware of their presence, till daylight, when they heard the heavy rolling of Mr. Gibbes' chair across the great hall towards the front door. Supposing the sound to be the rolling of a cannon, the soldiers advanced, and stood prepared with pointed bayonets to rush in, when the signal for assault should be given. But as the door was thrown open, and the stately form of the invalid presented itself, surrounded by women and children, they drew back, and—startled into an involuntary expression of respect—presented arms. Mr. Gibbes addressed them—yielding, of course, to the necessity that could not be resisted. The officers took immediate possession of the house, leaving the premises to their men, and extending no protection against pillage. The soldiers roved at their pleasure about the plantation, helping themselves to whatever they chose; breaking into the wine room, drinking to intoxication, and seizing upon and carrying off the negroes. A large portion of the plate was saved by the provident care of a faithful servant, who secretly buried it. Within the mansion, the energy and self-possession of Mrs. Gibbes still protected her family. The appearance of terror or confusion might have tempted the invaders to incivility; but it was impossible for them to treat otherwise than with deference, a lady whose calm and quiet deportment commanded their respect. Maintaining her place as mistress of her household, and presiding at her table, she treated her uninvited guests with a dignified courtesy that ensured civility while it prevented presumptuous familiarity. The boldest and rudest among them bowed involuntarily to an influence which fear or force could not have secured.

When the news reached Charlèston that the British had encamped on Mr. Gibbes's plantation, the authorities in that city despatched two galleys to dislodge them. These vessels ascended the river in the night, and arriving opposite, opened a heavy fire upon the invaders' encampment. The men had received strict injunctions not to fire upon the house, for fear of injury to any of the family. It could not, however, be known to Mr. Gibbes that such a caution had been given; and as soon as the Americans began their fire, dreading some accident, he proposed to his wife that they should take the children and seek a place of greater safety. Their horses being in the enemy's hands, they had no means of conveyance; but Mrs. Gibbes, with energies roused to exertion by the danger, and anxious only to secure shelter for her helpless charge, set off to walk with the children to an adjoining plantation situated in the interior. A drizzling rain was falling, and the weather was extremely chilly; the fire was incessant from the American guns, and sent—in order to avoid the house—in a direction which was in a range with the course of the fugitives. The shot, falling around them, cut the bushes, and struck the trees on every side. Exposed each moment to this imminent danger, they continued their flight with as much haste as possible, for about a mile, till beyond the reach of the shot.

Having reached the houses occupied by the negro laborers on the plantation, they stopped for a few

moments to rest. Mrs. Gibbes, wet, chilled, and exhausted by fatigue and mental anxiety, felt her strength
utterly fail, and was obliged to wrap herself in a blanket
and lie down upon one of the beds. It was at this
time, when the party first drew breath freely—with
thankfulness that the fears of death were over—that
on reviewing the trembling group to ascertain if all
had escaped uninjured, it was found that a little boy,
John Fenwick, was missing. In the hurry and terror
of their flight the child had been forgotten and left
behind! What was now to be done? The servants
refused to risk their lives by returning for him; and in
common humanity, Mr. Gibbes could not insist that
any one should undertake the desperate adventure.
The roar of the distant guns was still heard, breaking at
short intervals the deep silence of the night. The
chilly rain was falling, and the darkness was profound.
Yet the thought of abandoning the helpless boy to
destruction, was agony to the hearts of his relatives.
In this extremity the self-devotion of a young girl interposed to save him. Mary Anna, the eldest daughter of
Mrs. Gibbes—then only thirteen years of age, determined to venture back—in spite of the fearful peril—alone.
The mother dared not oppose her noble resolution,
which seemed indeed an inspiration of heaven; and
she was permitted to go. Hastening along the path
with all the speed of which she was capable, she reached
the house, still in the undisturbed possession of the
enemy; and entreated permission from the sentinel to
enter; persisting, in spite of refusal, till by earnest

10

importunity of supplication, she gained her object. Searching anxiously through the house, she found the child in a room in a third story, and lifting him joyfully in her arms, carried him down, and fled with him to the spot where her anxious parents were awaiting her return. The shot still flew thickly around her, frequently throwing up the earth in her way; but protected by the Providence that watches over innocence, she joined the rest of the family in safety.* The boy saved on this occasion by the intrepidity of the young girl, was the late General Fenwick, distinguished for his services in the last war with Great Britain. "Fenwick Place," still called "Headquarters," was three miles from "Peaceful Retreat."

* Major Garden, who after the war married Mary Anna Gibbes, mentions this intrepid action. There are a few errors in his account; he calls the boy who was left, "a distant relation," and says the dwelling-house was fired on by the Americans. The accomplished lady who communicated the particulars to me, heard them from her grandmother, Mrs. Gibbes; and the fact that the house was not fired upon, is attested by a near relative now living. The house never bore any marks of shot; though balls and grape-shot have been often found on the plantation. Again—Garden says the family "were allowed to remain in some of the upper apartments;" and were at last "ordered to quit the premises," implying that they were treated with some severity as prisoners. This could not have been the case; as Mrs. Gibbes constantly asserted that she presided at her own table, and spoke of the respect and deference with which she was uniformly treated by the officers. Her refusal to yield what she deemed a right, ensured civility towards herself and household.

The family Bible, from which the parentage of General Fenwick might have been ascertained, was lost during the Revolution, and only restored to the family in the summer of 1847.

Some time after these occurrences, when the family
were again inmates of their own home, a battle was
fought in a neighboring field. When the conflict was
over, Mrs. Gibbes sent her servants to search among
the slain left upon the battle-ground, for Robert Barnwell, her nephew, who had not returned. They discovered him by part of his dress, which one of the
blacks remembered having seen his mother making.
His face was so covered with wounds, dust and blood,
that he could not be recognised. Yet life was not
extinct; and under the unremitting care of his aunt and
her young daughter, he recovered. His son, Robert W.
Barnwell, was for some years president of the South
Carolina College. Scenes like these were often witnessed by the subject of this sketch, and on more than a
few occasions did she suffer acute anxiety on account
of the danger of those dear to her. She was accustomed to point out the spot where her eldest son, when only
sixteen years old, had been placed as a sentinel, while
British vessels were in the river, and their fire was
poured on him. She would relate how, with a mother's
agony of solicitude, she watched the balls as they struck
the earth around him, while the youthful soldier main-
tained his dangerous post, notwithstanding the entreaties of an old negro hid behind a tree, that he would
leave it. Through such trials, the severity of which we
who enjoy the peace so purchased cannot fully estimate,
she exhibited the same composure, and readiness to meet
every emergency, with the same benevolent sympathy
for others. During the struggle, while Carolina was

invaded or in a state of defence, her house was at different times the quarters of friend and foe.   The skirmishes
were frequent, and many who went forth in the morning in health and vigor, returned no more ; nor did she
know from day to day who were next to be her guests.

Mrs. Gibbes had a cultivated taste ; and amidst her
many cares, still found leisure for literary occupation.
Volumes of her writings remain, filled with well-selected
extracts from the many books she read, accompanied
by her own comments ; with essays on various subjects,
copies of letters to her friends, and poetry.   Everything
from her pen evinces delicacy as well as strength of
mind, extensive information, and refinement of taste,
with the tenderest sensibility, and a deep tone of piety.
Most of her letters were written after the war, and
throw no additional light on the feeling or manners of
that period.

She was in the habit of putting aside locks of hair
enclosed with appropriate poetical tributes, as memen-
toes of her departed friends ; and many of these touching memorials have been found among her papers.   For
fifteen years she was deprived of sight, but lost nothing
of her cheerfulness, or the engaging grace of her manner ;
nor was her conversation less interesting or entertaining to her visitors.   A stranger, who shortly before her
death was at her house with a party of friends, whom
she delighted by her conversation—expressed great
surprise on being informed she was blind.

During the latter part of her life, she resided at Wilton,
the country-seat of Mrs. Barnard Elliott, where she died

in 1825, at the age of seventy-nine. Her remains rest in the family burial-ground upon John's Island. A beautiful monumental inscription in St. Paul's church, Charleston, records the virtues that adorned her character, and the faith which sustained her under many afflictions.

XVII.

~~~~~~~~~~

ELIZA WILKINSON.

THE letters of Eliza Wilkinson present a lively picture of the situation of many inhabitants of that portion of country which was the scene of various skirmishes about the time of Lincoln's approach to relieve Charleston from Prevost, the retreat of that commander, and the engagement at Stono Ferry. The description given of occurrences, is not only interesting as a graphic detail, but as exhibiting traits of female character worthy of all admiration. It is much to be regretted that her records do not embrace a longer period of time.

Her father was an emigrant from Wales, and always had much pride in his Welsh name, Francis Yonge. He had three children, Eliza and two sons; and owned what is called Yonge's Island. He was old and infirm, and suffered much rough treatment at the hands of the British, from whom he refused to take a protection. Both his sons died—one the death of a soldier; and the old family name now lives in Charleston in the person of Francis Yonge Porcher, great grandchild of the subject of this notice.

Mrs. Wilkinson had been married only six months when her first husband died. At the period of the war, she was a young and beautiful widow, with fascinating manners, quick at repartee, and full of cheerfulness and good humor. Her place of residence, Yonge's Island, lies thirty miles south of Charleston. The Cherokee rose which still flourishes there in great abundance, hedging the long avenue, and the sight of the creek and causeway that separate the island from the mainland, call up many recollections of her. She bore her part in Revolutionary trials and privations, and was frequently a sufferer from British cruelty.

Mrs. Wilkinson was in Charleston when news came that a large party of the enemy had landed near Beaufort. With a few friends, she went over to her father's plantation, but did not remain there long; for upon receiving information that a body of British horse were within five or six miles, the whole party, with the exception of her father and mother, crossed the river to Wadmalaw, and went for refuge to the house of her sister. A large boat-load of women and children hurrying for safety to Charleston, stayed with them a day or two, and presented a sad spectacle of the miseries brought in the train of war. One woman with seven children, the youngest but two weeks old, preferred venturing her own life and that of her tender infant, to captivity in the hands of a merciless foe.

Mrs. Wilkinson remained at Wadmalaw for some time, and at length returned to her home on the island. The surrounding country was waiting in a distressed condition for the coming of General Lincoln, to whom the people looked for deliverance. Many painful days of suspense passed before tidings were received. All trifling discourse, she says, was laid aside—the ladies who gathered in knots talking only of political affairs. At last her brothers, with the Willtown troops, arrived from Charleston, and brought the joyful news of the approach of Lincoln. The dreaded enemy had not yet invaded the retirement of Yonge's Island; although it was suspected that spies were lurking about, and boat-loads of red coats were frequently seen passing and re-passing on the river. Mrs. Wilkinson retreated with her sister to an inland country-seat. There they were called on by parties of the Americans, whom they always received with friendly hospitality. "The poorest soldier," says one letter, "who would call at any time for a drink of water, I would take a pleasure in giving it to him myself; and many a dirty, ragged fellow have I attended with a bowl of water, or milk and water: they really merit every thing, who will fight from principle alone ; for from what I could learn, these poor creatures had nothing to protect, and seldom got their pay ; yet with what alacrity will they encounter danger and hardships of every kind!"

One night a detachment of sixty red coats passed the gate with the intention of surprising Lieutenant Morton Wilkinson at a neighboring plantation. A negro woman was their informer and guide; but their attempt was unsuccessful. On re-passing the avenue early the next morning, they made a halt at the head of it, but a negro man dissuaded them from entering, by telling them the place belonged to a decrepit old gentleman, who did not then live there. They took his word for it, and passed on.

On the second of June, two men belonging to the enemy, rode up to the house, and asked many questions, saying that Colonel M'Girth and his soldiers might be presently looked for, and that the inmates could expect no mercy. The family remained in a state of cruel suspense for many hours. The following morning a party of the whigs called at the gate, but did not alight. One of them, in leaping a ditch, was hurt, and taken into the house for assistance; and while they were dressing his wound, a negro girl gave the alarm that the "king's people" were coming. The two men mounted their horses and escaped: the women awaited the ene-my's approach. Mrs. Wilkinson writes to a friend:

"I heard the horses of the inhuman Britons coming in such a furious manner, that they seemed to tear up the earth, the riders at the same time bellowing out the most horrid curses imaginable—oaths and imprecations which chilled my whole frame. Surely, thought I, such horrid language denotes nothing less than death; but I had no time for thought—they were up to the house— entered with drawn swords and pistols in their hands: indeed they rushed in in the most furious manner, cry-ing out, 'Where are these women rebels?' That was

10*

the first salutation! The moment they espied us, off went our caps. (I always heard say none but women pulled caps!) And for what, think you? Why, only to get a paltry stone and wax pin, which kept them on our heads; at the same time uttering the most abusive language imaginable, and making as if they would hew us to pieces with their swords. But it is not in my power to describe the scene: it was terrible to the last degree; and what augmented it, they had several armed negroes with them, who threatened and abused us greatly. They then began to plunder the house of every thing they thought valuable or worth taking; our trunks were split to pieces, and each mean, pitiful wretch crammed his bosom with the contents, which were our apparel, &c.*

"I ventured to speak to the inhuman monster who had my clothes. I represented to him the times were such we could not replace what they had taken from us, and begged him to spare me only a suit or two: but I got nothing but a hearty curse for my pains; nay, so far was his callous heart from relenting, that casting his eyes towards my shoes, 'I want them buckles,' said he; and immediately knelt at my feet to take them out. While he was busy doing this, a brother villain, whose enormous mouth extended from ear to ear, bawled out, 'Shares there, I say! shares!' So they divided my buckles between them. The other wretches were employed in the same manner; they took my sister's ear-

* Letters of Eliza Wilkinson, arranged by Mrs. Gilman.

rings from her ears, her and Miss Samuells' buckles;
they demanded her ring from her finger; she pleaded
for it, told them it was her wedding-ring, and begged
they would let her keep it; but they still demanded it;
and presenting a pistol at her, swore if she did not deliver it immediately, they would fire. She gave it to
them; and after bundling up all their booty, they mounted their horses. But such despicable figures! Each
wretch's bosom stuffed so full, they appeared to be all
afflicted with some dropsical disorder. Had a party of
rebels (as they call us) appeared, we should have seen
their circumference lessen.

"They took care to tell us, when they were going
away, that they had favored us a great deal—that we
might thank our stars it was no worse. I had forgot to
tell you that upon their first entering the house, one of
them gave my arm such a violent grasp, that he left the
print of his thumb and three fingers in black and blue,
which was to be seen very plainly for several days afterwards. I showed it to one of our officers who dined
with us, as a specimen of British cruelty. After they
were gone, I began to be sensible of the danger I had
been in, and the thoughts of the vile men seemed worse
(if possible) than their presence; for they came so suddenly up to the house, that I had no time for thought;
and while they stayed, I seemed in amaze—quite stupid!
I cannot describe it. But when they were gone, and I
had time to consider, I trembled so with terror that I
could not support myself. I went into the room, threw

myself on the bed, and gave way to a violent burst of grief, which seemed to be some relief to my swollen heart."

This outrage was followed by a visit from M'Girth's men, who treated the ladies with more civility ; one of them promising to make a report at camp of the usage they had received. It was little consolation, however, to know that the robbers would probably be punished. The others, who professed so much feeling for the fair, were not content without their share of plunder, though more polite in the manner of taking it. " While the British soldiers were talking to us, some of the silent ones withdrew, and presently laid siege to a bee-hive, which they soon brought to terms. The others perceiving it, cried out, 'Hand the ladies a plate of honey.' This was immediately done with officious haste, no doubt thinking they were very generous in treating us with our own. There were a few horses feeding in the pasture. They had them driven up. ' Ladies, do either of you own these horses ?' ' No ; they partly belong to father and Mr. Smilie !' ' Well, ladies, as they are not *your* property, we will take them !' "

They asked the distance to the other settlements ; and the females begged that forbearance might be shown to the aged father. He was visited the same day by another body of troops, who abused him and plundered the house. " One came to search mother's pockets, too, but she resolutely threw his hand aside. ' If you must see what's in my pocket, I'll show you myself ,' and she took out a thread-case, which had thread, needles, pins, tape, &c. The mean wretch took it from her." * * "After drinking all the wine, rum, &c. they could find, and inviting the negroes they had with them, who were very insolent, to do the same—they went to their horses, and would shake hands with father and mother before their departure. Fine amends, to be sure!"

After such unwelcome visitors, it is not surprising that the unprotected women could not eat or sleep in peace. They lay in their clothes every night, alarmed by the least noise; while the days were spent in anxiety and melancholy. One morning, when Mrs. Wilkinson was coming out of her chamber, her eyes fixed on the window—for she was continually on the watch—she saw something glitter through a thin part of the wood bordering the road. It proved to be the weapons of a large body of soldiers. As they came from the direction of the enemy's encampment, she concluded they were British troops; and every one in the house took the alarm. "Never was there such a scene of confusion. Sighs, complaints, wringing of hands—one running here, another there, spreading the dreadful tidings; and in a little time the negroes in the field came running up to the house with a hundred stories. Table, tea-cups—all the breakfast apparatus, were immediately huddled together and borne off; and we watched sharply to see which way the enemy (as we supposed them) took. But, oh! horrible! in a minute or two we saw our avenue crowded with horsemen in uniform. Said I, 'that looks like our uniform—blue and red ;' but I immediately recollected to have heard that the Hessian uniform was much like ours ; so out of the house we went, into an out-house." Their excessive fright prevented the explanation attempted from being understood. While the officer was endeavoring to re-assure the terrified ladies, a negro woman came up, and tapping Mrs. Wilkinson on the shoulder, whispered, 'I don't like these men ; one of them gave me this piece of silver for some milk ; and I know our people don't have so much silver these times.' "

Their dismay and terror were groundless; for the horsemen were a party of Americans, under the command of Major Moore. The one taken for a Hessian was a French officer. The mistake had been mutual ; the distress shown at sight of them having caused the officer in command to conclude himself and his men unwelcome visitors to some tory family. The discovery that they were friends changed fear into delight. " They then laughed at me," says Mrs. Wilkinson, " heartily for my fright—saying that they really expected, by the time I had done wringing my hands, I would have no skin left upon them; but now they knew the reason they no longer wondered."

Word was presently brought that a number of the enemy were carrying provisions from a plantation about two miles distant. The whigs marched to the place, and returned with seven prisoners. Two of these were of M'Girth's party, who had treated the ladies so cruelly ; yet notwithstanding the injuries received, the

kind heart of Mrs. Wilkinson relented at the sight of
them. She expressed pity for their distress, calling them
friends, because they were in the power of her countrymen; and interceded for them with the captors. Enqui-
ring if they would like any thing to drink, she supplied
them with the water they craved, holding the glass to
their lips, as their hands were tied behind them. Several
of the American officers, who had gathered at the door
and window, were smiling at the unusual scene. "In
the meanwhile," she writes, "Miss Samuells was very
busy about a wounded officer, (one of M'Girth's,) who
had been brought to the house. He had a ball through
his arm; we could find no rag to dress his wounds,
every thing in the house being thrown into such confusion by the plunderers; but (see the native tenderness
of an American!) Miss Samuells took from her neck
the only remaining handkerchief the Britons had left
her, and with it bound up his arm."

Their friends having left them, Mr. Yonge sent for
his daughter to his own plantation. The ladies were
obliged to walk three miles, the horses having been
taken away; but umbrellas were sent for them, and
they were attended by two of Mr. Yonge's negro men
armed with clubs. While crossing a place called the
Sands, the blacks captured and wounded a negro belonging to the loyalists, who came out of the woods.
Mrs. Wilkinson interfered to save his life; and to insure
the safety of the poor creature, who claimed her protection, and who was dragged on rapidly by his captors
—they fearing pursuit—was obliged to walk very fast,

leaving the others behind, till she was ready to faint
from fatigue and the overpowering heat. They arrived
safe at her father's, whence they were driven ere long
by another alarm. This time their flight was in darkness, through bogs and woods, stumbling against the
stumps or each other. In their new abode they had
more security. Parties of friends were out continually,
keeping the enemy quiet; and sometimes in the night
soldiers would ride up, and bid the negroes tell the
ladies they might sleep soundly, for they were to maintain a patrol during the night.

At length the arrival of General Lincoln was announced; and he was joyfully welcomed by the inmates
of the house. That night two or three hundred men
were quartered on the plantation—some of the officers
sleeping in the hall. They refused to have beds made.
"Beds were not for soldiers; the floor or the earth
served them as well as any where else." At daybreak
they moved to camp. Another alarm occurred, and General Lincoln's defeat near Stono Ferry, caused the retreat of the family to Willtown. Our writer's pen had
thence to record only new aggressions and sufferings.

The siege and capitulation of Charleston brought the
evils under which the land had groaned, to their height.
The hardships endured by those within the beleagured
city—the gloomy resignation of hope—the submission
to inevitable misfortune, have been described by abler
chroniclers. The general feeling is expressed in a letter

from a soldier to his wife, written twelve days before
the event :

"Our affairs are daily declining; and not a ray of
hope remains to assure us of our success. *   * I
expect to have the liberty of soon returning to
you; but the army must be made prisoners of war.
This will give a rude shock to the independence of
America; and a Lincolnade will be as common a term
as a Burgoynade. * * A mortifying scene must be encountered; the thirteen stripes will be levelled in the dust;
and I owe my life to the clemency of the conqueror."

After the surrender, Mrs. Wilkinson visited the city,
went on board the prison-ship, and drank coffee with the
prisoners awaiting an exchange. She saw the departure of her friends who were driven into exile, and indulged herself occasionally in provoking her enemies by
sarcastic sallies. "Once," she writes, "I was asked by
a British officer to play the guitar.

"'I cannot play; I am very dull.'

"'How long do you intend to continue so,'Mrs.
Wilkinson?'

"'Until my countrymen return, sir!'

"'Return as what, madam?—prisoners or subjects?'

"'As conquerors, sir.'

"He affected a laugh. 'You will never see that,
madam!'

"'I live in hopes, sir, of seeing the thirteen stripes
hoisted once more on the bastions of this garrison.'

"'Do not hope so; but come, give us a tune on the
guitar.'

" ' I can play nothing but rebel songs.'

" ' Well, let us have one of them.'

" ' Not to-day—I cannot play—I will not play ; besides, I suppose I should be put into the Provost for such a heinous crime.'

" I have often wondered since, I was not packed off, too ; for I was very saucy, and never disguised my sentiments.

" One day," she continues, " Kitty and I were going to take a walk on the Bay, to get something we wanted. Just as we had got our hats on, up ran one of the Billets into the dining-room, where we were.

" ' Your servant, ladies.'

" ' Your servant, sir.'

" ' Going out, ladies ?'

" ' Only to take a little walk.'

" He immediately turned about, and ran down stairs. I guessed for what.   *   *   *   He offered me his hand, or rather arm, to lean upon.

" ' Excuse me, sir,' said I ; ' I will support myself, if you please.'

" ' No, madam, the pavements are very uneven ; you may get a fall ; do accept my arm.'

" ' Pardon me, I cannot.'

" 'Come, you do not know what your condescension may do.   I will turn rebel !'

" ' Will you ?' said I, laughingly—' Turn rebel first, and then offer your arm.'

" We stopped in another store, where were several British officers.   After asking for the articles I wanted,

I saw a broad roll of ribbon, which appeared to be of black and white stripes.

"'Go,' said I to the officer who was with us, 'and reckon the stripes of that ribbon; see if they are *thirteen!*' (with an emphasis I spoke the word)—and he went, too!

"'Yes, they are thirteen, upon my word, madam.'

"'Do hand it me.' He did so; I took it, and found that it was narrow black ribbon, carefully wound round a broad white. I returned it to its place on the shelf.

"'Madam,' said the merchant, 'you can buy the black and white too, and tack them in stripes.'

"'By no means, sir; I would not have them *slightly tacked,* but *firmly united.*' The above-mentioned officers sat on the counter kicking their heels. How they gaped at me when I said this! But the merchant laughed heartily."

Like many others, Mrs. Wilkinson refused to join in the amusements of the city while in possession of the British; but gave her energies to the relief of her friends. The women were the more active when military efforts were suspended. Many and ingenious were the contrivances they adopted, to carry supplies from the British garrison, which might be useful to the gallant defenders of their country. Sometimes cloth for a military coat, fashioned into an appendage to female attire, would be borne away, unsuspected by the vigilant guards whose business it was to prevent smuggling, and afterwards converted into regimental shape. Boots, "a world too wide" for the delicate wearer, were often transferred to the partisan who could not procure them for himself. A horseman's helmet has been concealed under a well-arranged head-dress; and epaulettes delivered from the folds of a matron's simple cap. Other articles in demand for military use, more easily conveyed, were regularly brought away by some stratagem or other. Feathers and cockades thus secured, and presented by the fair ones as a trophy, had an inestimable value in the eyes of those who received them; and useful apparel was worn with the greater satisfaction, that it had not been conveyed without some risk on the donor's part.

It was after the return of Mrs. Wilkinson to Yonge's Island, that news was received of the glorious victory of Washington over Cornwallis. Her last letter which is of any public interest, contains congratulations on this event.

The old family mansion has been removed from the island. But the burial-ground is still held sacred; and the memory of Eliza Wilkinson is cherished in the hearts of her kindred.

XVIII.

~~~~~~~~~~~

MARTHA BRATTON.

"THE memory of Mrs. Martha Bratton.—In the hands of an infuriated monster, with the instrument of death around her neck, she nobly refused to betray her husband; in the hour of victory she remembered mercy, and as a guardian angel, interposed in behalf of her inhuman enemies. Throughout the Revolution she encouraged the whigs to fight on to the last; to hope on to the end. Honor and gratitude to the woman and heroine, who proved herself so faithful a wife—so firm a friend to liberty!"

The above toast was drunk at a celebration of Huck's Defeat, given at Brattonsville, York District, South Carolina, on the twelfth of July, 1839. The ground of the battle that had taken place fifty-nine years before, was within a few hundred yards of Dr Bratton's residence, inherited from his father, one of the heroes of that day. He celebrated the anniversary of this triumph of the whigs. Tho cool spring of the battle-field, it is said, furnished the only beverage used on the occasion.

The victory gained at this spot had the most important effect on the destinies of the State. It was the first check given to the British troops—the first time after the fall of Charleston, that the hitherto victorious enemy had been met. It brought confidence to the drooping spirits of the patriots, and taught the invaders that freemen are not conquered while the mind is free. The whigs, inspired with new life and buoyant hopes, began to throng together; the British were again attacked and defeated; a band of resolute and determined spirits took the field, and kept it till victory perched upon their banners, and South Carolina became an independent State.

The year 1780 was a dark period for the patriots of Carolina. Charleston surrendered on the twelfth of May; and General Lincoln and the American army became prisoners of war. This success was followed up by vigorous movements. One expedition secured the important post of Ninety-Six; another scoured the country bordering on the Savannah; and Lord Cornwallis passed the Santee and took Georgetown. Armed garrisons were posted throughout the State, which lay at the mercy of the conqueror, to overawe the inhabitants, and secure a return to their allegiance. For several weeks all military opposition ceased; and it was the boast of Sir Henry Clinton, that here, at least, the American Revolution was ended. A proclamation was issued, denouncing vengeance on all who should dare appear in arms, save under the royal authority, and offering pardon, with a few exceptions, to those who would acknowledge it, and accept British protection.

The great body of the people, believing resistance unavailing and hopeless, took the offered protection, while those who refused absolute submission were exiled or imprisoned. But the fact is recorded that the inhabitants of York District never gave their paroles, nor accepted protection as British subjects; preferring resistance and exile to subjection and inglorious peace.* A few individuals, who were excepted from the benefits of the proclamation, with others in whose breasts the love of liberty was unconquerable, sought refuge in North Carolina. They were followed by the whigs of York, Chester, and some other districts bordering on that State, who fled from the British troops as they marched into the upper country to compel the entire submission of the conquered province. These patriot exiles soon organized themselves in companies, and under their gallant leaders, Sumter, Bratton, Wynn, Moffit and others, began to collect on the frontier, and to harass the victorious enemy by sudden and desultory attacks. At the time when this noble daring was displayed, the State was unable to feed or clothe or arm the soldiers. They depended on their own exertions for every thing necessary to carry on the warfare. They tabernacled in the woods and swamps, with wolves and other beasts

---

* This fact is dwelt upon in the oration delivered on the occasion by Colonel Beatty. Dr. Joseph Johnson of Charleston, to whom I am indebted for some of the particulars in Mrs. Bratton's history, thinks it due to the circumstance that a large proportion of the settlers in that part of the State were of Irish origin, and derived their distrust of British faith from traditions of violated rights, contrary to the stipulations of the treaty of Limerick.

of the forest; and frequently wanted both for food and clothing.

To crush this bold and determined spirit, British officers and troops were despatched, in marauding parties, to every nook and corner of South Carolina, authorised to punish every whig with the utmost rigor, and to call upon the loyalists to aid in the work of carnage. A body of these marauders, assembled at Mobley's Meeting-house in Fairfield District, were attacked and defeated in June by a party of whigs under the command of Colonel Bratton, Major Wynn, and Captain M'Clure. The report of this disaster being conveyed to Rocky Mount in Chester District, Colonel Turnbull, the commander of a strong detachment of British troops at that point, determined on summary vengeance, and for that purpose sent Captain Huck, at the head of four hundred cavalry, and a considerable body of tories, all well mounted, with the following order :

" To Captain Huyck—

" You are hereby ordered, with the cavalry under your command, to proceed to the frontier of the province, collecting all the royal militia with you on your march, and with said force to push the rebels as far as you may deem convenient."*

It was at this time that the heroism of the wife of Colonel Bratton was so nobly displayed. The evening

* The order was found in Huck's pocket after death, and is still preserved by one of his conquerors. His name is spelt as above in the manuscript.

preceding the battle, Huck arrived at Colonel Bratton's house. He entered rudely, and demanded where her husband was.

" He is in Sumter's army," was the undaunted reply.

The officer then essayed persuasion, and proposed to Mrs. Bratton to induce her husband to come in and join the royalists, promising that he should have a commission in the royal service. It may well be believed that arguments were used, which must have had a show of reason at the time, when the people generally had given up all hopes and notions of independence. But Mrs. Bratton answered with heroic firmness, that she would rather see him remain true to his duty to his country, even if he perished in Sumter's army.

The son of Mrs. Bratton, Dr. John S. Bratton, who was then a child, remembers that Huck was caressing him on his knee while speaking to his mother. On receiving her answer, he pushed the boy off so suddenly, that his face was bruised by the fall. At the same time, one of Huck's soldiers, infuriated at her boldness, and animated by the spirit of deadly animosity towards the whigs which then raged in its greatest violence, seized a reaping-hook that hung near them in the piazza, and brought it to her throat, with intention to kill her. Still she refused to give information that might endanger her husband's safety. There is no mention made of any interference on the part of Captain Huck to save her from the hands of his murderous ruffian. But the officer second in command interposed,

11

and compelled the soldier to release her. They took prisoners three old men, whom, with another they had captured during the day, they confined in a corn-crib.

Huck then ordered Mrs. Bratton to have supper prepared for him and his troopers. It may be conceived with what feelings she saw her house occupied by the enemies of her husband and her country, and found herself compelled to minister to their wants. What wild and gloomy thoughts had possession of her soul, is evident from the desperate idea that occurred to her of playing a Roman's part, and mingling poison, which she had in the house, with the food they were to eat; thus delivering her neighbors from the impending danger. But her noble nature shrank from such an expedient, even to punish the invaders of her home. She well knew, too, the brave spirit that animated her husband and his comrades. They might even now be dogging the footsteps of the enemy; they might be watching the opportunity for an attack. They might come to the house also. She would not have them owe to a cowardly stratagem the victory they should win in the field of battle. Having prepared the repast, she retired with her children to an upper apartment.

After they had supped, Huck and his officers went to another house about half a mile off, owned by James Williamson, to pass the night. His troops lay encamped around it. A fenced road passed the door, and sentinels were posted along the road. The soldiers slept in fancied security, and the guard kept negligent watch;

they dreamed not of the scene that awaited them; they knew not that defeat and death were impending. Colonel Bratton, with a party chiefly composed of his neighbors, had that day left Mecklenburg County, North Carolina, under the conviction that the royalists would shortly send forces into the neighborhood of their homes, to revenge the defeat of the tories at Mobley's Meeting-House. With a force of only seventy-five men—for about fifty had dropped off on the way—Colonel Bratton and Captain McClure, having received intelligence of the position and numbers of the enemy, marched to within a short distance of their encampment. The whigs arrived at night, and after concealing their horses in a swamp, Bratton himself reconnoitered the encampment, advancing within the line of sentinels. The party of Americans divided to enclose the enemy; one-half coming up the lane, the other being sent round to take the opposite direction. Huck and his officers were still sleeping when the attack commenced, and were aroused by the roar of the American guns. Huck made all speed to mount his horse, and several times rallied his men; but his efforts were unavailing : the spirit and determined bravery of the patriots carried all before them. The rout was complete. As soon as Huck and another officer fell, his men threw down their arms and fled.*

---

* It is said that Huck was shot by John Carrol, who, as well as his brother Thomas, was a brave and daring soldier, his valor being always of the most impetuous kind. A brief, but characteristic description of him has been given by another Revolutionary hero: " He was a

Some were killed, or mortally wounded; some perished in the woods; the rest escaped, or were made prisoners. In the pursuit the conflict raged around Bratton's house; and Mrs. Bratton and her children, anxious to look out, were in some danger from the shots. She made her little son, much against his will, sit within the chimney. While he was there, a ball struck against the opposite jam, and was taken up by him as a trophy. The battle lasted about an hour; it was bloody, though brief; and it is stated that the waters of the spring, which now gush forth so bright and transparent, on that memorable spot, were then crimsoned with the tide of human life. About daylight, when the firing had ceased, Mrs. Bratton ventured out, anxious, and fearful of finding her nearest and dearest relatives among the dead and wounded lying around her dwelling. But none of her loved ones had fallen. Her house was opened alike to the wounded on both sides; and she humanely attended the sufferers in person, affording them, indiscriminately, every relief and comfort in her power to bestow; feeding and nursing them, and supplying their wants with the kindest and most assiduous attention. Thus her lofty spirit was displayed no less by her humanity to the vanquished, than by her courage and resolution in the hour of danger. After the death of Huck in battle, the officer next in command became the leader of the troops. He was among the prisoners who surrendered to the whigs, and they were deter-

whig from the first—he was a whig to the last; he didn't believe in the tories, and he made the tories believe in him."

mined to put him to death. He entreated, as a last favor, to be conducted to the presence of Mrs. Bratton. She instantly recognized him as the officer who had interfered in her behalf and saved her life. Gratitude, as well as the mercy natural to woman's heart, prompted her now to intercede for him. She pleaded with an eloquence which, considering the share she had borne in the common distress and danger, could not be withstood. Her petition was granted; she procured his deliverance from the death that awaited him, and kindly entertained him till he was exchanged. There is hardly a situation in romance or dramatic fiction, which can surpass the interest and pathos of this simple incident.

The evening before the battle, Huck and his troops had stopped on their way at the house of Mrs. Adair, on South Fishing Creek, at the place where the road from Yorkville to Chester court-house now crosses that stream. They helped themselves to every thing eatable on the premises, and one Captain Anderson laid a strict injunction on the old lady, to bring her sons under the royal banner. After the battle had been fought, Mrs. Adair and her husband were sent for by their sons and Colonel Edward Lacy, whom they had brought up, for the purpose of sending them into North Carolina for safety. When Mrs. Adair reached the battle-ground, she dismounted from her horse, and passed round among her friends. Presently she came with her sons to a tent where several wounded men were lying—Anderson among them. She said to him, "Well, Captain, you ordered me last night to bring in my rebel sons.

Here are two of them; and if the third had been within a day's ride, he would have been here also." The chagrined officer replied, "Yes, madam, I have seen them." Mrs. Adair was the mother of the late Governor John Adair of Kentucky.

Instances of the noble daring of the women of that day, thus thrown "into the circle of mishap," and compelled to witness so many horrors, and share so many dangers, were doubtless of almost hourly occurrence But of the individuals whose faithful memory retained the impression of those scenes, how few survive throughout the land! Enquiries made on this subject are continually met by expressions of regret that some relative who has within a few years descended to the grave, was not alive to describe events of those trying times. "If you could only have heard —— or —— talk of Revolutionary scenes, volumes might have been filled with the anecdotes they remembered!" is the oft-repeated exclamation, which causes regret that the tribute due has been so long withheld from the memory of those heroines.

The defeat of Huck had the immediate effect of bringing the whigs together; and in a few days a large accession of troops joined the army of Sumter. The attack on the British at Rocky Mount was shortly followed by a complete victory over them at Hanging Rock.

Another anecdote is related of Mrs. Bratton. Before the fall of Charleston, when effectual resistance throughout the State was in a great measure rendered impossible

by the want of ammunition, Governor Rutledge had
sent a supply to all the regimênts, to enable them to
harass the invading army. Many of these supplies
were secured by the patriots in the back country, by
secreting them in hollow trees and the like hiding-places;
others fell into the hands of the enemy or were destroyed. The portion given to Colonel Bratton was in his
occasional absence from home confided to the care of
his wife. Some loyalists who heard of this, informed
the British officer in command of the nearest station,
and a detachment was immediately sent forward to
secure the valuable prize. Mrs. Bratton was informed
of their near approach, and was aware that there could be
no chance of saving her charge. She resolved that the
enemy should not have the benefit of it. She therefore
immediately laid a train of powder from the depot to
the spot where she stood, and, when the detachment
came in sight, set fire to the train, and blew it up. The
explosion that greeted the ears of the foe, informed
them that the object of their expedition was frustrated.
The officer in command, irritated to fury, demanded who
had dared to perpetrate such an act, and threatened
instant and severe vengeance upon the culprit. The
intrepid woman to whom he owed his disappointment
answered for herself. "It was I who did it," she replied.
"Let the consequence be what it will, I glory in having
prevented the mischief contemplated by the cruel enemies
of my country."

Mrs. Bratton was a native of Rowan County, North
Carolina, where she married William Bratton, a Penn-

sylvanian of Irish parentage, who resided in York
District in the State of South Carolina. The grant of
his land, which is still held by his descendants, was
taken out under George the Third. In the troubled
times that preceded the commencement of hostilities,
the decision of character exhibited by Mr. and Mrs.
Bratton, and their exemplary deportment, gave them
great influence among their neighbors. Colonel Bratton
continued in active service during the war, and was
prominent in the battles of Rocky Mount, Hanging Rock,
Guilford, etc., and in most of the skirmishes incident
to the partisan warfare under General Sumter. During
his lengthened absences from home, he was seldom
able to see or communicate with his family. A soldier's
perils add lustre to his deeds; but the heart of the
deeply anxious wife must have throbbed painfully when
she heard of them. She, however, never complained,
though herself a sufferer from the ravages of war; but
devoted herself to the care of her family, striving at the
same time to aid and encourage her neighbors. On
the return of peace, her husband resumed the cultivation
of his farm. Grateful for the preservation of their lives
and property, they continued industriously occupied in
agricultural pursuits to a ripe old age, enjoying to the
full

> " That which should accompany old age,
> As honor, love, obedience, troops of friends."

Colonel Bratton died at his residence two miles south

of Yorkville, now the seat of Mrs. Harriet Bratton; and his wife, having survived him less than a year, died at the same place in January, 1816. They were buried by the side of each other.

~~~~~

XIX

JANE THOMAS.

THE state of popular feeling after the occupation of Charleston by the British, and during the efforts made to establish an undisputed control over the State, might be in some measure illustrated by the life of Mrs. Thomas, were there materials for a full narrative of incidents in which she and her neighbors bore an active or passive part. It is in wild and stirring times that such spirits are nurtured, and arise in their strength. She was another of the patriotic females in whose breast glowed such ardent patriotism, that no personal hazard could deter from service, wherever service could be rendered. She was a native of Chester County, Pennsylvania, and the sister of the Reverend John Black, of Carlisle, the first president of Dickinson College. She was married about 1740, to John Thomas, supposed to be a native of Wales, who had been brought up in the same county. Some ten or fifteen years after his marriage, Mr. Thomas removed to South Carolina. His residence for some time was upon Fishing Creek in Chester District. About the year 1762, he removed to what is now called Spartanburg

District, and settled upon Fairforest Creek, a few miles above the spot where the line dividing that district from Union crosses the stream. Mrs. Thomas was much beloved and respected in that neighborhood. She was one of the first members of the Presbyterian congregation organized about that time, and known as Fairforest church, of which she continued a zealous and efficient member as long as she resided within its bounds.

For many years previous to the commencement of the Revolutionary war, Mr. Thomas was a magistrate and a captain of militia. Before hostilities began, he resigned both these commissions. When Colonel Fletcher refused to accept a commission under the authority of the province of South Carolina, an election was held, and John Thomas was chosen Colonel of the Spartan regiment. The proximity of this regiment to the frontier imposed a large share of active service on the soldiers belonging to it, and devolved great responsibilities upon its commander. Colonel Thomas led out his quota of men to repel the Indians in 1776, and shared the privations and dangers connected with the expedition under General Williamson into the heart of the Indian territory, in the autumn of that year. When that campaign terminated, and the Indians sued for peace, the protection of a long line of the frontier was intrusted to him. With diligence, fidelity and zeal did he perform this duty; and retained his command till after the fall of Charleston.

As soon as the news of the surrender of that city

reached the borders of the State, measures were concerted by Colonels Thomas, Brandon and Lysles, for the concentration of their forces with a view to protect the country. Their schemes were frustrated by the devices of Colonel Fletcher, who still remained in the neighborhood. Having discovered their intentions, he gave notice to some British troops recently marched into the vicinity, and to a body of tory cavalry thirty miles distant. These were brought together, and surprised the force collected by Brandon at the point designated, before the others had time to arrive. Within a short time after this event, almost every whig between the Broad and Saluda rivers was compelled to abandon the country or accept British protection. Numbers of them fled to North Carolina. Colonel Thomas, then advanced in life, with some others in like defenceless circumstances, took protection. By this course, they hoped to secure permission to remain unmolested with their families; but in this supposition they were lamentably mistaken. It was not long before Colonel Thomas was arrested, and sent to prison at Ninety-Six. Thence he was conveyed to Charleston, where he remained in durance till near the close of the war.

It was the policy of Cornwallis, whom Sir Henry Clinton, on his departure to New York, had left in command of the royal army, to compel submission by the severest measures. The bloody slaughter under Tarleton at Waxhaw Creek, was an earnest of what those who ventured resistance might expect. This course was pursued with unscrupulous cruelty, and the unfortunate patriots were made to feel the vengeance of exasperated tyranny. He hoped thus eventually to crush and extinguish the spirit still struggling and flashing forth, like hidden fire, among the people whom the arm of power had for a season brought under subjection. But the oppressor, though he might overawe, could not subdue the spirit of a gallant and outraged people. The murmur of suffering throughout the land rose ere long into a mighty cry for deliverance. The royal standard became an object of execration. And while brave leaders were at hand—while the fearless and determined Sumter could draw about him the hardy sons of the upper and middle country—while the patriotic Marion, ever fertile in resource, could harass the foe from his impenetrable retreat in the recesses of forests and swamps; while the resolute and daring Pickens could bring his bold associates to join in the noble determination to burst the chains riveted on a prostrate land—and others of the same mould, familiar with difficulties, accustomed to toil and danger, and devoted to the cause of their suffering country, were ready for prompt and energetic action—hope could be entertained that all was not yet lost. The outrages committed by the profligate and abandoned, whose loyalty was the cover for deeds of rapine and blood, served but to bind in closer union the patriots who watched their opportunity for annoying the enemy, and opening a way for successful resistance.

One of the congenial co-operators in these plans of the British commander, was Colonel Ferguson. He

encouraged the loyalists to take arms, and led them to
desolate the homes of their neighbors. About the last
of June he came into that part of the country where
the family of Colonel Thomas lived, and caused great
distress by the pillage and devastation of the bands of
tories who hung around his camp. The whigs were
robbed of their negroes, horses, cattle, clothing, bedding,
and every article of property of sufficient value to take
away. These depredations were frequent, the expeditions for plunder being sometimes weekly; and were
continued as long as the tories could venture to show
their faces. In this state of things, while whole families
suffered, female courage and fortitude were called into
active exercise; and Mrs. Thomas showed herself a
bright example of boldness, spirit and determination.

While her husband was a prisoner at Ninety-Six,
she paid a visit to him and her two sons, who were his
companions in rigorous captivity. By chance she
overheard a conversation between some tory women,
the purport of which deeply interested her. One said
to the others : "To-morrow night the loyalists intend to
surprise the rebels at Cedar Spring."

The heart of Mrs. Thomas was thrilled with alarm
at this intelligence. The Cedar Spring was within a
few miles of her house; the whigs were posted there,
and among them were some of her own children.

Her resolution was taken at once; for there was no
time to be lost. She determined to apprise them of the
enemy's intention, before the blow could be struck.
Bidding a hasty adieu to her husband and sons, she

was upon the road as quickly as possible; rode the
intervening distance of nearly sixty miles the next day,
and arrived in time to bring information to her sons
and friends of the impending danger. The moment
they knew what was to be expected, a brief consultation
was held; and measures were immediately taken for
defence. The soldiers withdrew a short distance from
their camp-fires, which were prepared to burn as brightly
as possible. The men selected suitable positions in the
surrounding woods.

Their preparations were just completed, when they
heard in the distance, amid the silence of night, the
cautious advance of the foe. The scene was one which
imagination, far better than the pen of the chronicler,
can depict. Slowly and warily, and with tread as
noiseless as possible, the enemy advanced; till they
were already within the glare of the blazing fires, and
safely, as it seemed, on the verge of their anticipated
work of destruction. No sound betrayed alarm; they
supposed the intended victims wrapped in heavy
slumbers; they heard but the crackling of the flames,
and the hoarse murmur of the wind as it swept through
the pine trees. The assailants gave the signal for the
onset, and rushed towards the fires—eager for indis-
criminate slaughter. Suddenly the flashes and shrill
reports of rifles revealed the hidden champions of liberty.
The enemy, to their consternation, found themselves
assailed in the rear by the party they had expected to
strike unawares. Thrown into confusion by this unex-
pected reception, defeat, overwhelming defeat, was

the consequence to the loyalists. They were about one hundred and fifty strong, while the whigs numbered only about sixty. The victory thus easily achieved they owed to the spirit and courage of a woman! Such were the matrons of that day.

Not merely upon this occasion was Mrs. Thomas active in conveying intelligence to her friends, and in arousing the spirit of Independence among its advocates. She did, as well as suffered much, during the period of devastation and lawless rapine. One instance of her firmness is well remembered. Early in the war Governor Rutledge sent a quantity of arms and ammunition to the house of Colonel Thomas, to be in readiness for any emergency that might arise on the frontier. These munitions were under a guard of twenty-five men; and the house was prepared to resist assault. Colonel Thomas received information that a large party of tories, under the command of Colonel More of North Carolina, was advancing to attack him. He and his guard deemed it inexpedient to risk an encounter with a force so much superior to their own; and they therefore retired, carrying off as much ammunition as possible. Josiah Culbertson, a son-in-law of Colonel Thomas, who was with the little garrison, would not go with the others, but remained in the house. Besides him and a youth, the only inmates were women. The tories advanced, and took up their station; but the treasure was not to be yielded to their demand. Their call for admittance was answered by an order to leave the premises; and their fire was re-

ceived without much injury by the logs of the house.
The fire was quickly returned from the upper story,
and proved much more effectual than that of the assailants. The old-fashioned "batten door," strongly barri-
caded, resisted their efforts to demolish it. Meanwhile
Culbertson continued to fire, the guns being loaded as
fast as he discharged them, by the ready hands of Mrs.
Thomas and her daughters, aided by her son William;
and this spirited resistance soon convinced the enemy
that further effort was useless. Believing that many
men were concealed in the house, and apprehending a
sally, their retreat was made as rapidly as their wounds
would permit. After waiting a prudent time, and re-
connoitering as well as she could from her position
above, Mrs. Thomas descended the stairs, and opened
the doors. When her husband made his appearance,
and knew how gallantly the plunderers had been repulsed, his joy was only equalled by admiration of his
wife's heroism. The powder thus preserved constituted
the principal supply for Sumter's army in the battles at
Rocky Mount and Hanging Rock.

Mrs. Thomas was the mother of nine children; and
her sons and sons-in-law were active in the American
service. John, the eldest son, rose during the war
from the rank of captain till he succeeded his father in
the command of the Spartan regiment. This he commanded at the battle of the Cowpens, and elsewhere.
He was with Sumter in several of his most important
engagements. Robert, another son, was killed in Roebuck's defeat. Abram, who was wounded at Ninety-Six

and taken prisoner, died in the enemy's hands. William, the youth who had assisted in defending his home on the occasion mentioned, took part in other actions. Thus Mrs. Thomas was liable to some share of the enmity exhibited by the royalists towards another matron, against whom the charge, " She has seven sons in the rebel army," was an excuse for depredations on her property. If she had but four sons, she had sons-in-law who were likewise brave and zealous in the cause. Martha, one of the daughters, married Josiah Culbertson, who was the most effective scout in the country. He fought the Indians single-handed and in the army ; was in nearly every important battle ; and killed a number of celebrated tories in casual encounter. He seems to have been a special favorite with Colonel Isaac Shelby, in whose regiment he served in the battle at Musgrove's Mill, King's Mountain, and elsewhere. To this officer his daring spirit and deadly aim with the rifle, especially commended him ; and he was employed by Shelby in the execution of some important trusts. He received a captain's commission towards the close of the war.

Ann was the wife of Joseph McJunkin, who entered the service of his country as a private, at the age of twenty, and rose to the rank of major before the close of 1780. He was in most of the battles before March, 1781, and contributed much to the success of those fought at Hanging Rock, Musgrove's Mill, Blackstock's Ford, and the Cowpens. This brave and faithful officer died in 1840. A sketch of his life, by the Rev. James

H. Saye, of South Carolina, is in preparation, and has in part been published.

Jane, the third daughter, married Captain Joseph McCool; and Letitia was the wife of Major James Lusk. Both these were brave and efficient patriots; but the scenes of their exploits, and the success that attended them, are now remembered but in tradition. Of how many who deserve the tribute of their country's gratitude, is history silent! Every member of this family, it will thus be seen, had a personal interest in the cause of the country.

Not only was Mrs. Thomas distinguished for her indomitable perseverance where principle and right were concerned, and for her ardent spirit of patriotism, but for eminent piety, discretion, and industry. Her daughters exhibited the same loveliness of character, with the uncommon beauty of person which they inherited from her. All accounts represent Mrs. Culbertson as a woman of great beauty; and her sister Ann is said to have been little inferior to her in personal appearance. Mrs. Thomas herself was rather below the ordinary stature, with black eyes and hair, rounded and pleasing features, fair complexion, and countenance sprightly and expressive.

Soon after the close of the war, Colonel Thomas removed into Greenville district, where he and his wife resided till their death. But few of their descendants remain in the section of country where their parents lived, being scattered over the regions of the far West. To the gentleman already mentioned as the biographer of McJunkin, I am indebted for all these details, ascertained from authentic papers in his possession.

~~~~~~~~~~~~~~~~~~

A FEW anecdotes of other women in the region where Mrs. Thomas lived during the war, are of interest as showing the state of the times. Isabella Sims, the wife of Captain Charles Sims, resided on Tyger River, six or seven miles below the scene of Brandon's defeat, above mentioned, on Fairforest Creek. When she heard of that disaster, she went up and devoted herself for several days to nursing the wounded soldiers. Daniel McJunkin shared her maternal care, and recovered to render substantial service afterwards.

On another occasion, having heard the noise of battle during the afternoon and night, she went up early in the morning to Leighton's. A scout consisting of eight whigs had been surrounded by a very large body of tories. Some of the scouts made their escape by charging through the line; four defended themselves in the house till after dark, when they surrendered. Mrs. Sims, on her arrival, found that John Jolly, a whig officer who belonged to the vicinity, had been shot in attempting to escape. She sent for his wife, and made the necessary arrangements for his decent burial. Sarah, his widow, was left with five children; and for a time had great difficulty in procuring a subsistence. Her house was visited almost weekly by plundering parties, and robbed of food and clothing. At one time one of the robbers remained after the others had gone ; and to an order to depart returned a refusal, with abusive and profane language. The exasperated mother seized a stick, with which she broke his arm, and drove him from the premises.

Not long after the death of Jolly, the famous Cunningham, a tory colonel who acted a prominent part in the partisan warfare of Laurens, Newberry, and Edgefield districts, came with a squadron of cavalry to the house of Captain Sims, who was gone for safety to North Carolina. Calling Mrs. Sims to the door, Cunningham ordered her to quit the place in three days ; saying if he found the family there on his return, he would shut them in the house and burn it over them. Mrs. Sims fled with her family across the country to the house of a friendly old man ; and remained there till her husband came and took them to York District, and thence to Virginia.

The wife of Major Samuel Otterson, a distinguished patriot, who lived also on Tyger River, chanced to know the place where a barrel of powder was concealed in the woods close at hand. She received intelligence one night that a party of tories would come for the treasure the next morning. Resolved that it should not fall into their hands, she prepared a train immediately, and blew up the powder. In the morning came the enemy, and on their demand for it, were told by Mrs. Otterson what she had done. They refused to believe her, but cut off her dress at the waist, and drove her before them to show the place of deposit. The evidence of its fate was conclusive, when they reached the spot.

Other instances of female intrepidity are rife in popular memory. Miss Nancy Jackson, who lived in the Irish settlement near Fairforest Creek, kicked a tory down the steps as he was descending loaded with plunder. In a great rage he threatened to send the Hessian troops there next day; which obliged her to take refuge with an acquaintance several miles distant. On one occasion the house of Samuel McJunkin, a stout patriot, but too old for the battle-field, was visited by a party under the noted Colonel Patrick Moore. They stayed all night; and when about to depart, stripped the house of bed-clothes and wearing apparel. The last article taken was a bed-quilt, which one Bill Haynesworth placed upon his horse. Jane, Mr. McJunkin's daughter, seized it, and a struggle ensued. The soldiers amused themselves by exclaiming, "Well done, woman!"—"Well done, Bill!" For once the colonel's feelings of gallantry predominated; and he swore if Jane could take the quilt from the man, she should have it. Presently in the contest, Bill's feet slipped from under him, and he lay panting on the ground. Jane placed one foot upon his breast and wrested the quilt from his grasp.

XX.

~~~~~~~~

DORCAS RICHARDSON.*

FRUITFUL in noble spirits were those wild and gloomy
times; and woman's high truth and heroic devotion
poured a solemn radiance over the dreary and appalling
scenes of civil war. No pen has recorded the instances
innumerable in which her virtues shone conspicuous;
they are forgotten by those who enjoy the benefits thus
secured; or but a vague recollection remains—or an
example is here and there remembered in family tradition. Even to these examples what meagre justice
can be done by the few scattered and desultory anecdotes which must take the place of a complete history!

Living in the midst of the storm and struggle, and
bearing more than her own share of the terrible trials
which fell to woman's lot, Mrs. Richardson afforded an
example of modest heroism, and of humble, cheerful
faith. Her residence was in Clarendon, Sumter District. She was the daughter of Captain John Nelson,

* For the details of this sketch I am indebted to the kindness of
DR. JOSEPH JOHNSON, of Charleston, who has collected and pre
served many interesting anecdotes of the war in South Carolina.

a native of Ireland, who married Miss Brownson, of
South Carolina.   The ferry over the Santee River,
established and kept for several years by them, is still
called Nelson's Ferry ; and many of their descendants
continue to live on both sides of the river.   It is said
that Lord Cornwallis, on his march into the interior,
after the fall of Charleston, established his head-quarters
at this ferry, at the house of the widow Nelson.   She
received from him an assurance that her property
should be protected.   When a large quantity of plate
which she had buried for security was discovered and
claimed as a prize by the captors, she reminded his
lordship of his promise ; but he refused to order the restoration of the plate, saying that the protection he had
pledged extended only to things above ground !

Dorcas was married at the age of twenty, in 1761,
and removed to her husband's plantation, situated about
twenty miles further up the river, on the east side, near
the junction of the Congaree and Wateree.   In this
home of peace, contentment, and abundance, she enjoyed all the comforts of southern country life among
the prosperous class, till the outburst of that storm in
which the fortunes and happiness of so many patriots
were wrecked.

At the commencement of the war Richard Richardson was captain of a company of militia in the brigade
of his father General Richardson ; and with him em-
braced the quarrel of the Colonies, in defence of their
chartered rights.   Both were zealous, firm, and influ-
ential officers.   The captain was frequently called out

with his company by order of the new government; and his first expedition was against the loyalists in the upper districts, incited by the royal governor, Lord William Campbell. General Richardson commanded, and was aided by Colonel William Thompson with his regiment of regulars called the Rangers. The enemy was dispersed, most of their leaders captured, and the arms and ammunition they had seized recovered. Captain Richardson was appointed with his mounted men to guard the prisoners to Charleston. This occurrence took place at the close of 1775; and the winter having set in earlier than usual with uncommon severity, the young soldiers suffering much from the cold, sleet, and snow, it was called the Snow Campaign.

When the three regiments of regulars were raised and officered in 1775, Captain Richardson and his father were retained in the militia on account of their great popularity and influence; Edward, a younger brother, being appointed captain of the Rangers under Colonel Thompson. A second regiment of riflemen, however, was raised in March of the following year; and Richard Richardson was appointed captain under Colonel Thomas Sumter. From this time, during the six succeeding years, he was able to be very little at home with his family. At the surrender of Charleston he was taken prisoner with his father and brother. In violation of the terms of capitulation, Richard was sent to a military station on John's Island, where he nearly fell a victim to the small-pox. The British having failed to observe the conditions on which he had

12

surrendered, as soon as he recovered sufficiently to move about, he made his escape ; and being disguised by the effects of the disease, returned to the neighborhood of his home, where he concealed himself in the Santee Swamp.   This extensive swamp-land borders the river for many miles, presenting to the view a vast plain of dense woods which seem absolutely impervious.   The recesses of those dark thickets, where the trees grow close together, and are interlaced by a luxuriant growth of giant creepers, often afforded hiding-places for the hunted Americans.   At this time the British troops had overrun the State ; and Colonel Tarleton had made the house of Captain Richardson, with some others, a station for his regiment of cavalry. They lived luxuriously on the abundance of his richly-stocked and well-cultivated plantation ; while Mrs. Richardson and her children, it is said, were restricted to a single apartment, and allowed but a scanty share of the provisions furnished from her own stores.   Here was an occasion for the exercise of self-denial, that the wants of one dear to her might be supplied.   Every day she sent food from her small allowance to her husband in the swamp, by an old and faithful negro, in whose care and discretion she could implicitly trust. She had expected the seizure of her horses and cattle by the British, and had sent Richardson's favorite riding-horse into the swamp for concealment, with a few cattle which she wished to save for future need. Every thing that fell into the enemy's hands was consumed.   The horse was shut up in a covered pen in the woods, which had once been used for holding corn ; and he thence received the name of Corncrib. He was subsequently killed in the battle of Eutaw.

Mrs. Richardson not only sent provisions to her husband in his place of shelter, but sometimes ventured to visit him, taking with her their little daughter. These stolen meetings were full of consolation to the fugitive soldier. The spot he had chosen for his retreat was a small knoll or elevation in the heart of the swamp, called " John's Island," by way of, distinction from another in the neighborhood, occupied by other whigs, which bore the name of " Beech Island." On this many of their initials may still be seen, carved on the bark of the trees.

It was not long before the British had information of Richardson's escape. They naturally concluded that he was somewhere in the vicinity of his family and relatives. A diligent search was instituted ; scouts were sent in every direction, and they watched to surprise him, or find some clue to his retreat. In secret and publicly rewards were offered for his apprehension ; but without success. One day an officer, caressing the little girl, asked when she had seen her papa ; the mother grew pale, but dared not speak, for a short time only had elapsed since the child had been taken on a visit to her father. The thoughtless prattler answered promptly, that she had seen him only a few days before. " And where ?" asked the officer, eager to extract information from innocent lips that might betray the patriot. The child replied without hesitation, " On

John's Island." The officer knew of no place so called except the large sea island from which Richardson had escaped. After a moment's reflection, he came to the conclusion that the child had been dreaming, and relieved the mother's throbbing heart by saying, " Pshaw, that was a long time ago!" It may well be believed that the little tell-tale was not trusted with another visit to the spot.

Not unfrequently did the officers, in the most unfeeling manner, boast in the presence of the wife, of what they would do to her husband when they should capture him. Once only did she deign the reply, "I do not doubt that men who can outrage the feelings of a woman by such threats, are capable of perpetrating any act of treachery and inhumanity towards a brave but unfortunate enemy. But conquer or capture my husband, if you can do so, before you boast the cruelty you mean to mark your savage triumph! And let me tell you, meanwhile, that some of you, it is likely, will be in a condition to implore *his* mercy, before he will have need to supplicate, or deign to accept yours." This prediction was literally verified in more than one instance during the eventful remainder of the war.

Tarleton himself was frequently present during these scenes, apparently a pleased, though generally a silent spectator. He would remark at times, in the way of self-vindication, "that he commiserated the trials, and wondered at the endurance, of this heroic woman ; but that his sanction of such proceedings was necessary to the success of His Majesty's cause." Weak cause, indeed, that was constrained to wring the cost of its maintenance from the bleeding hearts of wives and mothers!

On one occasion some of the officers displayed in the sight of Mrs. Richardson, their swords reeking with blood—probably that of her cattle—and told her it was the blood of Captain Richardson, whom they had killed. At another time they brought intelligence that he had been taken and hanged. In this state of cruel suspense she sometimes remained for several successive days, unable to learn the fate of her husband, and not knowing whether to believe or distrust the horrible tales brought to her ears.

One day, when the troops were absent on some expedition, Captain Richardson ventured on a visit to his home. A happy hour was it to the anxious wife and faithful domestics, when they could greet him once more in his own mansion. But before he thought of returning to his refuge in the forest, a patrolling party of the enemy appeared unexpectedly at the gate. Mrs. Richardson's presence of mind and calm courage were in instant requisition, and proved the salvation of the hunted patriot. Seeing the British soldiers about to come in, she pretended to be intently busy about something in the front door, and stood in the way, retarding their entrance. The least appearance of agitation or fear—the least change of color—might have betrayed all by exciting suspicion. But with a self-control as rare as admirable, she hushed even the wild beating of her heart, and continued to stand in the way, till her husband had time to retire through the back door, into the swamp near at hand. The brave captain was not idle in his seclusion; but collecting around him the whigs of his acquaintance who remained firm in their devotion to their native land, he trained them daily in cavalry exercise. When Tarleton ravaged the plantation and burnt the dwelling of his deceased father, General Richardson, he passed so near the ruins as to see the extent of the desolation. General Marion happened at that time to be in a very critical situation, and unaware of the great superiority of the enemy's force close at hand. The gallant Richardson hastened to his aid; joined him, and conducted the retreat of his army, which was immediately commenced and successfully executed. The British were not long in discovering that the captain had joined the forces of Marion; and their deportment to his wife was at once changed. One and all professed a profound respect for her brave and worthy husband, whose services they were desirous of securing. They endeavored to obtain her influence to prevail on him to join the royal army, by promises of pardon, wealth, and honorable promotion. The high-spirited wife treated all such offers with the contempt they deserved, and refused to be made instrumental to their purposes. They then despatched his brother Edward, who was a prisoner on parole upon the adjoining plantation, to be the bearer of their offers. By him Mrs. Richardson also sent a message to her husband. It was to assure him that she did not join in British solicitations; that she and her children were well, and provided with abundance of every thing necessary for their comfort. Thus with heroic art did she conceal the privations and wants she was suffering, lest her husband's solicitude for her and his family might tempt him to waver from strict obedience to the dictates of honor and patriotism.

Edward went as directed to the American camp, took his brother into Marion's presence, and there faithfully delivered both messages with which he had been charged. The specious offers from the enemy were of course rejected, and the messenger, conceiving himself absolved from his parole by the treatment he had received, remained with Marion till the termination of hostilities in the State.

Several times after this did Richard place his life in peril to visit his amiable family. Hearing that Tarleton's troop had been ordered away from his plantation, he obtained permission to go thither for a short time. He arrived in safety; but had been seen on his way by a loyalist. A party of them was immediately assembled, and was soon to be seen drawn up in front of his house. Corncrib, the faithful steed, was hitched outside the gate; his master hastily came forth, leaped on him, and galloping up the avenue, where the enemy were posted, passed through the midst of them without receiving either a shot or a sabre wound. Just as he passed their ranks, one of his well-known neighbors fired at him, but missed the aim. All this took place in the sight of his terrified family, who often afterwards described his danger and providential escape. His wife could only account for this by conjecturing that the party had determined to take Richardson alive, and thus claim the reward offered for his apprehension; and that when in their midst, they could not shoot him without the risk of killing some of their comrades. His daring gallantry entirely disconcerted them, and saved his life.

Some time after this he again asked the indulgence of a visit to his family; but General Marion in granting it, mindful of the danger he had before encountered, insisted that he should be accompanied by an escort. The party had scarcely reached the house of Richardson, when, as before, a large body of British and tories was seen advancing rapidly down the avenue, eager to surprise their intended victims. To remount in all haste their wearied steeds, and rush down the bank at the rear of the house, seeking concealment in the swamp, offered the only chance for escape. In this they all succeeded, except a young man named Roberts, with whom Mrs. Richardson was well acquainted, and who was taken prisoner. In vain did she intercede for him with the British officers, and with streaming eyes implore them to spare the life of the unfortunate youth. They hanged him on a walnut tree only a few paces from her door, and compelled her to witness the revolting spectacle! When she complained with tears of anguish, of this cruelty to herself, and barbarity towards one who had offended by risking his life in defence of her husband, they jeeringly told her they "would soon have him also, and then she should see him kick like that fellow." To such atrocities could the passions of brutalized men lead them, even in an age and nation that boasted itself the most enlightened on earth!

When peace returned to shed blessings over the land, Mrs. Richardson continued to reside in the same house, with her family. Tarleton and his troopers had wasted the plantation, and destroyed every thing moveable about the dwelling; but the buildings had been spared, because they were spacious, and afforded a convenient station for the British, about midway between Camden and Fort Watson on Scott's Lake. Colonel Richardson, who had been promoted for his meritorious service in the field, cheerfully resumed the occupations of a planter. His circumstances were much reduced by the chances of war; but a competence remained, which he and his wife enjoyed in tranquillity and happiness, surrounded by affectionate relatives and friendly neighbors. Of their ten children, four died young; the rest married and reared families.

Mrs. Richardson survived her husband many years, and died at the advanced age of ninety-three, in 1834. She was remarkable throughout life for the calm judgment, fortitude, and strength of mind, which had sustained her in the trials she suffered during the war, and protected her from injury or insult when surrounded by a lawless soldiery. To these elevated qualities she united unostentatious piety, and a disposition of uncommon serenity and cheerfulness. Her energy and consolations, through the vicissitudes of life, were derived from religion; it was her hope and triumph in the hour of death.

12*

XXI.

~~~~~~~~~

ELIZABETH, GRACE, AND RACHEL MARTIN.

THE daring exploit of two women in Ninety-Six District, furnishes an instance of courage as striking as any remembered among the traditions of South Carolina. During the sieges of Augusta and Cambridge, the patriotic enthusiasm that prevailed among the people prompted to numerous acts of personal risk and sacrifice. This spirit, encouraged by the successes of Sumter and others over the British arms, was earnestly fostered by General Greene, whose directions marked at least the outline of every undertaking. In the efforts made to strike a blow at the invader's power, the sons of the Martin family were among the most distinguished for active service rendered, and for injuries sustained at the enemy's hands. The wives of the two eldest, during their absence, remained at home with their mother-in-law. One evening intelligence came to them that a courier, conveying important despatches to one of the upper stations, was to pass that night along the road, guarded by two British officers. They determined to waylay the party, and at the risk of their lives, to obtain possession of the papers. For this purpose the two

young women disguised themselves in their husbands'
clothes, and being well provided with arms, took their
station at a point on the road which they knew the
escort must pass. It was already late, and they had
not waited long before the tramp of horses was heard
in the distance. It may be imagined with what anxious
expectation the heroines awaited the approach of the
critical moment on which so much depended. The
forest solitude around them, the silence of night, and the
darkness, must have added to the terrors conjured up
by busy fancy. Presently the courier appeared, with
his attendant guards. As they came close to the spot,
the disguised women leaped from their covert in the
bushes, presented their pistols at the officers, and demanded the instant surrender of the party and their despatches.
The men were completely taken by surprise, and in
their alarm at the sudden attack, yielded a prompt submission. The seeming soldiers put them on their parole,
and having taken possession of the papers, hastened
home by a short cut through the woods. No time was lost
in sending the important documents by a trusty messenger to General Greene. The adventure had a singular
termination. The paroled officers, thus thwarted in
their mission, returned by the road they had taken, and
stopping at the house of Mrs. Martin, asked accommodation as weary travellers, for the night. The hostess
inquired the reason of their returning so soon after
they had passed. They replied by showing their paroles,
saying they had been taken prisoners by two rebel lads.
The ladies rallied them upon their want of intrepidity.

" Had you no arms ?" was asked.   The officers answered that they had arms, but had been suddenly taken off their guard, and were allowed no time to use their weapons.   They departed the next morning, having no suspicion that they owed their capture to the very women whose hospitality they had claimed.

The mother of this patriotic family was a native of Caroline County, Virginia.   Her name was Elizabeth Marshall, and she was probably of the same family with Chief Justice Marshall, as she belonged to the same neighborhood.   After her marriage to Abram Martin, she removed to his settlement bordering on the Indian nation, in Ninety-Six, now Edgefield District, South Carolina.   The country at that time was sparsely settled, most of its inhabitants being pioneers from other States, chiefly from Virginia; and their neighborhood to the Indians had caused the adoption of some of their savage habits.   The name Edgefield is said to have been given because it was at that period the edge or boundary of the respectable settlers and their cultivated fields.   Civilization, however, increased with the population ; and in the time of the Revolution, Ninety-Six was among the foremost in sending into the field its quota of hardy and enterprising troops, to oppose the British and their savage allies.

At the commencement of the contest, Mrs. Martin had nine children, seven of whom were sons old enough to bear arms.   These brave young men, under the tuition and example of their parents, had grown up in attachment to their country, and ardently devoted to its service, were ready on every occasion to encounter the dangers of border warfare. When the first call for volunteers sounded through the land, the mother encouraged their patriotic zeal. "Go, boys," she said; "fight for your country! fight till death, if you must, but never let your country be dishonored. Were I a man I would go with you."

At another time, when Colonel Cruger commanded the British at Cambridge, and Colonel Browne in Augusta, several British officers stopped at her house for refreshment; and one of them asked how many sons she had. She answered—eight; and to the question, where they all were, replied promptly: "Seven of them are engaged in the service of their country." "Really, madam," observed the officer, sneeringly, "you have enough of them." "No sir," said the matron, proudly, "I wish I had fifty."

Her house in the absence of the sons was frequently exposed to the depredations of the tories. On one occasion they cut open her feather beds, and scattered the contents. When the young men returned shortly afterwards, their mother bade them pursue the marauders. One of the continental soldiers having been left at the house badly wounded, Mrs. Martin kindly attended and nursed him till his recovery. A party of loyalists who heard of his being there, came with the intention of taking his life; but she found means to hide him from their search.

The only daughter of Mrs. Martin, Letitia, married Captain Edmund Wade, of Virginia, who fell with his commander, General Montgomery, at the siege of Quebec. At the time of the siege of Charleston by Sir Henry Clinton, the widow was residing with her mother at Ninety-Six. Her son Washington Wade was then five years old, and remembers many occurrences connected with the war.* The house was about one hundred miles in a direct line west of Charleston. He recollects walking in the piazza on a calm evening, with his grandmother. A light breeze blew from the east; and the sound of heavy cannon was distinctly heard in that direction.† The sound of cannon heard at that time, and in that part of the State, they knew must come from the besieged city. As report after report reached their ears, the agitation of Mrs. Martin increased. She knew not what evils might be announced; she knew not but the sound might be the knell of her sons, three of whom were then in Charleston. Their wives were with her, and partook of the same heart-chilling fears. They stood still for a few minutes, each wrapped in her own painful and silent reflections, till the mother at length, lifting her hands and eyes towards heaven—exclaimed fervently :—"THANK GOD, THEY ARE THE CHILDREN OF THE REPUBLIC!"

Of the seven patriot brothers, six were spared through all the dangers of partisan warfare in the region of the "dark and bloody ground." The eldest, William

* Most of the particulars relating to this family were furnished by him to DR. JOHNSON, of Charleston, who kindly communicated them to me, with additional ones obtained from other branches of the family.

† This statement has been repeatedly confirmed by others in the neighborhood.

M. Martin, was a captain of artillery; and after having served with distinction in the sieges of Savannah
and Charleston, was killed at the siege of Augusta,
just after he had obtained a favorable position for his
cannon, by elevating it on one of the towers constructed by General Pickens.   It is related that not
long after his death, a British officer passing to Fort
Ninety-Six, then in possession of the English, rode out
of his way to gratify his hatred to the whigs by carrying the fatal news to the mother of this gallant young
man.   He called at the house, and asked Mrs. Martin
if she had not a son in the army at Augusta.   She
replied in the affirmative.   " Then I saw his brains
blown out on the field of battle," said the monster, who
anticipated his triumph in the sight of a parent's agony.
But the effect of the startling announcement was other
than he expected.   Terrible as was the shock, and
aggravated by the ruthless cruelty with which her
bereavement was made known, no woman's weakness
was suffered to appear.   After listening to the dreadful
recital, the only reply made by this American dame
was, "He could not have died in a nobler cause!"
The evident chagrin of the officer as he turned and
rode away, is still remembered in the family tradition.

This eldest son married Grace Waring, of Dorchester,
when she was but fourteen years of age.   She was the
daughter of Benjamin Waring, who afterwards became
one of the earliest settlers of Columbia when established
as the seat of government in the State.   The principles
of the Revolution had been taught her from childhood;

and her efforts to promote its advancement were joined
with those of her husband's family. She was one of
the two who risked their lives to seize upon the despatches, as above related. Her husband's untimely
death left her with three young children—two sons and
a daughter; but she never married again.

Her companion in that daring and successful enterprise was the wife of Barkly Martin, another son. She
was Rachel Clay, the daughter of Henry Clay, Jun., of
Mecklenburg County, Virginia, and first cousin to
Henry Clay, of Kentucky. She is said to be still living in Bedford County, Tennessee; is about eighty-six
years of age, and never had any children. Her sister
married Matthew, another of the brothers, and removed
to Tennessee. Their family was large and of high
respectability. One of the sons is the Hon. Barkly
Martin, late member of Congress from that State. His
father lived to a great age, and died in Tennessee in
October, 1847, about seventy-six years after his first
battle-field. The decendants of the other brothers are
numerous and respectable in the different southern
States.

A TRIBUTE is due to the fortitude of those who suffered
when the war swept with violence over Georgia. After
Colonel Campbell took possession of Savannah in 1778,
the whole country was overrun with irregular marauders, wilder and more ruthless than the Cossacks of the
Don. As many of the inhabitants as could retire from

the storm did so, awaiting a happier time to renew the
struggle. One of those who had sought refuge in
Florida, was Mr. Spalding, whose establishments were
on the river St. John's. He had the whole Indian
trade from the Altamaha to the Apalachicola. His
property, with his pursuits, was destroyed by the war;
yet his heart was ever with his countrymen, and the
home he had prepared for his wife was the refuge of
every American prisoner in Florida. The first Assembly that met in Savannah re-called him and restored
his lands; but could not give back his business, nor
secure the debts due; while his British creditors, with
their demands for accumulated interest, pressed upon
the remnant of his fortune. Under these adverse circumstances, and distressed on account of the losses of her
father and brothers, who had taken arms in the American cause, Mrs. Spalding performed her arduous duties with a true woman's fidelity and tenderness. She
followed her husband with her child, when flight became necessary; and twice during the war traversed
the two hundred miles between Savannah and St.
John's River in an open boat, with only black servants
on board, when the whole country was a desert, without
a house to shelter her and her infant son. The first of
these occasions was when she visited her father and
brothers while prisoners in Savannah; the second,
when in 1782, she went to congratulate her brothers
and uncle on their victory. This lady was the daughter of Colonel William McIntosh, and the niece of

General Lachlan McIntosh.   Major Spalding, of Georgia, is her son.

Mrs. Spalding's health was seriously impaired by the anxieties endured during the struggle, and many years afterwards it was deemed necessary for her to try the climate of Europe.   In January, 1800, she, with her son and his wife, left Savannah in a British ship of twenty guns, with fifty men, built in all points to resemble a sloop of war, without the appearance of a cargo. When they had been out about fifteen days, the captain sent one morning at daylight, to request the presence of two of his gentlemen passengers on deck.   A large ship, painted black and showing twelve guns on a side, was seen to windward, running across their course. She was obviously a French privateer.   The Captain announced that there was no hope of out-sailing her, should their course be altered; nor would there be hope in a conflict, as those ships usually carried one hundred and fifty men.   Yet he judged that if no effort were made to shun the privateer, the appearance of his ship might deter from an attack.   The gentlemen were of the same opinion.   Mr. Spalding, heart-sick at thought of the perilous situation of his wife and mother, and unwilling to trust himself with an interview till the crisis was over, requested the captain to go below and make what preparation he could for their security. After a few minutes' absence the captain returned to describe a most touching scene.   Mrs. Spalding had placed her daughter-in-law and the other inmates of the cabin for safety in the two state-rooms, filling the berths with the cots and bedding from the outer cabin. She had then taken her own station beside the scuttle, which led from the outer cabin to the magazine, with two buckets of water. Having noticed that the two cabin boys were heedless, she had determined herself to keep watch over the magazine. She did so till the danger was past. The captain took in his light sails, hoisted his boarding nettings, opened his ports, and stood on upon his course. The privateer waited till the ship was within a mile, then fired a gun to windward, and stood on her way. This ruse preserved the ship. The incident may serve to show the spirit of this matron, who also bore her high part in the perils of the Revolution.

XXII.

~~~~~

DICEY LANGSTON.

THE portion of South Carolina near the frontier, watered by the Pacolet, the Tyger, and the Ennoree, comprising Spartanburg and Union Districts, witnessed many deeds of violence and blood, and many bold achievements of the hardy partisans. It could also boast its full complement of women whose aid in various ways was of essential service to the patriots. So prevalent was loyalism in the darkest of those days, so bitter was the animosity felt towards the whigs, and so eager the determination to root them from the soil, that the very recklessness of hate gave frequent opportunities for the betrayal of the plans of their enemies. Often were the boastings of those who plotted some midnight surprise, or some enterprise that promised rare pillage—uttered in the hearing of weak and despised women—unexpectedly turned into wonder at the secret agency that had disconcerted them, or execrations upon their own folly. The tradition of the country teems with accounts of female enterprise in this kind of service, very few instances of which were recorded in the military journals.

The patriots were frequently indebted for important information to one young girl, fifteen or sixteen years old at the commencement of the war. This was Dicey, the daughter of Solomon Langston of Laurens District. He was in principle a stout liberty man, but incapacitated by age and infirmities from taking any active part in the contest. His son was a devoted patriot, and was ever found in the field where his services were most needed. He had his home in the neighborhood, and could easily receive secret intelligence from his sister, who was always on the alert. Living surrounded by loyalists, some of whom were her own relatives, Miss Langston found it easy to make herself acquainted with their movements and plans, and failed not to avail herself of every opportunity to do so, and immediately to communicate what she learned to the whigs on the other side of the Ennoree River. At length suspicion of the active aid she rendered was excited among the tory neighbors. Mr. Langston was informed that he would be held responsible thenceforward, with his property, for the conduct of his daughter. The young girl was reproved severely, and commanded to desist from her patriotic treachery. For a time she obeyed the parental injunction ; but having heard by accident that a company of loyalists, who on account of their ruthless cruelty had been commonly called the " Bloody Scout," intent on their work of death, were about to visit the " Elder settlement" where her brother and some friends were living, she determined at all hazards to warn them of the intended expedition. She had none in whom to confide ; but was obliged to leave her home alone, by stealth, and at the dead hour of night. Many miles were to be traversed, and the road lay through woods, and crossed marshes and creeks, where the conveniences of bridges and foot-logs were wanting. She walked rapidly on, heedless of slight difficulties; but her heart almost failed her when she came to the banks of the Tyger—a deep and rapid stream, which there was no possibility of crossing except by wading through the ford. This she knew to be deep at ordinary times, and it had doubtless been rendered more dangerous by the rains that had lately fallen. But the thought of personal danger weighed not with her, in comparison to the duty she owed her friends and country. Her momentary hesitation was but the shrinking of nature from peril encountered in darkness and alone, when the imagination conjures up a thousand appalling ideas, each more startling than the worst reality. Her strong heart battled against these, and she resolved to accomplish her purpose, or perish in the attempt. She entered the water; but when in the middle of the ford, became bewildered, and knew not which direction to take. The hoarse rush of the waters, which were up to her neck—the blackness of the night—the utter solitude around her—the uncertainty lest the next step should ingulph her past help, confused her ; and losing in a degree her self-possession, she wandered for some time in the channel without knowing whither to turn her steps. But the energy of a resolute will, under the care of Providence, sustained her. Having with difficulty reached the other side, she lost no time in hastening to her brother, informed him and his friends of the preparations made to surprise and destroy them, and urged him to send his men instantly in different directions to arouse and warn the neighborhood. The soldiers had just returned from a fatiguing excursion, and complained that they were faint from want of food. The noble girl, not satisfied with what she had done at such risk to herself, was ready to help them still further by providing refreshment immediately. Though wearied, wet, and shivering with cold, she at once set about her preparations. A few boards were taken from the roof of the house, a fire was kindled with them, and in a few minutes a hoe-cake, partly baked, was broken into pieces, and thrust into the shot pouches of the men. Thus provisioned, the little company hastened to give the alarm to their neighbors, and did so in time for all to make their escape. The next day, when the "scout" visited the place, they found no living enemy on whom to wreak their vengeance.

At a later period of the war, the father of Miss Langston incurred the displeasure of the loyalists in consequence of the active services of his sons in their country's cause. They were known to have imbibed their principles from him; and he was marked out as an object of summary vengeance. A party came to his house with the desperate design of putting to death all the men of the family. The sons were absent; but the feeble old man, selected by their relentless hate as a

victim, was in their power. He could not escape or
resist ; and he scorned to implore their mercy. One of
the company drew a pistol, and deliberately levelled it
at the breast of Lansgton. Suddenly a wild shriek was
heard ; and his young daughter sprang between her
aged parent and the fatal weapon. The brutal soldier
roughly ordered her to get out of the way, or the contents of the pistol would be instantly lodged in her own
heart. She heeded not the threat, which was but too
likely to be fulfilled the next moment. Clasping her
arms tightly round the old man's neck, she declared
that her own body should first receive the ball aimed at
his heart ! There are few human beings, even of the
most depraved, entirely insensible to all noble and generous impulses. On this occasion the conduct of the
daughter, so fearless, so determined to shield her father's
life by the sacrifice of her own, touched the heart even
of a member of the " Bloody Scout." Langston was
spared; and the party left the house filled with admiration
at the filial affection and devotion they had witnessed.

At another time the heroic maiden showed herself as
ready to prevent wrong to an enemy as to her friends.
Her father's house was visited by a company of whigs,
who stopped to get some refreshment, and to feed their
wearied horses. In the course of conversation one of
them mentioned that they were going to visit a tory
neighbor, for the purpose of seizing his horses. The
man whose possessions were thus to be appropriated
had been in general a peaceable citizen; and Mr.
Langston determined to inform him of the danger in

which his horses stood of having their ownership
changed. Entering cordially into her father's design,
Miss Langston set off immediately to carry the information. She gave it in the best faith ; but just before
she started on her return home, she discovered that the
neighbor whom she had warned was not only taking
precautions to save his property, but was about to send
for the captain of a tory band not far distant, so that
the "liberty men" might be captured when intent on
their expedition, before they should be aware of their
danger. It was now the generous girl's duty to perform a like friendly act towards the whigs. She lost
no time in conveying the intelligence, and thus saved
an enemy's property, and the lives of her friends.

Her disregard of personal danger, where service
could be rendered, was remarkable. One day, returning from a whig neighborhood in Spartanburg District,
she was met by a company of loyalists, who ordered
her to give them some intelligence they desired respecting those she had just left. She refused ; whereupon
the captain of the band held a pistol to her breast, and
ordered her instantly to make the disclosures, or she
should "die in her tracks." Miss Langston only replied,
with the cool intrepidity of a veteran soldier: "Shoot
me if you dare! I will not tell you," at the same time
opening a long handkerchief which covered her neck
and bosom, as if offering a place to receive the contents
of the weapon. Incensed by her defiance, the officer
was about to fire, when another threw up his hand, and
saved the courageous girl's life.

13

On one occasion, when her father's house was visited on a plundering expedition by the noted tory Captain Gray with his riflemen, and they had collected and divided every thing they thought could be of use, they were at some loss what to do with a large pewter basin. At length the captain determined on taking that also, jeeringly remarking, "it will do to run into bullets to kill the rebels." " Pewter bullets, sir," answered Miss Langston, " will not kill a whig." " Why not?" inquired Captain Gray. " It is said, sir," replied she, "that a witch can be shot only with a silver bullet; and I am sure the whigs are more under the protection of Providence." At another time when a company of the enemy came to the house they found the door secured. To their demand for admission and threats of breaking down the door, Miss Langston answered by sternly bidding them begone. Her resolute language induced the company to "hold a parley;" and the result was, that they departed without further attempt to obtain an entrance.

One more anecdote is given to illustrate her spirit and fearlessness. Her brother James had left a rifle in her care, which she was to keep hid till he sent for it. He did so, by a company of "liberty men," who were to return by his father's dwelling. On arriving at the house, one of them asked the young girl for the gun. She went immediately, and brought it; but as she came towards the soldiers, the thought struck her that she had neglected to ask for the countersign agreed upon between her brother and herself. Advancing more cautiously—she observed to them that their looks were suspicious; that for aught she knew they might be a set of tories; and demanded the countersign. One of the company answered that it was too late to make conditions; the gun was in their possession, and its holder, too. "Do you think so," cried she, cocking it, and presenting the muzzle at the speaker. "If the gun is in your possession, *take charge of her!*" Her look and attitude of defiance showed her in earnest; the countersign was quickly given; and the men, laughing heartily, pronounced her worthy of being the sister of James Langston.

After the war was ended, Miss Langston married Thomas Springfield, of Greenville, South Carolina. She died in Greenville District, a few years since. Of her numerous descendants then living, thirty-two were sons and grandsons capable of bearing arms, and ready at any time to do so in the maintenance of that liberty which was so dear to the youthful heart of their ancestor.*

THE recollection of the courage and patriotism of Mrs. Dillard is associated with the details of a battle of considerable importance, which took place in Spartanburg District, at the Green Spring, near Berwick's iron works. The Americans here gained great honor.

* The preceding anecdotes were furnished by Hon. B. F. Perry, of Greenville, South Carolina, who received them from one of Mrs. Springfield's family.

Colonel Clarke, of the Georgia volunteers, joined with Captains McCall, Liddle, and Hammond, in all about one hundred and ninety-eight men—having received intelligence that a body of tory militia, stated to be from two to five hundred, commanded by Colonel Ferguson, were recruiting for the horse service—determined to attempt to rout them.* They marched accordingly; and hearing that a scouting party was in advance of Ferguson's station, prepared to give them battle. Colonel Clarke, with his forces, encamped for the night at Green Spring.

On that day the Americans had stopped for refreshment at the house of Captain Dillard, who was with their party as a volunteer. They had been entertained by his wife with milk and potatoes—the simple fare which those hardy soldiers often found it difficult to obtain. The same evening Ferguson and Dunlap, with a party of tories, arrived at the house. They inquired of Mrs. Dillard whether Clarke and his men had not been there; what time they had departed; and what were their numbers? She answered that they had been at the house; that she could not guess their numbers; and that they had been gone a long time. The officers then ordered her to prepare supper for them with all possible despatch. They took possession of the house, and took some bacon to be given to their men. Mrs. Dillard set about the preparations for supper. In going backwards and forwards from the kitchen, she overheard much of their conversation. It will be re-

* Mills' Statistics of South Carolina, p. 738.

membered that the kitchens at the South are usually separate from the dwelling-houses. The doors and windows of houses in the country being often slightly constructed, it is also likely that the loose partitions afforded facilities for hearing what might be said within. Besides, the officers probably apprehended no danger from disclosing their plans in the presence of a lonely woman.

She ascertained that they had determined to surprise Clarke and his party ; and were to pursue him as soon as they had taken their meal. She also heard one of the officers tell Ferguson he had just received the information that the rebels, with Clarke, were to encamp that night at the Great Spring. It was at once resolved to surprise and attack them before day. The feelings may be imagined with which Mrs. Dillard heard this resolution announced. She hurried the supper, and as soon as it was placed upon the table, and the officers had sat down, slipped out by a back way. Late and dark as it was, her determination was to go herself and apprize Clarke of his danger, in the hope of being in time for him to make a safe retreat ; for she believed that the enemy were too numerous to justify a battle.

She went to the stable, bridled a young horse, and without saddle, mounted and rode with all possible speed to the place described. It was about half an hour before day when she came in full gallop to one of the videttes, by whom she was immediately conducted to Colonel Clarke. She called to the colonel, breathless with eagerness and haste, " Be in readiness either to fight or run ; the enemy will be upon you immediately, and they are strong !"

In an instant every man was up, and no moments were lost in preparing for action. The intelligence came just in time to put the whigs in readiness. Ferguson had detached Dunlap with two hundred picked mounted men, to engage Clarke and keep him employed till his arrival. These rushed in full charge into the American camp ; but the surprise was on their part. They were met hand to hand, with a firmness they had not anticipated. Their confusion was increased by the darkness, which rendered it hard to distinguish friend from foe. The battle was warm for fifteen or twenty minutes, when the tories gave way. They were pursued nearly a mile, but not overtaken. Ferguson came " too late for the frolic ;" the business being ended. Clarke and his little band then returned to North Carolina for rest and refreshment ; for the whole of this enterprise was performed without one regular meal, and without regular food for their horses.

Mrs. Angelica Nott, widow of the late Judge Nott, of South Corolina, remembers some illustrative incidents which occurred in the section where she resided with her aunt, Mrs. Potter, near the Grindal Shoal, a little south of Pacolet River. The whig population in this portion of the State, were exposed during part of 1780 and 1781 to incredible hardships. The breezes of fortune which had fanned into life the expiring embers of opposition to English tyranny, had been so variable that the wavering hopes of the people were often trembling on the verge of extinction. The reverses of the British arms had exasperated the loyalists, and embittered the enmity felt towards the stubborn people who refused to be conquered. Such was the state of feeling when the destiny of the South was committed to the hands of a soldier of consummate genius, in whom the trust of all was implicitly placed.

When Tarleton was on his march against Morgan, just before their encounter at the Cowpens, a party of loyalists came to the place where Mrs. Potter lived, and committed some depredations. They burned the straw covering from a rude hut, in which the family lodged, while a relative ill of the small-pox occupied the house. Mrs. Potter and her children had built this lodge of rails, for their temporary accommodation. The soldiers attempted to take off her wedding-ring, which, as it had been worn for years, became imbedded under the skin, in the effort to force it from her finger. They swore it should be cut off, but finally desisted from the attempt. On the same march, Tarleton encamped at the house of John Beckham, whose wife was the sister of Colonel Henderson of the continental army. Mrs. Beckham saw for the first time this renowned officer while standing in her yard, and ordering his men to catch her poultry for supper. She spoke civilly to him, and hastened to prepare supper for him and his suite, as if they had been honored guests. When about to leave in the morning, he ordered the house to be burnt, after being given up to pillage; but on her remonstrance, recalled the order. All her bedding was taken, except one quilt, which soon shared the same fate. At another time Mrs. Beckham went to Granby, eighty miles distant, for a bushel of salt, which she brought home on the saddle under her. The guinea appropriated for the purchase, was concealed in the hair braided on the top of her head.

Mrs. Potter was visited by the famous tory, Colonel Cunningham, commonly called "Bloody Bill Cunningham," on one occasion, with a party of two hundred and fifty men. They arrived after dark; and as green corn happened to be in season, encamped by one of her fields, fed their horses with the corn, built fires with the rails, and roasted the ears for themselves. At that time, the family lived chiefly on roasted corn, without bread, meat, or salt. Hickory ashes were used, with a small quantity of salt, for preserving beef when it could be had. Leather shoes were replaced by woolen rags sewed round the feet; and of beds or bedding none were left. The beds were generally ripped open by the depredators, the feathers scattered, and the ticking used for tent-cloths. The looms were robbed of cloth found in them; and hence the women of the country resorted to various expedients to manufacture clothing, and preserve it for their own use and that of their friends. A family residing on the Pacolet, built a loom between four trees in the forest, and wove in fair weather, covering the loom and web with cow-hides when it rained.

XXIII.

ELIZABETH STEELE.

THE long, arduous, and eventful retreat of General Greene through the Carolinas, after the battle of the Cowpens, that retreat on whose issue hung the fate of the South—with the eager pursuit of Cornwallis, who well knew that the destruction of that army would secure his conquests—is a twice-told tale to every reader. The line of march lay through Salisbury, North Carolina; and while the British commander was crossing the Catawba, Greene was approaching this village. With the American army were conveyed the prisoners taken by Morgan in the late bloody and brilliant action, the intention being to convey them to Virginia. Several of these were sick and wounded, and among them were some British officers, unable, from loss of strength, to proceed further on the route.

General Greene, aware of the objects of Cornwallis, knew his design, by a hurried march to the ford, to cross the Catawba before opposition could be made; and had stationed a body of militia there to dispute the passage. Most anxiously did the General await their arrival, before he pursued his route. The day gradually

13*

wore away, and still no signs appeared of the militia; and it was not till after midnight that the news reached him of their defeat and dispersion by the British troops, and the death of General Davidson, who had commanded them. His aids having been despatched to different parts of the retreating army, he rode on with a heavy heart to Salisbury. It had been raining during the day, and his soaked and soiled garments and appearance of exhaustion as he wearily dismounted from his jaded horse at the door of the principal hotel, showed that he had suffered much from exposure to the storm, sleepless fatigue, and harassing anxiety of mind. Dr. Reed, who had charge of the sick and wounded prisoners, while he waited for the General's arrival was engaged in writing the paroles with which it was necessary to furnish such officers as could not go on. From his apartment overlooking the main street, he saw his friend, unaccompanied by his aids, ride up and alight; and hastened to receive him as he entered the house. Seeing him without a companion, and startled by his dispirited looks—the doctor could not refrain from noticing them with anxious inquiries; to which the wearied soldier replied: "Yes—fatigued—hungry—alone, and penniless!"

The melancholy reply was heard by one determined to prove, by the generous assistance proffered in a time of need, that no reverse could dim the pure flame of disinterested patriotism. General Greene had hardly taken his seat at the well-spread table, when Mrs. Steele, the landlady of the hotel, entered the room, and carefully closed the door behind her. Approaching her distinguished guest, she reminded him of the despondent words he had uttered in her hearing, implying, as she thought, a distrust of the devotion of his friends, through every calamity, to the cause. Money, too, she declared he should have; and drew from under her apron two small bags full of specie, probably the earnings of years. "Take these," said she, "for you will want them, and I can do without them."

Words of kindness and encouragement accompanied this offering of a benevolent heart, which General Greene accepted with thankfulness. "Never," says his biographer, "did relief come at a more propitious moment; nor would it be straining conjecture to suppose that he resumed his journey with his spirits cheered and lightened by this touching proof of woman's devotion to the cause of her country."[*]

General Greene did not remain long in Salisbury; but before his departure from the house of Mrs. Steele, he left a memorial of his visit. He took from the wall of one of the apartments a portrait of George III., which had come from England as a present from a person at court to one of Mrs. Steele's connections attached to an embassy, wrote with chalk on the back, " O, George, hide thy face and mourn;" and replaced it with the face to the wall. The picture, with the writing uneffaced, is still in possession of a granddaughter of Mrs. Steele, a daughter of Dr. McCorkle, and may be seen in Charlotte.

[*] Greene's Life of Nathanael Greene. See also Foote's Sketches North Carolina. p. 355.

Elizabeth Steele was distinguished not only for her attachment to the American cause during the war, but for the piety that shone brightly in her useful life. Among her papers was found after her death a written dedication of herself to her Creator, and a prayer for support in the practice of Christian duty; with a letter, left as a legacy to her children, enjoining it upon them to make religion the great work of life. She was a tender mother, and beloved for her constant exercise of the virtues of kindness and charity. She was twice married, and died in Salisbury, in 1791. Her son, the Hon. John Steele, conspicuous in the councils of the State and Nation, was one whose public services offer materials for an interesting biography. A collection of his correspondence has lately been added to the treasures of the Historical Society of the University of North Carolina; and it is to be hoped that under its auspices, justice will be done to his memory at no distant period. Margaret, Mrs. Steele's daughter, was the wife of the Rev. Samuel E. McCorkle.

It was in the same pursuit of Greene and Morgan by Cornwallis, that the British destroyed the property of the Widow Brevard, in Centre congregation. "She has seven sons in the rebel army," was the reason given by the officer for permitting her house to be burned and her farm plundered. One of her sons, Captain Alexander Brevard, took part in nine battles; and the youngest was at seventeen first lieutenant of a company of horse. Ephraim Brevard, another son, having graduated at Princeton College, and completed a course of medical studies, fixed his residence at Charlotte. Mr. Foote says, "His talents, patriotism, and education, united with his prudence and practical sense, marked him as a leader in the councils that preceded the convention held in Queen's Museum; and on the day of meeting designated him as secretary and draughtsman of that singular and unrivalled DECLARATION, which alone is a passport to the memory of posterity through all time."

It will be borne in mind that it was in Charlotte, the county town of Mecklenburg County, that the bold idea of National Independence was first proclaimed to the world. On the 19th May, 1775, an immense concourse of people was assembled in this frontier settlement—all agitated with the excitement which had plunged the whole land into commotion; on that day came the first intelligence of the commencement of hostilities at Lexington; and when the convention and the people were addressed, the universal cry was, "Let us be independent! Let us declare our independence, and defend it with our lives and fortunes!" The resolutions drawn up by Dr. Brevard were discussed; and by their unanimous adoption, the day following, by the convention and the approving multitude, the citizens of Mecklenburg County declared themselves a free and independent people. Due honor is awarded to him who took so active a part in that memorable transaction; but where is the tribute that should be paid to the widowed mother who sowed the seeds which on that day yielded fruit—who implanted in her son's mind those sterling principles, the guidance of which rendered his life one of eminent usefulness?

When the southern States became the arena of war, Dr. Brevard entered the army as surgeon, and was taken prisoner at the surrender of Charleston. In that city he was seized with a fatal disease, to which he fell a victim after being set at liberty, and permitted to place himself under the care of friends.

The deplorable sufferings of the unfortunate prisoners in Charleston, moved the sympathy of the inhabitants of Western Carolina; for news came that many were perishing in captivity of want and disease. The men could not go thither to visit their friends and relatives, without insuring their own destruction; but the women gathered clothing, medicines, and provisions, and travelled long journeys, encountering danger as well as hardship, to minister in person to those who so sorely needed their succor. Much relief was brought to the sufferers by these visits of mercy; although the lives preserved were sometimes saved at the sacrifice of the noble benefactors. The mother of Andrew Jackson, returning to the Waxhaw, after a journey to Charleston— to carry clothing and other necessaries to some friends on board the prison ship, was seized with the prison-fever, and died in a tent, in the midst of the wide, sandy wilderness of pines. Her lonely grave by the road-side, were the spot known, would speak mournfully of woman's self-immolating heroism. Mrs. Jackson, with her children, had quitted their home on the Waxhaw, where she had buried her husband, after the rout and slaughter of Buford's regiment by the forces of Tarleton, when the women and children fled from the ravages of the merciless enemy. They had found a place of refuge in Sugar Creek congregation, where they remained during part of the summer. Part of the the foundations of the log meeting-house where the congregation met for worship may still be seen.

Other widowed mothers were there in North Carolina, who trained their sons to become zealous patriots and efficent statesmen. The names of Mrs. Flinn, Mrs. Sharpe, Mrs. Graham, and Mrs. Hunter, are worthy of remembrance. The great principles proclaimed at the Mecklenburg Convention, were acted out in the noblest efforts of patriotism by their sons.

Mr. Caruthers, the biographer of the Rev. David Caldwell, states, that while all the active men in his congregations were engaged with the army at the battle of Guilford Court-house, there were two collections of females, one in Buffalo, and the other in Alamance, engaged in earnest prayer for their families and their country; and that many others sought the divine aid in solitary places. One pious woman sent her son frequently during the afternoon, to the summit of a little hill near which she spent much time in prayer, to listen and bring her word which way the firing came—from the southward or the northward. When he returned and said it was going northward, " Then," exclaimed she, "all is lost! Greene is defeated." But all was not lost ; the God who hears prayer remembered his people.

XXIV.

~~~~~~~~~~

MARY SLOCUMB.

The first expedition into North Carolina projected by Lord Cornwallis, was baffled by the fall of Colonel Ferguson at King's Mountain. The disaster at the Cowpens forbade perseverance in the second attempt, and was followed by the memorable retreat of Greene. The battle of Guilford took place in March, 1781 ; and towards the end of April, while Lord Rawdon encountered Greene at Hobkirk's Hill, Cornwallis set out on his march from Wilmington, bent on his avowed purpose of achieving the conquest of Virginia. On his march towards Halifax, he encamped for several days on the river Neuse, in what is now called Wayne County, North Carolina. His head-quarters were at Springbank, while Colonel Tarleton, with his renowned legion, encamped on the plantation of Lieutenant Slocumb. This consisted of level and extensive fields, which at that season presented a most inviting view of fresh verdure from the mansion-house. Lord Cornwallis himself gave it the name of " Pleasant Green," which it ever afterwards retained. The owner of this fine estate held a subaltern's commission in the State line under Colonel Washington, and was in command of a troop of light horse, raised in his own neighborhood, whose general duty it was to act as Rangers, scouring the country for many miles around, watching the movements of the enemy, and punishing the loyalists when detected in their vocation of pillage and murder. These excursions had been frequent for two or three years, and were often of several weeks' duration. At the present time Slocumb had returned to the vicinity, and had been sent with twelve or fifteen recruits to act as scouts in the neighborhood of the British General. The morning of the day on which Tarleton took possession of his plantation, he was near Springbank, and reconnoitered the encampment of Cornwallis, which he supposed to be his whole force. He then, with his party, pursued his way slowly along the south bank of the Neuse, in the direction of his own house, little dreaming that his beautiful and peaceful home, where, some time before, he had left his wife and child, was then in the possession of the terrible Tarleton.

During these frequent excursions of the Rangers, and the necessary absence of her husband, the superintendence of the plantation had always devolved upon Mrs. Slocumb. She depended for protection upon her slaves, whose fidelity she had proved, and upon her own fearless and intrepid spirit. The scene of the occupation of her house, and Tarleton's residence with her, remained through life indelibly impressed on her memory, and were described by her to one who enjoyed the honor of her intimate friendship. I am permitted to give his account, copied almost verbatim from notes taken at the time the occurrences were related by Mrs. Slocumb.

It was about ten o'clock on a beautiful spring morning, that a splendidly-dressed officer, accompanied by two aids, and followed at a short distance by a guard of some twenty troopers, dashed up to the piazza in front of the ancient-looking mansion. Mrs. Slocumb was sitting there, with her child and a near relative young lady, who afterwards became the wife of Major Williams. A few house servants were also on the piazza.

The officer raised his cap, and bowing to his horse's neck, addressed the lady, with the question—

"Have I the pleasure of seeing the mistress of this house and plantation!"

"It belongs to my husband."

"Is he at home?" "He is not." "Is he a rebel?" "No sir. He is in the army of his country, and fighting against our invaders; therefore not a rebel." It is not a little singular, that although the people of that day gloried in their rebellion, they always took offence at being called rebels.

"I fear, madam," said the officer, "we differ in opinion." A friend to his country will be the friend of the king, our master."

"Slaves only acknowledge a master in this country," replied the lady.

A deep flush crossed the florid cheeks of Tarleton, for he was the speaker; and turning to one of his aids, he ordered him to pitch the tents and form the encampment in the orchard and field on their right. To the other aid his orders were to detach a quarter guard and station piquets on each road. Then bowing very low, he added: "Madam, the service of his Majesty requires the temporary occupation of your property; and if it would not be too great an inconvenience, I will take up my quarters in your house."

The tone admitted no controversy. Mrs. Slocumb answered: "My family consists of only myself, my sister and child, and a few negroes. We are your prisoners."

From the piazza where he seated himself, Tarleton commanded a view of the ground on which his troops were arranging their camp. The mansion fronted the east, and an avenue one hundred and fifty feet wide, and about half a mile in length, stretched to the eastern side of the plantation, where was a highway, with open grounds beyond it, partly dry meadow and partly sand barren. This avenue was lined on the south side by a high fence, and a thick hedge-row of forest trees. These are now removed, and replaced by the Pride of India and other ornamental trees. On the north side extended the common rail-fence seven or eight feet high, such as is usually seen on plantations in the low country. The encampment of the British troops being on that part of the plantation lying south of the avenue, it was completely screened by the fences and hedge-row from the view of any one approaching from down the country.

While the men were busied, different officers came up at intervals, making their reports and receiving orders. Among others, a tory captain, whom Mrs. Slocumb immediately recognized—for before joining the royal army, he had lived fifteen or twenty miles below—received orders in her hearing to take his troop and scour the country for two or three miles round.

In an hour every thing was quiet, and the plantation presented the romantic spectacle of a regular encampment of some ten or eleven hundred of the choicest cavalry of the British monarch.

Mrs. Slocumb now addressed herself to the duty of preparing for her uninvited guests. The dinner set before the king's officers was, in her own words to her friend, "as a good dinner as you have now before you, and of much the same materials." A description of what then constituted a good dinner in that region may not be inappropriate. "The first dish, was, of course, the boiled ham, flanked with the plate of greens. Opposite was the turkey, supported by the laughing baked sweet potatoes ; a plate of boiled beef, another of sausages, and a third with a pair of baked fowls, formed a line across the centre of the table ; half a dozen dishes of different pickles, stewed fruit, and other condiments filled up the interstices of the board." The dessert, too, was abundant and various. Such a dinner, it may well be supposed, met the particular approbation of the royal officers, especially as the fashion of that day introduced stimulating drinks to the table, and the peach brandy prepared under Lieutenant Slocumb's own supervision, was of the most excellent sort. It received the unqualified praise of the party; and its merits were freely discussed. A Scotch officer, praising it by the name of whiskey, protested that he had never drunk as good out of Scotland. An officer speaking with a slight brogue, insisted it was not whiskey, and that no Scotch drink ever equalled it. "To my mind," said he, "it tastes as yonder orchard smells."

"Allow me, madam," said Colonel Tarleton, to inquire where the spirits we are drinking is procured."

"From the orchard where your tents stand," answered Mrs. Slocumb.

"Colonel," said the Irish captain, "when we conquer this country, is it not to be divided out among us?"

"The officers of this army," replied the Colonel, "will undoubtedly receive large possessions of the conquered American provinces."

Mrs. Slocumb here interposed. "Allow me to observe and prophesy," said she, "the only land in these United States which will ever remain in possession of a British officer, will measure but six feet by two."

"Excuse me, madam," remarked Tarleton. "For your sake I regret to say—this beautiful plantation will be the ducal seat of some of us."

"Don't trouble yourself about me," retorted the spirited lady. "My husband is not a man who would allow a duke, or even a king, to have a quiet seat upon his ground."

At this point the conversation was interrupted by rapid volleys of fire-arms, appearing to proceed from the

wood a short distance to the eastward. One of the
aids pronounced it some straggling scout, running from
the picket-guard; but the experience of Colonel Tarleton could not be easily deceived.

"There are rifles and muskets," said he, "as well as
pistols; and too many to pass unnoticed. Order boots
and saddles, and you—Captain, take your troop in the
direction of the firing."

The officer rushed out to execute his orders, while
the Colonel walked into the piazza, whither he was
immediately followed by the anxious ladies. Mrs.
Slocumb's agitation and alarm may be imagined; for
she guessed but too well the cause of the interruption.
On the first arrival of the officers she had been impor-
tuned, even with harsh threats—not, however, by Tarleton—to tell where her husband, when absent on duty,
was likely to be found; but after her repeated and
peremptory refusals, had escaped further molestation on
the subject. She feared now that he had returned
unexpectedly, and might fall into the enemy's hands
before he was aware of their presence.

Her sole hope was in a precaution she had adopted
soon after the coming of her unwelcome guests. Having heard Tarleton give the order to the tory captain
as before-mentioned, to patrol the country, she immediately sent for an old negro, and gave him directions
to take a bag of corn to the mill about four miles distant, on the road she knew her husband must travel if
he returned that day. "Big George" was instructed to
warn his master of the danger of approaching his

home. With the indolence and curiosity natural to his race, however, the old fellow remained loitering about the premises, and was at this time lurking under the hedge-row, admiring the red coats, dashing plumes, and shining helmets of the British troopers.

The Colonel and the ladies continued on the look-out from the piazza. "May I be allowed, madam," at length said Tarleton, "without offence, to inquire if any part of Washington's army is in this neighborhood.

"I presume it is known to you," replied Mrs. Slocumb, "that the Marquis and Greene are in this State. And you would not of course," she added, after a slight pause, "be surprised at a call from Lee, or your old friend Colonel Washington, who, although a perfect gentleman, it is said shook your hand (pointing to the scar left by Washington's sabre) very rudely, when you last met."*

This spirited answer inspired Tarleton with apprehensions that the skirmish in the woods was only the prelude to a concerted attack on his camp. His only reply was a loud order to form the troops on the right; and springing on his charger, he dashed down the avenue a few hundred feet, to a breach in the hedge-

* As I cannot distrust the authority on which I have received this anecdote, it proves that on more than one occasion the British colonel was made to feel the shaft of female wit, in allusion to the unfortunate battle of the Cowpens. It is said that in a close encounter between Washington and Tarleton during that action, the latter was wounded by a sabre cut on the hand. Colonel Washington, as is well known, figured in some of the skirmishes in North Carolina.

row, leaped the fence, and in a moment was at the head of his regiment, which was already in line.

Meanwhile, Lieutenant Slocumb, with John Howell, a private in his band, Henry Williams, and the brother of Mrs. Slocumb, Charles Hooks, a boy of about thirteen years of age, was leading a hot pursuit of the tory captain who had been sent to reconnoitre the country, and some of his routed troop. These were first discerned in the open grounds east and northeast of the plantation, closely pursued by a body of American mounted militia; while a running fight was kept up with different weapons, in which four or five broad swords gleamed conspicuous. The foremost of the pursuing party appeared too busy with the tories to see any thing else; and they entered the avenue at the same moment with the party pursued. With what horror and consternation did Mrs. Slocumb recognize her husband, her brother, and two of her neighbors, in chase of the tory captain and four of his band, already half-way down the avenue, and unconscious that they were rushing into the enemy's midst!

About the middle of the avenue one of the tories fell; and the course of the brave and imprudent young officers was suddenly arrested by "Big George," who sprang directly in front of their horses, crying, "Hold on, massa! de debbil here! Look yon!"* A glance to the left showed the young men their danger: they were within pistol shot of a thousand men drawn up in order of battle. Wheeling their horses, they discovered a

* Yon, for yonder.

troop already leaping the fence into the avenue in their rear. Quick as thought they again wheeled their horses, and dashed down the avenue directly towards the house, where stood the quarter-guard to receive them. On reaching the garden fence—a rude structure formed of a kind of lath, and called a wattled fence— they leaped that and the next, amid a shower of balls from the guard, cleared the canal at one tremendous leap, and scouring across the open field to the northwest, were in the shelter of the wood before their pursuers could clear the fences of the enclosure. The whole ground of this adventure may be seen as the traveller passes over the Wilmington railroad, a mile and a half south of Dudley depôt.

A platoon had commenced the pursuit; but the trumpets sounded the recall before the flying Americans had crossed the canal. The presence of mind and lofty language of the heroic wife, had convinced the British Colonel that the daring men who so fearlessly dashed into his camp were supported by a formidable force at hand. Had the truth been known, and the fugitives pursued, nothing could have prevented the destruction not only of the four who fled, but of the rest of the company on the east side of the plantation.

Tarleton had rode back to the front of the house, where he remained eagerly looking after the fugitives till they disappeared in the wood. He called for the tory captain, who presently came forward, questioned him about the attack in the woods, asked the names of

14

the American officers, and dismissed him to have his wounds dressed, and see after his men. The last part of the order was needless; for nearly one-half of his troop had fallen. The ground is known to this day as the Dead Men's Field.

As Tarleton walked into the house he observed to Mrs. Slocumb, "Your husband made us a short visit, madam. I should have been happy to make his acquaintance, and that of his friend, Mr. Williams."

"I have little doubt," replied the wife, "that you will meet the gentlemen, and they will thank you for the polite manner in which you treat their friends."

The Colonel observed apologetically, that necessity compelled them to occupy her property; that they took only such things as were necessary to their support, for which they were instructed to offer proper remuneration; and that every thing should be done to render their stay as little disagreeable as possible. The lady expressed her thankfulness for his kindness, and withdrew to her room, while the officers returned to their peach-brandy and coffee, and closed the day with a merry night.

Slocumb and his companions passed rapidly round the plantation, and returned to the ground where the encounter had taken place, collecting on the way the stragglers of his troop. Near their bivouac he saw the tory captain's brother, who had been captured by the Americans, hanging by a bridal rein from the top of a sapling bent down for the purpose, and struggling in the agonies of death. Hastening to the spot, he severed the rein with a stroke of his sword, and with much difficulty restored him to life. Many in the lower part of North Carolina can remember an old man whose protruded eyes and suffused countenance presented the appearance of one half strangled. He it was who thus owed his life and liberty to the humanity of his generous foe.

Mr. Slocumb, by the aid of Major Williams, raised about two hundred men in the neighborhood, and with this force continued to harass the rear of the royal army, frequently cutting off foraging parties, till they crossed the Roanoke, when they joined the army of La Fayette at Warrenton. He remained with the army till the surrender at Yorktown.

It need hardly be mentioned that "Big George" received his reward for this and other services. His life with his master was one of ease and indulgence. On the division of Colonel Slocumb's estate some years since, a considerable amount was paid to enable the faithful slave to spend the remnant of his days with his wife, who belonged to another person.

Another anecdote, communicated by the same friend of Mrs. Slocumb, is strikingly illustrative of her resolution and strength of will. The occurrence took place at a time when the whole country was roused by the march of the British and loyalists from the Cape Fear country, to join the royal standard at Wilmington. The veteran Donald McDonald issued his proclamation at Cross Creek, in February, 1776, and having assembled his Highlanders, marched across rivers and through forests, in haste to join Governor Martin and Sir Henry Clinton, who were already at Cape Fear. But while he had eluded the pursuit of Moore, the patriots of New-bern and Wilmington Districts were not idle. It was a time of noble enterprise, and gloriously did leaders and people come forward to meet the emergency. The gallant Richard Caswell called his neighbors hastily together; and they came at his call as readily as the clans of the Scotch mountains mustered at the signal of the burning cross. The whole county rose in mass; scarce a man able to walk was left in the Neuse region. The united regiments of Colonels Lillington and Cas-well encountered McDonald at Moore's Creek;* where, on the twenty-seventh, was fought one of the bloodiest battles of the Revolution. Colonel Slocumb's recollec-tions of this bravely-contested field were too vivid to be dimmed by the lapse of years. He was accustomed to dwell but lightly on the gallant part borne by himself in that memorable action; but he gave abundant praise to his associates; and well did they deserve the tribute. "And," he would say—"*my wife was there!*" She was indeed; but the story is best told in her own words:

"The men all left on Sunday morning. More than eighty went from this house with my husband; I looked at them well, and I could see that every man had mischief in him. I know a coward as soon as I set my eyes upon him. The tories more than once 'ried

---

* Moore's Creek, running from north to south, empties into the South River, about twenty miles above Wilmington. See sketch of Flora McDonald.

to frighten me, but they always showed coward at the bare insinuation that our troops were about.

" Well, they got off in high spirits ; every man stepping high and light. And I slept soundly and quietly that night, and worked hard all the next day; but I kept thinking where. they had got to—how far; where and how many of the regulars and tories they would meet; and I could not keep myself from the study. I went to bed at the usual time, but still continued to study. As I lay—whether waking or sleeping I know not—I had a dream ; yet it was not all a dream. (She used the words, unconsciously, of the poet who was not then in being.) I saw distinctly a body wrapped in my husband's guard-cloak—bloody—dead ; and others dead and wounded on the ground about him. I saw them plainly and distinctly. I uttered a cry, and sprang to my feet on the floor ; and so strong was the impression on my mind, that I rushed in the direction the vision appeared, and came up against the side of the house. The fire in the room gave little light, and I gazed in every direction to catch another glimpse of the scene. I raised the light; every thing was still and quiet. My child was sleeping, but my woman was awakened by my crying out or jumping on the floor. If ever I felt fear it was at that moment. Seated on the bed, I reflected a few moments—and said aloud: ' I must go to him.' I told the woman I could not sleep and would ride down the road. She appeared in great alarm; but I merely told her to lock the door after me, and look after the child. I went to the stable, saddled my mare—as fleet and easy a nag as ever travelled; and in one minute we were tearing down the road at full speed. The cool night seemed after a mile or two's gallop to bring reflection with it; and I asked myself where I was going, and for what purpose. Again and again I was tempted to turn back; but I was soon ten miles from home, and my mind became stronger every mile I rode. I should find my husband dead or dying—was as firmly my presentiment and conviction as any fact of my life. When day broke I was some thirty miles from home. I knew the general route our little army expected to take, and had followed them without hesitation. About sunrise I came upon a group of women and children, standing and sitting by the road-side, each one of them showing the same anxiety of mind I felt. Stopping a few minutes I inquired if the battle had been fought. They knew nothing, but were assembled on the road to catch intelligence. They thought Caswell had taken the right of the Wilmington road, and gone towards the northwest (Cape Fear). Again was I skimming over the ground through a country thinly settled, and very poor and swampy; but neither my own spirits nor my beautiful nag's failed in the least. We followed the well-marked trail of the troops.

" The sun must have been well up, say eight or nine o'clock, when I heard a sound like thunder, which I knew must be cannon. It was the first time I ever heard a cannon. I stopped still; when presently the cannon thundered again. The battle was then fighting. What a fool! my husband could not be dead last night, and the battle only fighting now! Still, as I am so near, I will go on and see how they come out. So away we went again, faster than ever; and I soon found by the noise of guns that I was near the fight. Again I stopped. I could hear muskets, I could hear rifles, and I could hear shouting. I spoke to my mare and dashed on in the direction of the firing and the shouts, now louder than ever. The blind path I had been following brought me into the Wilmington road leading to Moore's Creek Bridge, a few hundred yards below the bridge. A few yards from the road, under a cluster of trees were lying perhaps twenty men. They were the wounded. I knew the spot; the very trees; and the position of the men I knew as if I had seen it a thousand times. I had seen it all night! I saw all at once; but in an instant my whole soul was centred in one spot; for there, wrapped in his bloody guard-cloak, was my husband's body! How I passed the few yards from my saddle to the place I never knew. I remember uncovering his head and seeing a face clothed with gore from a dreadful wound across the temple. I put my hand on the bloody face; 'twas warm; and an *unknown voice* begged for water. A small camp-kettle was lying near, and a stream of water was close by. I brought it; poured some in his mouth; washed his face; and behold—it was Frank Cogdell. He soon revived and could speak. I was washing the wound in his head. Said he, 'It is not that; it is that hole in my leg that is killing me.' A puddle of blood was standing on the ground about his feet. I took his knife, cut away his trousers and stocking, and found the blood came from a shot-hole through and through the fleshy part of his leg. I looked about and could see nothing that looked as if it would do for dressing wounds but some heart-leaves. I gathered a handful and bound them tight to the holes; and the bleeding stopped. I then went to the others; and—Doctor! I dressed the wounds of many a brave fellow who did good fighting long after that day! I had not inquired for my husband; but while I was busy Caswell came up. He appeared very much surprised to see me; and was with his hat in hand about to pay some compliment: but I interrupted him by asking—'Where is my husband ?'

"'Where he ought to be, madam; in pursuit of the enemy. But pray,' said he, 'how came you here ?'

"'Oh, I thought,' replied I, 'you would need nurses as well as soldiers. See! I have already dressed many of these good fellows; and here is one'—going to Frank and lifting him up with my arm under his head so that he could drink some more water—'would have died before any of you men could have helped him.'

"'I believe you,' said Frank. Just then I looked up, and my husband, as bloody as a butcher, and as muddy as a ditcher,* stood before me.

"'Why, Mary!'' he exclaimed, 'What are you doing there ? Hugging Frank Cogdell, the greatest reprobate in the army ?'

* It was his company that forded the creek, and penetrating the swamp, made the furious charge on the British left and rear, which decided the fate of the day.

" ' I don't care,' I cried. 'Frank is a brave fellow, a good soldier, and a true friend to Congress.'

" ' True, true! every word of it!' said Caswell. 'You are right, madam!' with the lowest possible bow.

"I would not tell my husband what brought me there. I was so happy; and so were all! It was a glorious victory; I came just at the height of the enjoyment. I knew my husband was surprised, but I could see he was not displeased with me. It was night again before our excitement had at all subsided. Many prisoners were brought in, and among them some very obnoxious; but the worst of the tories were not taken prisoners. They were, for the most part, left in the woods and swamps wherever they were overtaken. I begged for some of the poor prisoners, and Caswell readily told me none should be hurt but such as had been guilty of murder and house-burning. In the middle of the night I again mounted my mare and started for home. Caswell and my husband wanted me to stay till next morning and they would send a party with me; but no! I wanted to see my child, and I told them they could send no party who could keep up with me. What a happy ride I had back! and with what joy did I embrace my child as he ran to meet me!"

What fiction could be stranger than such truth! And would not a plain unvarnished narrative of the sayings and doings of the actors in Revolutionary times, unknown by name, save in the neighborhood where they lived, and now almost forgotten even by their de-

14*

scendants, surpass in thrilling interest any romance
ever written! In these days of railroads and steam, it
can scarcely be credited that a woman actually rode
alone, in the night, through a wild unsettled country,
a distance—going and returning—of a hundred and
twenty-five miles; and that in less than forty hours,
and without any interval of rest! Yet even this fair
equestrian, whose feats would astonish the modern
world, admitted that one of her acquaintances was a
better horsewoman than herself. This was Miss Esther
Wake, the beautiful sister-in-law of Governor Tryon,
after whom Wake County was named. She is said to
have rode eighty miles—the distance between Raleigh
and the Governor's head-quarters in the neighborhood
of Colonel Slocumb's residence—to pay a visit; returning the next day. Governor Tryon was here
several days, at the time he made the famous foray
against the Regulators. What would these women
have said to the delicacy of modern refinement in the
southern country, fatigued with a moderate drive in a
close carriage, and looking out on woods and fields from
the windows!

The physiologist may explain the vision that produced an impression so powerful as to determine this
resolute wife upon her nocturnal expedition to Moore's
Creek. The idea of danger to her husband, which
banished sleep, was sufficient to call up the illusion to
her excited imagination; and her actions were decided
by the impulse of the moment, prompting her to hasten
at once to his assistance.

This is not the place to record the Revolutionary services of Colonel Slocumb. The aid of one of his descendants enables me to add some notice of the personal history of his wife to the foregoing anecdotes. Her maiden name was Hooks. She was born in the county of Bertie, North Carolina, in 1760. When she was about ten years of age, her father, after a tour of exploration in search of a portion of country which combined the advantages of fertility and healthful air, removed his family to the county of Duplin. He was an open-hearted, hospitable man; and was one of a number bearing the same character, who settled a region of country called Goshen, still famous in North Carolina for the frank simplicity of the manners of its inhabitants, and for their profuse and generous hospitality. Here were nurtured some of the noblest spirits of the Revolution. The names of Renau, Hill, Wright, Pearsall, Hooks, and Slocumb, among others, are remembered with pride. The constant presence of the loyalists or tories in the neighborhood, and their frequent depredations, called for vigilance as well as bravery. Many a tale of treachery and cruelty, enough to freeze the blood with horror, is this day told at the fireside. Sometimes the barn or dwelling of the doomed whig, wrapped in lurid flames, lighted up the darkness of the night; sometimes his fate was to be hung to a sapling; and not unfrequently these atrocities were in like manner avenged upon the aggressors. Accustomed to hear of such things, and inured to scenes of danger, it cannot be wondered, that the gay and sprightly Mary

Hooks should acquire a degree of masculine energy and independence, with many of the accomplishments of the bolder sex. She was at this time in the early bloom of youth, with slender and symmetrical form and pleasing features, animated by blue, expressive, laughing eyes. If not absolutely beautiful, her face could not fail to charm; for it beamed with the bright soul that knew not what it was to fear. Her playful wit and repartee, rendered piquant by her powers of sarcasm, were rarely equalled.

Soon after the removal of the family to Goshen, her mother died; and in 1777, her father married the widow of John Charles Slocumb, who resided in the locality above-described, on the Neuse. At the time of their marriage, the parties had each three children. Ezekiel Slocumb was the eldest son, and as the law then stood, inherited the whole of his father's real estate. Of the two plantations to which he was entitled, however, he gave one to his brother. Though but a youth of seventeen, the management of the property devolved on him; while the other children of the united family lived together at Goshen. In due time for a " course of love," Ezekiel Slocumb and Mary Hooks were married, both being about eighteen years of age. The lovely and spirited bride immediately entered upon her duties at her husband's home on the Neuse; but they were not allowed to remain long in untroubled security. To prevent or punish the frequent depredations of the tories, the boy-husband joined a troop of light-horse, who, acting on their own responsibility, performed the duty of scouts, scouring the country wherever they had notice of any necessity for their presence. In these prolonged absences, Mrs. Slocumb took the entire charge of the plantation, being obliged to perform many of the duties which usually fall to the lot of the rougher sex. She used to say, laughingly, that she had done in those perilous times all that a man ever did, except "mauling rails;" and to take away even that exception she went out one day and *split a few.* She was a graceful and fearless rider; and Die Vernon herself never displayed more skillful horsemanship in scampering over the hills of Scotland, than did the subject of this memoir, in her excursions through the wild woods of Neuse. Not only was this southern accomplishment then in vogue among the women, but it was not thought unfeminine to chase the fox. Many a time and oft has our heroine been in at the death, and won the honor. Nor could the stag say confidently, 'this day he would not die,' if Mary Slocumb chanced to be mounted on "Old Roan," with her light unerring "Joe Manton" slung at her side!

But those were not days for sport and pleasure alone. In the knowledge how to spin, sew, and weave, our fair equestrian was perfect. She could also wash and cook; and it was her pride to excel in all she did. In those days matrons of condition disdained not labor with their hands; nor were affluent circumstances an excuse for idleness or extravagance. The results of her persevering industry and that of her domestics appeared at her death in curtains, quilts, and cloths of various sorts and patterns, sufficient in quantity to furnish a country store. Let our indolent fine ladies blush for themselves when they learn that a woman of mind and intelligence, whose rare powers of conversation charmed the social circle, actually carded, spun, wove, cut and made all the clothes worn by an officer of the army in active service during the southern campaign, including his guard-cloak; and that the material of her own dress was manufactured by her own hands!*

* The following picture of a housewife of the olden time is taken from the MS. " Remembrancer" of Christopher Marshall, Member of the Committee of Observation, &c., &c. These curious manuscript papers have been arranged by William Duane, jun., of Philadelphia:

"As I have in this memorandum taken scarcely any notice of my wife's employments, it might appear as if her engagements were very trifling; the which is not the case, but the reverse; and to do her that justice which her services deserved, by entering them minutely, would take up most of my time, for this genuine reason, how that from early in the morning till late at night, she is constantly employed in the affairs of the family, which for four months has been very large; for besides the addition to our family in the house, [is] a constant resort of comers and goers, which seldom go away with dry lips and hungry bellies. This calls for her constant attendance, not only to provide, but also to attend at getting prepared in the kitchen, baking our bread and pies, meat, &c., and also on the table. Her cleanliness about the house, her attendance in the orchard, cutting and drying apples, of which several bushels have been procured; add to which, her making of cider without tools, for the constant drink of the family, her seeing all our washing done, and her fine clothes and my shirts, the which are all smoothed by her; add to this, her making of twenty large cheeses, and that from one cow, and daily using with milk and cream, besides her sewing, knitting, &c. Thus she looketh well to the ways of her household, and eateth not the bread of idle

Mrs. Slocumb's was a happy girlhood and youth. She always recurred to its history with delight; and retained the fashion of dress then prevalent with a fond pertinacity amusing to others. She scorned ever to wear any other than the long tight-waisted habit worn in her youthful days; and however costly the material, it had to be cut in the good old way. For almost sixty years she never did, and never would, allow herself to vary one iota from the fashion of Seventy-Six. It was with her a matter of pride no less than taste; it was a relic of the Revolution; and it would have savored of ingratitude, if not of impiety, to cast it away.

The true dignity of an American matron was shown in Mrs. Slocumb's reception and entertainment of the British officers, as already related. Her deportment was uniformly calm and self-possessed; her lofty spirit gave to her slender and fragile form a majesty that secured the respect of all the officers, and protected her from the slightest approach towards insolent familiarity. She presided at her table with dignity and courtesy, extending open hospitality to all her unbidden guests. Her liberality was acknowledged by strict orders that no depredations should be committed on any thing belonging to the house or plantation. These orders were in general successfully enforced; but even military authority could not save the farm-yard poultry or stock from a hungry soldiery. Not a feather was left, and

ness; yea, she also stretcheth out her hand, and she reacheth forth her hand to her needy friends and neighbors. I think she has not been above four times since her residence has been here, to visit her neighbors.

many a fine bullock was knocked in the head. But in
other things the protection availed her. On the news
of the army's approach, she had taken the precaution to
bury in the edge of a marsh near at hand, her plate and
other valuables. The soldiers suspected the place of
deposit, and plunged their pike-staffs into the ground
about the spot, until they discovered the treasure.
They were compelled to restore it to the rightful owner.

Mrs. Slocumb's little son, at this time two or three
years old, became a pet with several of the officers.
The little fellow was permitted to share with them the
pleasure and pride of prancing about on their splendid
chargers. Perhaps to some of them his childish glee
recalled their own domestic circles, and awakened in
their stern hearts the holy feelings of home. They
seemed delighted when the infant equestrian thus
playing dragoon, would clap his little hands and shout
in his innocent mirth. This child was the Hon. Jesse
Slocumb, member of Congress, who died full of honors in
early manhood. His remains rest in the Congressional
burial-ground at Washington. The brother of Mrs.
Slocumb already mentioned, was at the same time a
member from the Wilmington District. He died two
or three years since in Alabama.

When the British army broke up their encampment
at the plantation, a sergeant was ordered by Colonel
Tarleton to stand in the door till the last soldier had
gone out, to ensure protection to a lady whose noble
bearing had inspired them all with the most profound
respect. This order was obeyed; the guard brought

up the rear of that army in their march northward. Mrs. Slocumb saw them depart with tears of joy; and on her knees gave thanks, with a full heart, to the Divine Being who had protected her. A day or two afterwards, her husband returned to her arms and a happy home. They lived together for sixty years in unbroken harmony, the patriarchs of all that country, and looked up to by the inhabitants with unbounded love and respect. Many a traveller has been entertained at this hospitable mansion. A chapter might here be written on the subject of that ancient hospitality now so nearly obsolete in regions of country visited by the march of improvement. It was preserved in all its primitive exuberance in the house of Colonel Slocumb; there was always provision in his larder, and a place at his board for the chance guest, who was certain of a cordial welcome, and wine which a connoisseur would have pronounced of the choicest vintage of Europe. If it be asked how this unbounded hospitality was sup- ported—the answer is, every thing used was of home manufacture; nothing being purchased except those few essentials which are not the produce of our country.

Mrs. Slocumb possessed a strong and original mind, a commanding intellect and clear judgment, which she retained unimpaired to the time of her death. Among her friends she was remarkable for vivid powers of con- versation, while those less familiarly acquainted thought her reserved, and some fancied her severe and sarcastic. In this respect she was misjudged, for her severity was aimed only at folly or misconduct.

Her characteristic fortitude in the endurance of bodily pain—so great that it seemed absolute stoicism—should be noticed.   In her seventy-second year she was afflicted with a cancer on her hand, which the surgeon informed her must be removed with the knife.   At the time appointed for the operation she protested against being held by the assistants, telling the surgeon, "it was his business to cut out the cancer; she would take care of her arm."   He insisted, however, on her submitting to be held.   At the first incision, one of the assistants complained of faintness; Mrs. Slocumb bade him go away; and driving them off, braced her arm on the table, and never moved a muscle nor uttered a groan during the operation.

In her last years she was visited with a complication of disorders, enough to have broken the stoutest spirit; but bore all with Christian patience, and at the age of seventy-six sank quietly to rest.   She died on the sixth of March, 1836.   Her venerable husband survived her about five years.   Both now slumber together near the home where they lived and loved so long.   Pleasant Green has passed into the hands of other owners; the noble old oaks that surrounded the mansion and lined the avenue, have been girdled, and seem to lift their bare arms in lamentation for their ancient possessors.   But the memory of those who dwelt there is linked with glorious recollections, which time can never efface from American hearts.

Mention has been made of Esther Wake, the sister of Lady Tryon. These two lovely and accomplished women exercised great influence, according to tradition, in matters of state.* The gallantry of a warm-hearted people perhaps inclined them to estimate the character of their governor by the grace, beauty and accomplishment that adorned his domestic circle. The governor's dinners were princely, and the fascination of the ladies irresistible. In his attempt to obtain an appropriation from the assembly for building a splendid palace, female genius and influence rose superior to his official consequence and political manœuvres. Though the colony was poor, their management obtained a second grant. The admiration they commanded helped to sustain Governor Tryon's waning authority. When the royal government was annihilated, and the motion to change the name of Tryon County was under consideration, the resolution to alter that of Wake was rejected by acclamation. Thus the county in which the city of Raleigh is located, is consecrated to the memory of beauty and virtue.

* Sabine's American Loyalists. Jones' Defence of North Carolina.

XXV.

SARĀH BACHE.*

SARAH, the only daughter of Benjamin Franklin, was born at Philadelphia, on the eleventh of September, 1744. Of her early years no particulars can now be obtained; but from her father's appreciation of the importance of education, and the intelligence and information that she displayed through life, we may presume that her studies were as extensive as were then pursued by females in any of the American colonies.

In 1764, she was called to part with her father, sent to Europe for the first time in a representative capacity. The people of Pennsylvania were at that time divided into two parties—the supporters and the opponents of the proprietaries. The sons of Penn, as is known, had left the religion of their father, and joined the Church of England; and the bulk of that persuasion were of the proprietary party. The mass of the Quakers were in opposition, and with them Franklin had acted. After having been for fourteen years a

* Mr. William Duane, Jr., to whose pen the reader is indebted for this sketch—is the grandson of Mrs Bache.

SARAH BACHE.

S Bache

member of the Assembly, he lost his election to that
body in the autumn of 1764, by a few votes ; but his
friends being in the majority in the House, immediately
elected him the agent of the province in England. The
proprietary party made great opposition to his appointment ; and an incident occurred in connection with it
that shows us how curiously the affairs of Church and
State were intermingled in those days. A petition or
remonstrance to the Assembly against his being chosen
agent, was laid for signature upon the communion-table
of Christ Church, in which he was a pew-holder, and
his wife a communicant. His daughter appears to
have resented this outrage upon decency and the
feelings of her family, and to have spoken of leaving
the church in consequence ; which gave occasion to the
following dissuasive in the letter which her father wrote
to her from Reedy Island, November 8th, 1764, on his
way to Europe : "Go constantly to church whoever
preaches. The act of devotion in the common prayer-
book is your principal business there ; and if properly
attended to, will do more towards amending the heart
than sermons generally can do; for they were composed by men of much greater piety and wisdom than
our common composers of sermons can pretend to be ;
and therefore I wish you would never miss the prayer
days. Yet I do not mean you should despise sermons,
even of the preachers you dislike, for the discourse is
often much better than the man, as sweet and clear
waters come through very dirty earth. I am the more
particular on this head, as you seemed to express a lit-

tle before I came away some inclination to leave our church, which I would not have you do."*

The opinion entertained by many that a disposition to mobbing is of modern growth in this country is erroneous. In Colonial times outrages of this character were at least as frequent as now. Dr. Franklin had not been gone a year before his house was threatened with an attack. Mrs. Franklin sent her daughter to Governor Franklin's in Burlington, and proceeded to make preparation for the defence of her "castle." Her letter detailing the particulars may be found in the last edition of Watson's Annals of Philadelphia.

The first letter from Sarah Franklin to her father that has been preserved, was written after her return from this visit to Burlington. In it she says, "The subject now is Stamp Act, and nothing else is talked of. The Dutch talk of the 'Stamp tack,' the negroes of the 'tamp'—in short, every body has something to say." The commissions which follow for gloves, lavender, and tooth-powder, give us a humble idea of the state of the supplies in the Colonies at that day. The letter thus concludes: "There is not a young lady of my acquaintance but what desires to be remembered to you. I am, my dear, your very dutiful daughter,

"SALLY FRANKLIN."

In a letter dated on the 23d of the following March (1765), the Stamp Act is again mentioned: "We have

* The manuscript letters from which extracts are made in this memoir, are in the possession of Mrs. Bache's descendants in Philadelphia.

heard by a round-about way that the Stamp Act is repealed. The people seem determined to believe it, though it came from Ireland to Maryland. The bells rung, we had bonfires, and one house was illuminated. Indeed I never heard so much noise in my life; the very children seem distracted. I hope and pray the noise may be true."

A letter to her brother, written September 30th, 1766, speaks thus of some political movements in Philadelphia at that time : " The letter from Mr. Sergeant was to Daniel Wistar. I send you the Dutch paper, where I think there is something about it. On Friday night there was a meeting of seven or eight hundred men in Hare's brew-house, where Mr. Ross, mounted on a bag of grain, spoke to them a considerable time. He read Sergeant's letter, and some others, which had a good effect, as they satisfied many. Some of the people say he outdid Whitfield; and Sir John says he is in a direct line from Solomon. He spoke several things in favor of his absent friend, whom he called the good, the worthy Dr. Franklin, and his worthy friend. After he was gone, Hugh Roberts stood up and proposed him in Willing's place, and desired those who were for him to stand up ; and they all rose to a man."

On the 29th of October, 1767, Sarah Franklin was married to Richard Bache, a merchant of Philadelphia, and a native of Settle, in Yorkshire, England. After their marriage, Mr. and Mrs. Bache appear to have resided with Mrs. Franklin in the house built by her in the year 1765, upon ground over which Franklin Place now runs.*

Mrs. Franklin died on the 19th of December, 1774, having been attacked by paralysis four days previously. The mansion house continued to be occupied by Mr. Bache and his family. In the garden a willow tree was planted by Mrs. Bache on the 4th of July, 1776.

The approach of the British army through New Jersey in December, 1776, induced Mr. Bache to remove his family to Goshen township in Chester County, from which place the following letter was addressed by Mrs. Bache to her father, who, in the previous October, had been sent to France by the American Congress. Mrs. Bache's eldest son accompanied him, and was educated in France and Geneva under the supervision of his grandfather.

" GOSHEN, *February* 23d, 1777.

" HONORED SIR—

" We have been impatiently waiting to hear of your arrival for some time. It was seventeen weeks yesterday since you left us—a day I shall never forget.

---

* This house, in which Franklin died, stood rather nearer to Chestnut Street than to Market Street. The original entrance to it was over the ground upon which No. 112 Market Street is now built. On Franklin's return from Europe, he opened a new entrance to it between Nos. 106 and 108, under the archway still remaining, the house No. 106, and that lately No. 108, being built by him. His house was torn down about the year 1813, when Franklin Court was built upon the ground occupied by it—the court in front and the garden in the rear.

How happy shall we be to hear you are all safe arrived
and well. You had not left us long before we were
obliged to leave town. I never shall forget nor forgive
them for turning me out of house and home in the middle of winter, and we are still about twenty-four miles
from Philadephia, in Chester County, the next plantation to where Mr. Ashbridge used to live. We have
two comfortable rooms, and we are as happily situated
as I can be separated from Mr. Bache ; he comes to
see us as often as his business will permit. Your library
we sent out of town well packed in boxes, a week before us, and all the valuable things, mahogany excepted,
we brought with us. There was such confusion that
it was a hard matter to get out at any rate ; when we
shall get back again I know not, though things are
altered. much in our favor since we left town. I think
I shall never be afraid of staying in it again, if the
enemy were only three miles instead of thirty from it,
since our cowards, as Lord Sandwich calls them, are so
ready to turn out against those heroes who were to
conquer all before them, but have found themselves so
much mistaken; their courage never brought them to
Trenton, till they heard our army were disbanded. I
send you the newspapers ; but as they do not always
speak true, and as there may be some particulars in
Mr. Bache's letters to me that are not in them, I will
copy those parts of his letters that contain the news. I
think you will have it more regular.

"Aunt has wrote to you, and sent it to town. She
is very well, and desires her love to you and Temple.
15

We have wished much for him here when we have
been a little dull; he would have seen some characters
here quite new to him.   It's lucky for us Mr. George
Clymer's, Mr. Meredith's, and Mr. Budden's families
are moved so near us.   They are sensible and agreeable
people, and are not often alone.   I have refused dining
at Mr. Clymer's to-day, that I might have the pleasure
of writing to you and my dear boy, who, I hope, be-
haves so as to make you love him.   We used to think
he gave little trouble at home; but that was, perhaps,
a mother's partiality.   I am in great hopes that the first
letter of Mr. Bache will bring me news of your arrival.
I shall then have cause to rejoice.   I am, my dear papa,
as much as ever, your dutiful and affectionate daughter,
                                              "S. BACHE."

Mrs. Bache returned home with her family shortly
after, but in the following autumn the approach of the
British army after their victory on the Brandywine,
again drove them from Philadelphia.   On the 17th of
September, 1777, four days after the birth of her eldest
daughter, Mrs. Bache left town, taking refuge at first in
the hospitable mansion of her friend Mrs. Duffield, in
Beasalem Township, Bucks County.   They afterwards
removed to Manheim Township in Lancaster County,
where they remained until the evacuation of Philadelphia by the British forces.   The following extracts are
from letters written to Dr. Franklin after their return.
On the 14th July, 1778, Mr. Bache writes: "Once
more I have the happiness of addressing you from this

dearly beloved city, after having been kept out of it more than nine months. * * * I found your house and furniture upon my return to town, in much better order than I had reason to expect from the hands of such a rapacious crew; they stole and carried off with them some of your musical instruments, viz: a Welsh harp, ball harp, the set of tuned bells which were in a box, viol-de-gamba, all the spare armonica glasses and one or two spare cases. Your armonica is safe. They took likewise the few books that were left behind, the chief of which were Temple's school books and the History of the Arts and Sciences in French, which is a great loss to the public; some of your electric apparatus is missing also—a Captain André also took with him the picture of you which hung in the dining-room. The rest of the pictures are safe and met with no damage, except the frame of Alfred, which is broken to pieces."*

André was quartered in Franklin's house during the sojourn of the British in Philadelphia. In the following letter from Mrs. Bache, his future acquaintance Arnold is mentioned. It is dated October 22, 1778, Mrs. Bache having remained at Manheim with her children until the autumn. "This is the first opportunity I have had since my return home of writing to you. We found the house and furniture in much better order than we could expect, which was owing to the care the

---

* The postscript to this letter is curious: " I wish I could have sent to me from France two dozen of padlocks and keys fit for mails, and a dozen post-horns; they are not to be had here."

Miss Cliftons took of all we left behind; my being removed four days after my little girl was born, made it impossible for me to remove half the things we did in our former flight." After describing her little girl, she adds: "I would give a good deal you could see her; you can't think how fond of kissing she is, and gives such old-fashioned smacks, General Arnold says he would give a good deal to have her for a school mistress, to teach the young ladies how to kiss." * * * There is hardly such a thing as living in town, every thing is so high, the money is old tenor to all intents and purposes. If I was to mention the prices of the common necessaries of life it would astonish you. I have been all amazement since my return; such an odds have two years made, that I can scarcely believe I am in Philadelphia. * * * They really ask me six dollars for a pair of gloves, and I have been obliged to pay fifteen pounds for a common calamanco petticoat without quilting, that I once could have got for fifteen shillings."

These high prices were owing to the depreciation of the Continental money, but it subsequently was much greater. The time came when Mrs. Bache's domestics were obliged to take two baskets with them to market, one empty to contain the provisions they purchased, the other full of continental money to pay for them.

On the 17th of January, 1779, after speaking of the continued rise of prices, she writes, that "there never was so much dressing and pleasure going on; old friends meeting again, the whigs in high spirits and strangers

of distinction among us." Speaking of her having met
with General and Mrs. Washington several times, she
adds: "He always inquires after you in the most
affectionate manner, and speaks of you highly. We
danced at Mrs. Powell's on your birth-day, or night I
should say, in company together, and he told me it was
the anniversary of his marriage; it was just twenty years
that night."

With this letter a piece of American silk was sent as
a present to the Queen of France, Maria Antionette.

Dr. Franklin in his reply seems to have expressed
some dissatisfaction at the gaiety of his countrymen,
which he considered unseasonable. Mrs. Bache thus
excuses herself for participating in it in a letter dated
September 14, 1779: "I am indeed much obliged to
you for your very kind present. It never could have
come at a more seasonable time, and particularly so as
they are all necessary.   *   *   *   But how could
my dear papa give me so severe a reprimand for wishing a little finery. He would not, I am sure, if he
knew how much I have felt it. Last winter was a season of triumph to the whigs, and they spent it gaily.
You would not have had me, I am sure, stay away from
the Ambassador's or General's entertainments, nor when
I was invited to spend the day with General Washington and his lady; and you would have been the last
person, I am sure, to have wished to see me dressed
with singularity. Though I never loved dress so much
as to wish to be particularly fine, yet I never will go out
when I cannot appear so as do credit to my family

and husband. *   *   * I can assure my dear
papa that industry in this country is by no means laid
aside; but as to spinning linen, we cannot think of that
till we have got that wove which we spun three years
ago. Mr. Duffield has bribed a weaver that lives on
his farm to weave me eighteen yards, by making him
three or four shuttles for nothing, and keeping it a secret
from the country people, who will not suffer them to
weave for those in town. This is the third weaver's it
has been at, and many fair promises I have had about
it. 'Tis now done. and whitening, but forty yards of
the best remains at Liditz yet, that I was to have had
home a twelvemonth last month. Mrs. Keppele, who
is gone to Lancaster, is to try to get it done there for
me; but not a thread will they weave but for hard
money. My maid is now spinning wool for winter
stockings for the whole family, which will be no difficulty in the manufactory, as I knit them myself. I only
mention these things that you may see that balls are
not the only reason that the wheel is laid aside.   *
    *   * This winter approaches with so many
horrors that I shall not want any thing to go abroad in,
if I can be comfortable at home. My spirits, which I
have kept up during my being drove about from place
to place, much better than most people's I meet with,
have been lowered by nothing but the depreciation of
the money, which has been amazing lately, so that home
will be the place for me this winter, as I cannot get a
common winter cloak and hat but just decent under
two hundred pounds; as to gauze now, it is fifty dollars

a yard; 'tis beyond my wish, and I should think it not
only a shame but a sin to buy it if I had millions. It
is indeed, as you say, that money is too cheap; for
there are so many people that are not used to have it,
nor know the proper use of it, that get so much, that
they care not whether they give one dollar or a hundred for any thing they want; but to those whose
every dollar is the same as a silver one, which is our
case, it is particularly hard; for Mr. Bache could not
bear to do business in the manner it has been done in
this place, which has been almost all by monopolizing
and forestalling."

In the patriotic effort of the ladies of Philadelphia to furnish the destitute American soldiers with
money and clothing during the year 1780, Mrs. Bache
took a very active part. After the death of Mrs.
Reed, the duty of completing the collections and
contributions devolved on her and four other ladies,
as a sort of Executive Committee. The shirts
provided were cut out at her house. A letter
to Dr. Franklin, part of which has been published,
shows how earnestly she was engaged in the work.
The Marquis de Chastellux thus describes a visit which
he paid her about this time: "After this slight repast,
which only lasted an hour and a half, we went to visit
the ladies, agreeable to the Philadelphia custom, where
the morning is the most proper hour for paying visits.
We began by Mrs. Bache. She merited all the anxiety
we had to see her, for she is the daughter of Mr. Franklin. Simple in her manners, like her respected father,

she possesses his benevolence. She conducted us into
a room filled with work, lately finished by the ladies of
Philadelphia. This work consisted neither of embroidered tambour waistcoats, nor of net-work edging, nor
of gold and silver brocade. It was a quantity of shirts
for the soldiers of Pennsylvania. The ladies bought
the linen from their own private purses, and took a
pleasure in cutting them out and sewing them themselves. On each shirt was the name of the married or
unmarried lady who made it; and they amounted to
twenty-two hundred.

Mrs. Bache writes to Mrs. Meredith, at Trenton;
"I am happy to have it in my power to tell you that
the sums given by the good women of Philadelphia for
the benefit of the army have been much greater than
could be expected, and given with so much cheerfulness and so many blessings, that it was rather a pleasing
than a painful task to call for it. I write to claim you
as a Philadelphian, and shall think myself honored in
your donation."

A letter of M. de Marbois to Dr. Franklin, the
succeeding year—thus speaks of his daughter: "If
there are in Europe any women who need a model of
attachment to domestic duties and love for their country,
Mrs. Bache may be pointed out to them as such. She
passed a part of the last year in exertions to rouse the
zeal of the Pennsylvania ladies, and she made on this
occasion such a happy use of the eloquence which you
know she possesses, that a large part of the American
army was provided with shirts, bought with their

money, or made by their hands. In her applications
for this purpose, she showed the most indefatigable
zeal, the most unwearied perseverance, and a courage
in asking, which surpassed even the obstinate reluctance
of the Quakers in refusing."

The letters of Mrs. Bache show much force of character, and an ardent, generous and impulsive nature. She
has a strong remembrance of kindness, and attachment
to her friends; and in writing to her father her veneration for him is ever apparent, combined with the confidence and affection of a devoted daughter. Her beloved
children are continually the theme on which her pen
delights to dwell. Again and again the little family
group is described to her father when abroad; and it is
pleasing to dwell on the picture of the great philosopher
and statesman reading with parental interest domestic
details like the following; "Willy begins to learn his
book very well, and has an extraordinary memory. He
has learned, these last holidays, the speech of Anthony
over Cæsar's body, which he can scarcely speak without tears. When Betsy looks at your picture here,
she wishes her grandpapa had teeth, that he might be
able to talk to her; and has frequently tried to tempt
you to walk out of the frame with a piece of apple pie,
the thing of all others she likes best. Louis is remarkable for his sweet temper and good spirits." To her son
she says: "There is nothing would make me happier than
your making a good and useful man. Every instruction
with regard to your morals and learning I am sure
you have from your grandpapa: I shall therefore only

add my prayers that all he recommends may be strictly attended to."

In September, 1785, after an absence of nearly seven years at the Court of France, Dr. Franklin returned to his home in Philadelphia. He spent the last years of his life amidst the family of his daughter and the descendants of the friends of his early years, the most of whom he had survived.

In 1792, Mr. and Mrs. Bache visited England, and would have extended their tour to France, had it not been for the increasing troubles of the French Revolution. They were absent about a year.

Mr. Bache, having relinquished commercial pursuits, removed in 1794 to a farm upon the river Delaware, sixteen miles above Philadelphia, which he named Settle, after his birthplace. Here they spent upwards of thirteen years, making their residence the seat of hospitality.

In 1807, Mrs. Bache was attacked by cancer, and removed to Philadelphia in the winter of 1807–8, for the benefit of medical attendance. Her disease proved incurable, and on the 5th of October, 1808, she died in the house in Franklin Court, aged sixty-four years. Her remains, with those of her husband, who survived her a few years only, are interred in the Christ Church burial-ground, beside those of her parents.

In person, Mrs. Bache was rather above the middle height, and in the latter years of her life she became very stout. Her complexion was uncommonly fair, with much color; her hair brown, and her eyes blue, like those of her father.

Strong good sense, and a ready flow of wit, were among the most striking features of her mind. Her benevolence was very great, and her generosity and liberality were-eminent. Her friends ever cherisnea a warm affection for her.

It has been related that her father, with a view of accustoming her to bear disappointments with patience, was sometimes accustomed to request her to remain at home, and spend the evening over the chess-board, when she was on the point of going out to some meeting of her young friends. The cheerfulness which she displayed in every turn of fortune, proves that this discipline was not without its good effect.

Many of her witticisms have been remembered, but few of which, owing to the local events that gave rise to them, and the mention of individuals, would bear being now repeated. She took a great interest through life in political affairs, and was a zealous republican. Having learned that the English lady to whom some of her daughters were sent to school, had placed the pupils connected with persons in public life (her children amongst the number) at the upper end of the table, upon the ground that the young ladies of rank should sit together, Mrs. Bache sent her word that in this country there was no rank but rank mutton.

Her remark concerning the Carolinians has been remembered. She said she " hated them all from Bee to Izard." Mr. Izard's sentiments, as is known, were anti-Franklinean, and he lost no opportunity of inveighing against the philosopher.

Mrs. Bache had eight children, of whom a daughter died very young, and her eldest son in 1798, of the yellow fever, then prevailing in Philadelphia. Three sons and three daughters survived her.

END OF VOL. I.